POLAR PEOPLES

SELF-DETERMINATION
&
DEVELOPMENT

Minority Rights Group is an international, non-governmental organization whose aims are to ensure justice for minority (and non-dominant majority) groups suffering discrimination by:

1. Researching and publishing the facts as widely as possible to raise public knowledge and awareness of minority issues worldwide.

2. Advocating on all aspects of human rights of minorities to aid the prevention of dangerous and destructive conflicts.

3. Educating through its schools programme on issues relating to prejudice, discrimination and group conflicts.

If you would like to know more about the work of the Minority Rights Group, please contact Alan Phillips (Director), MRG, 379 Brixton Road, London SW9 7DE, United Kingdom.

m

Minority Rights Publications is a series of books from Minority Rights Group. Through the series, we aim to make available to a wide audience reliable data on, and objective analyses of, specific minority issues. The series draws on the expertise and authority built up by Minority Rights Group over two decades of publishing. Further details on MRG's highly acclaimed series of reports can be found at the end of this book. Other titles in the book series are:

The Balkans: Minorities and States in Conflict, 2nd Edition
by Hugh Poulton (1993)

Armenia and Karabagh: The Struggle for Unity
Edited by Christopher J. Walker (1991)

The Kurds: A Nation Denied
by David McDowall (1992)

Refugees: Asylum in Europe?
by Danièle Joly et al (1992)

POLAR PEOPLES

SELF-DETERMINATION
&
DEVELOPMENT

Edited by
Minority Rights Group

Minority Rights Publications

First published in the United Kingdom
in 1994 by
Minority Rights Publications
379 Brixton Road
London SW9 7DE

British Library Cataloguing in Publication Data
A CIP catalogue record of this book is available from the British Library.

93-4059

ISBN 1 873194 51 X paper
ISBN 1 873194 56 0 hardback

Library of Congress Cataloguing in Publication Data
CIP Data available from the Library of Congress

Designed and typeset by Brixton Graphics
Printed and bound in the UK by Redwood Books

Cover photo of Northern Minorities in Russia
Petrotchuk Nickolay/UNEP-Select

CONTENTS

PREFACE

olar Peoples takes its place in a long line of reports, books and papers which MRG has published to draw attention to minorities and their rights. As the eyes of the world focus on the high-profile conflicts in the former Yugoslavia, Somalia, Haiti and elsewhere, it is easy for the struggles of minority groups in other parts of the globe to be forgotten. This book attempts to redress the balance for the indigenous peoples of the North and to give an update on their contemporary situation.

These indigenous groups are often quite dissimilar in terms of their culture, language and the terrain in which they live. Yet they are similar in that most have lost a great deal over the years through contact with incomers who have respected neither their customs nor their land.

Recently, however, there has been a resurgence of indigenous political activity at local, regional, national and international levels. This trend can also be seen amongst the peoples of the North who are now seeking the restoration of their lands and the operation of their rights. Some of these are now being granted, in part, by the national governments within whose boundaries they live. Yet in other sections of this vast area, their rights and resources are diminishing very rapidly.

Polar Peoples cannot offer ethnographic completeness since the result would be a book of immense length. Instead, its aim is to outline and explain the main issues affecting these people today, rather than to include details of each single group. (This is especially true, for example, of the chapter on the Alaska Natives.) Thus the authors describe the historical contexts, general trends and some of the most important cases concerning native status and rights in this part of the world which, technologically and politically speaking, is changing very fast.

The region itself has been loosely defined and includes those indigenous groups living in the southern part of Siberia. These are still 'Northern Minorities', as a result of Soviet policies, and face many of the same problems as their fellow communities on the Arctic Rim.

Similarly, some Eskimos live well below the polar zone but are as affected by the policies of their national governments as are those living further north.

The chapters on *Native Peoples of the Russian Far North* and *The Inuit of Canada* have both been published recently by MRG as separate reports, in 1992 and 1993 respectively. That on *The Saami* was previously in similar report form but has been fully revised and updated for inclusion here. *The Alaska Natives* and *Greenland: Emergence of an Inuit Homeland* have been specially commissioned for this book. The publishing provenance of the individual chapters means they have different structures but they offer, nevertheless, a welcome contribution to our understanding of the achievements and difficulties faced by the minority peoples of the North.

About the authors

Hugh Beach is Associate Professor in the Department of Cultural Anthropology at Uppsala University, Sweden. He has written extensively on the Saami and circumpolar region, and is a specialist on the social effects of the Chernobyl disaster on the Swedish Saami. One of his most recent publications has been 'Filtering Mosquitoes and Swallowing Reindeer: the politics of ethnicity and environmentalism in northern Sweden', in G. Dahl (ed.) *Environmental Arguments and Subsistence Producers*, published in the Stockholm Series in Social Anthropology.

Ian Creery has worked with Inuit at Frobisher Bay and Broughton Island in the Northwest Territories, and as Fieldwork Coordinator for the Land Claims Project of the Inuit Tapirisat of Canada. For several years he worked with CBC Northern Service, producing documentaries and implementing training projects.

Fae L. Korsmo is Assistant Professor of Political Science at the University of Alaska Fairbanks. Her recent publications include 'Evaluative Discourse, Tribal Sovereignty, and the Alaska Native Claims Settlement Act' in *Minority Group Influence: Agenda Setting, Formulation and Public Policy* (forthcoming from Greenwood Press) and 'Problem Definition and the Alaska Natives: Ethnic Identity and Policy Formation' in Policy Studies Review.

Mark Nuttall is Lecturer in Social Anthropology at the Department of Human Sciences, Brunel University, UK. He has done extensive fieldwork in Greenland and is currently focussing on political and cultural understandings of natural resources and the environment in the Arctic. His book, *Arctic Homeland: Kinship, Community & Development in Northwest Greenland* was published by Belhaven Press in 1992.

Nikolai Vakhtin is a linguist and ethnologist based at the Institute of Linguistic Research, Academy of Sciences in St Petersburg. He specializes in the study of the languages and cultures of the indigenous peoples of the northeast, in particular the Eskimos of the Chukotka Peninsula and the Aleuts of the Commander Islands. He is the author of numerous books and articles in Russian.

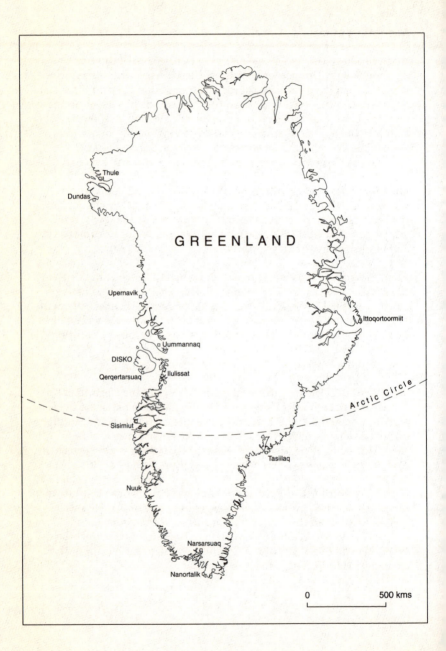

GREENLAND

Thule
Dundas

Upernavik

Uummannaq

DISKO
Qerqertarsuaq   Ilulissat

Ittoqqortoormiit

Arctic Circle

Sisimiut

Tasiilaq

Nuuk

Narsarsuaq
Nanortalik

0   500 kms

1

GREENLAND: EMERGENCE OF AN INUIT HOMELAND

by Mark Nuttall

Introduction

This chapter provides an overview of some of the social, political and economic changes experienced in Greenland both before and since Home Rule. When Home Rule was achieved from Denmark in 1979, the Greenland Inuit became the first population of Inuit to achieve a degree of self-government. Since then, Greenland has set a precedent for aboriginal self-determination not only in the circumpolar north, but worldwide, and has provided a model for the inclusion of indigenous values in social and economic development and in the design and implementation of environmental policy. While Greenland remains part of the Kingdom of Denmark, the Greenland Home Rule Authorities have assumed control over and responsibility for a number of public institutions, and have undertaken policies that aim to develop the country in terms of its own social and economic conditions and available natural resources. But self-government alone is not a panacea for the immense social, economic, health and environmental problems that Inuit in Greenland face in a rapidly modernizing world. Rather, it has given them the political and legislative means to find solutions to such problems.

It is no longer tenable to view the Greenland Inuit, unlike some other aboriginal peoples, as an oppressed minority in relation to a dominant nation-state. The Greenland Inuit have embarked on a course of nation-building and, because of the extensive system of self-government that has developed under Home Rule, they have more constitutionally protected rights than many other indigenous peoples. Yet, while indigenous rights are rather more protected than they have

1

been in the past (and Greenland Home Rule is recognized by the United Nations for this), threats to Inuit cultural integrity and to Greenland's Arctic environment still come from areas outside the control of the Greenland Inuit. Animal-rights activists and environmental groups, for example, are influential and powerful pressure groups that have mobilized public opinion and political action against Inuit subsistence hunting. Furthermore, international attention is now focused even more on the Arctic because it is regarded as a critical zone for global environmental change by international scientists and environmentalists. As a result, international environmental agencies are devoting much energy to designing appropriate resource management systems and environmental protection strategies. All this affects the rights of Inuit to continue customary subsistence activities, although the Greenland authorities and environmental agencies have been developing a workable participatory approach to the sustainable management of resources.

As of 1 January 1991, the population of Greenland was 55,533, of which 29,880 were males and 25,653 were females. Out of the total population, 46,691 persons were born in Greenland. The category 'persons born in Greenland' does not distinguish between Inuit and non-Inuit, but refers to all those subject to Danish law; yet even allowing for Danes who have been born in Greenland, it is generally accepted that the Inuit population numbers some 45,000, while Danes number approximately 10,000.

The majority Inuit population comprises three distinct linguistic groups: Kalaallit along the west coast, Inughuit (popularly known as Polar Eskimos and famous for being the world's most northerly indigenous inhabitants) in the far north around Thule, and Iit on the east coast. Since Home Rule, Greenland has been known officially as Kalaallit Nunaat (the 'Greenlanders' Land'), and collectively the Inuit population is known as Kalaallit. Yet, both the Inughuit and Iit do not always refer to themselves as Kalaallit, and in this chapter both 'Inuit' and 'Greenlanders' are used as more generic and interchangeable terms of reference. To avoid confusion, for the purposes of this discussion when 'Greenlander' is used as a term of reference for Inuit, it should not be taken to include Danes, although many Danes born and brought up in Greenland may consider themselves to be Greenlanders.

History and Danish colonization

Greenland is a land of superlatives. With an area of 2,175,000 sq. km. it is the world's largest island. Permanent human habitation is only possible along the ice-free coastal areas, which cover 341,700 sq. km. or one-sixth of the total area. The other five-sixths of the country are covered by the immense inland ice, which in some places rises to well over 3,000 metres. Along many parts of the coast, the inland ice reaches down to the sea and glaciers continually calve icebergs into the fjords. These then drift with the currents and make navigation hazardous. Greenland is also a land of extremes in temperature. In the far north, the mean temperature in January, in deep winter, ranges between -15°C to -30°C, while in July, at the height of the Arctic summer, the mean temperature is +5°C. In the far south, some 2,000 km. away, the mean temperature in January is -15°C and in July can reach +8°C or 10°C. Throughout Greenland, vegetation tends to be sparse. There are no vast tracts of forest to be found, as in Alaska, Siberia, Scandinavia or Canada, although it is not unknown for willow scrub to reach a height of two or three metres. Other vegetation includes lichens, dwarf willow and dwarf birch, grasses and many varieties of flowering plants that carpet the landscape in summer. Sea mammals, such as seals, whales, walrus and narwhals, and land mammals such as caribou and musk-ox, thrive in abundance and have provided the mainstay of the subsistence economy. This will be discussed in more detail below.

Greenland's coastal areas have been inhabited for about four-and-a-half thousand years. Archaeological knowledge of the earliest Inuit settlements in Greenland is detailed and provides insight into the Inuit way of life before extensive European contact.[1] The first Paleo-Eskimo groups arrived in the far north of the island between 2500–2000 BC. These people were nomadic migrants from the Canadian High Arctic who hunted mainly land mammals such as musk-ox. Successive groups of migrants continued to harvest both land and sea resources, such as caribou, seals, whales and walrus. As will be shown later, many communities continue to rely on terrestrial and marine resources for subsistence purposes.

European settlement in Greenland began *c.* AD 985, when the Norseman Erik the Red sailed from Iceland and established two colonies in the south and southwest. For almost 500 years the Norse settlements subsisted from farming and from keeping cattle, sheep and goats. During the early part of the 15th Century, however, contact between Greenland and the rest of the Scandinavian world was severed, and the fate of the Norse settlements has long been a matter for conjecture. The Icelandic sagas record that the Norsemen in Greenland knew of, and came into contact with, people they called *Skraelings*, and this in fact is probably the earliest known contact between Norsemen and Inuit. Theories that account for the demise of the Norse settlements vary from an emphasis on climatic deterioration, disease and starvation to one on conflict with the *Skraelings*, who may have come into direct competition with the Norsemen for scarce resources.

Later European interest in Greenland was mercantile. Early English explorers, such as Martin Frobisher and John Davis in the 16th Century, met with groups of Inuit along the west coast (in fact, Davis produced the first written description of the West Greenland Inuit), but it was European whaling activity which was to have the first significant impact on the native population. Competitive whaling between the English and the Dutch off the coast of Spitzbergen in the early 17th Century had resulted in the depletion of whale stocks, and this led to the seeking out and exploitation of new whaling grounds in Davis Strait and Baffin Bay, between Greenland and Canada. In pursuit of the Greenland Right whale, Scottish, English and Dutch whalers became regular visitors to the coasts of Greenland and Baffin Island, making contact with the Inuit and trading with them at their settlements and hunting camps. Knives, woollen clothes, tea, sugar, pots, pans and kettles were among the most common items that whalers traded in return for seal and whale blubber, for narwhal tusks and for seal, caribou and fox skins. But while such material impact on Inuit culture is difficult to assess, the whalers also brought diseases, such as influenza and various venereal diseases, to which the Inuit had no immunity.

In 1721 Hans Egede, a Norwegian-Danish Lutheran priest, arrived on Greenland's west coast, hoping to find the remnants of the Norse colony. Encountering nomadic Inuit groups instead, he established a trade and mission station near present-day Nuuk (the Greenland capital), and so began over 230 years of Danish colonial rule. Success in converting the Inuit to Christianity was due in part to Egede and his missionaries learning the language of the Inuit. Within a few years, Danish priests training in Copenhagen were receiving language instruction in Greenlandic and young Inuit were being trained as catechists. Egede's son and successor, Poul, was responsible for many important Biblical translations. By 1744 the four Gospels had been translated into Greenlandic and the translation of the entire New Testament was completed by 1766.[2]

Knowledge of pre-Christian Inuit religious belief comes primarily from the accounts of Inuit life written by the missionaries themselves, and from early ethnographers and travellers. Inuit cosmology was underpinned by an elaborate system of beliefs and moral codes that acted to regulate a complexity of relationships between people, animals, the environment and the spirit forces believed to be inherent in natural phenomena. For the Inuit, the environment was one of risk, fraught with danger and uncertainty. Part of this danger was due to the fact that the Inuit relied on hunting animals that had souls that needed to be propitiated by the hunter after being killed. Lack of success in hunting, illness, misfortune, famine and bad weather were all understood to come about because this elaborate moral code had been contravened in some way, resulting in a violation of the relations between Inuit and the natural world. Offences by an individual against animals and spirits in the natural world would put the entire community at risk. The transgression of the complexity of taboos necessary for ensuring the regulation of relationships between the human and natural worlds either could cause pain to the souls of recently killed animals, or could cause vindictive and malevolent spirits to bring illness. A return to human well-being was possible through the intervention of the *angakkut* (shamans), who acted as curers of illness, affliction and misfortune.

The Lutheran missionaries dismissed such beliefs as held by the Inuit as superstition, denounced their apparent lack of belief in a Creator[3] and concentrated on teaching them about such theological concepts as sin, purgatory, salvation and eternal life. At this time, Inuit communities in Greenland had no tradition of formal leadership, yet the *angakkut* held a certain amount of power. Egede and his successors denounced the *angakkut* as liars and identified their helping and oracular spirits (necessary for assisting the *angakkut* in their journeys to the spirit world) as manifestations of the Devil.

While the Inuit rejected their own religious beliefs in favour of Christianity, and Egede was able to undermine the secular and spiritual authority of the *angakkut*, his commercial activity did not yield the same results as his missionary zeal. Because of this the Danish government took over responsibility for trade in 1726. From the beginning, the Danes hoped to create a viable trade network by transferring trading rights in Greenland to independent companies. Danish merchants did not have too much commercial success, however, so in 1776 the Danish government formed the Royal Greenland Trade Company (known as the KGH: Det Kongelige Grønlandske Handelskompagni) and established a Danish Greenland trade monopoly which was to last until the end of the Second World War. During the 18th Century there was a progressive northwards expansion and establishment of colonies (which were later to grow into the large towns of the west coast). As well as the colonies, trading posts, or *udsteder* (lit. 'outposts' or 'out places') were established by the KGH to serve the small settlements and hunting camps known as *boplads* ('dwelling places'). The *udsteder* were to become the larger villages now called *bygd* in Danish and *nunaqarfiit* in Greenlandic.

By 1782 the Inuit population along the west coast, from Cape Farewell in the south to Upernavik in the north, had come into permanent contact with Danes and other Europeans. The year-round presence of Danes was felt in the hierarchy of authority that, as well as the missionaries, included inspectors, traders and their assistants. In each settlement the trader occupied a position of power over the lives of the Inuit, based on his responsibility for distributing trade goods and for paying wages in kind. The trader and other Danes who came to work in the settlements seldom stayed for longer than a few years, before returning to Denmark and being replaced by new employees of the KGH.

The Danish colonial attitude towards Greenland was isolationist and paternal, and aimed to protect the Inuit hunting culture. Rather than being exploitative, any trade had to benefit the indigenous population, and this certainly was a significantly different attitude from other imperial powers embarking on expansionist enterprises in different regions of the globe. In their Trade Instructions of 1782 the KGH laid down rules for the practical and moral conduct of KGH employees in their interaction with the Inuit. In particular, Danes were forbidden from having sexual intercourse with Inuit women and banned from supplying the Inuit with any form of alcohol. It was possible for KGH employees to marry native women, however, provided those women were of mixed Inuit and European descent.

By the end of the 18th Century the fortunes of the missionaries, traders and Inuit were inextricably bound up with the hunting way of life. As a result, the KGH attempted to prevent the Inuit from becoming too dependent on the Danes by ensuring that all basic necessities could be satisfied by hunting. However, by this time the Inuit were well and truly in a trading economy which was based on whale blubber and sealskins, and did become dependent on trade goods to supplement their diet and technology. Occasionally, people abandoned subsistence activities to seek employment with the KGH. Dependency on the trading economy also meant that in times of scarcity, poor hunting and famine, the missionary and trade manager were responsible for social welfare. However, the majority of the Inuit population were able to continue their small-scale subsistence hunting lifestyle. Seals provided the mainstay of the local economy, with the skin and blubber underpinning the trade network.[4]

The first major revision of Danish policy became necessary as a result of climatic change. The early part of the 19th Century was characterized by a gradual warming of Greenland's southern coastal waters, resulting in migration of seals to colder waters along the west coast. This disrupted the subsistence economy of many settlements, but with several species of fish, most notably cod, having appeared in the now warmer waters of the south a major transition from hunting to fishing was encouraged by the Danes. A modest cod fishery began in 1911 and expanded rapidly over the next 20 to 30 years. Yet this was not without its cultural and ideological problems, as Inuit had traditionally regarded fishing as a lowly pursuit. While it was important as a subsistence activity, it did not bring the prestige associated with the hunting of sea mammals. Nonetheless, many Inuit were unable to continue sealing and whaling activities and were forced to change their attitude towards fishing. Traditional hunting camps were abandoned as people not only moved to other areas in search of good fishing grounds, but moved to larger settlements in search of employment. By the outbreak of the Second World War, the cod fishery was capital-intensive and had brought some prosperity to Greenland.

But after the end of the Second World War, Denmark ended its isolationist policy towards Greenland. Emphasis was placed on social welfare and on infrastructural change as part of a process of 'modernization'. Colonial status was abolished in 1953 and Greenland became an integral part of the Kingdom of Denmark, thus giving the Greenland Inuit equal status to Danes. The ending of colonial rule marked the beginning of another era characterized by extensive changes in Greenlandic society. A massive construction programme was undertaken, to cater for the health, educational and housing needs of a growing population, and the increased rationalization of the fishing industry was placed at the centre of economic development. During the 1960s, as part of a policy of centralization and urbanization, people were 'encouraged' to migrate from outlying areas to west coast towns by the closing down of what the Danish authorities regarded as 'unprofitable' settlements.

The road to Home Rule

By the late 1960s and early 1970s, Greenlandic society had been overwhelmingly transformed from one based primarily on small-scale subsistence hunting and fishing to a modern, export-oriented economy. The majority of the population was now living in the fast-growing west coast towns and this demographic transition brought its own problems. Life in the settlements had been characterized by, and organized around, kinship and other networks of close social association.

But movement to the towns led to the fragmentation of kin-based groups and individuals now experienced alienation, social and economic marginality and discrimination, accentuated by ethnic divisions between Inuit and Danes. The presence of the latter had increased significantly because of the need for workers in construction and in services such as health and education.

As a direct result of the changes and upheavals during this period, Greenland experienced an emerging and unprecedented Inuit political awareness. This was nurtured by the members of a relatively young Danish-speaking Greenland Inuit elite who had been educated in both Greenland and Denmark during the 1950s, 1960s and 1970s. A Home Rule movement began and this was strengthened by the formation of the left-wing Siumut (Forward) party. This was made up of a small group of Inuit critical in their opposition to the Danish administration and confident in airing their views. Most were men, although women are now more prominent in Greenlandic politics than they have been in the past. While in Denmark, Greenlandic students had formed the Young Greenlanders' Council, which was able to put across its views on the nature of the relationship between Greenland and Denmark at rallies organized by left-wing groups who regarded an emerging Greenland Home Rule movement as linked to a worldwide struggle against imperialism.[5]

The increasing articulation and forcefulness of indigenous opinion regarding the Danish administration could not be ignored. It found expression in such things as Greenland's reluctance to join the European Economic Community in 1973. Although the Greenland electorate voted against joining the EEC, Greenland had to follow Denmark into the Community because of the majority Danish decision in favour of membership. Other things added to the dissatisfaction with the Danish administration of Greenland, such as the granting of concessions to multinational oil companies to explore for oil in the fishing grounds off the west coast of Greenland in 1974. Slowly, the Danes, who were well aware of this increasing dissatisfaction, recognized that a changed relationship between Greenland and Denmark was necessary.

A Home Rule commission was set up by the Danes in 1975, and this was followed by the passing of the Home Rule Act three years later. Greenlandic Home Rule came into force in 1979 after a referendum held in January of that year resulted in an overwhelming vote in favour. Following its success in the first general election, Siumut formed a majority government, with Atassut (Solidarity), a party favouring links with Denmark and the EEC, in opposition. The other main political party, Inuit Ataqatigiit (Inuit Brotherhood), was later to hold the balance of power following the next election in 1983. In 1991 a coup within Siumut replaced Jonathan Motzfeldt, the party's leader and Greenland's first Prime Minister, with Lars Emil Johansen. Following the elections in March 1991, Johansen formed a coalition with Inuit Ataqatigiit. The Greenland Parliament is known as the *Landsting*, and the government is known as the *Landsstyre*. There are 27 seats in the *Landsting* and following the 1991 elections the breakdown by party has been as follows: Siumut, 11 seats; Atassut, 8 seats; Inuit Ataqatigiit, 5 seats; Akulliit Partiiaat (Centre Party), 2 seats; Issittup Partiia (Polar Party), 1 seat.

Because Home Rule was defined in territorial terms rather in terms of ethnic or racial criteria, it is important to point out that the Greenlandic electorate consists of both Inuit and Danes resident in the country. Furthermore, both Inuit and Danes have the right to stand for election to the *Landsting*, although there are no Danes sitting in the *Landsting* as yet. With around 10,000 Danes living in Greenland, making up almost one-fifth of the total population of 55,000, this is a striking figure compared with the fact that Danes only made up a few per cent of the population during the final years of colonial rule.[6] Although many come on short-term contracts and stay for one or two years, others make their homes in Greenland, often marrying Greenlanders. While Danes are a minority group, they are very much a part of Greenlandic society, owning businesses, and working alongside Greenlanders. This structural rather than cultural dimension to Home Rule illustrates how the various Inuit land claims agreements are results of different social, economic and political circumstances. In contrast to the Alaska Native Claims Settlement Act, or Nunavut in the Canadian East Arctic, Greenland Home Rule, to quote Jens Dahl, 'was a political reform, recognizing a politically, geographically and demographically undivided Greenland'.[7]

Under Home Rule, Greenland is divided administratively into 18 districts or municipalities which each have a municipal centre, or town. The largest municipality is Nuuk, the capital, which has a population of over 12,000. Each district has a municipal council called a *kommune*, which has a degree of autonomy in managing district affairs. The towns are the administrative centres which serve the villages in each district. Local income tax and payments from the Home Rule Authorities are the main source for municipal revenues. Municipal government allows for a less centralized form of administration and gives the municipalities much responsibility for social services, education and housing.

Under the Home Rule Act, legislative and administrative powers in a large number of areas were to be transferred to the Home Rule Authorities. By 1993, the Home Rule Authorities had assumed control of such areas as health, taxation, industry, transportation, social services and education, thereby making the transition of these powers complete. The Danish government still retains control of defence and foreign affairs. The Danes maintain Greenland Command in south Greenland, which is mainly concerned with fisheries protection. Greenlanders are not liable for military service, but as part of the Kingdom of Denmark Greenland is a member of NATO.

The nurturing of Greenlandic identity

In the years leading to Home Rule, Greenlandic politicians took an explicit anti-European stance and focused their attention on the working out and defining of a Greenlandic national identity. As a reaction to external control, and in order to emphasize that Greenland was not a part of Europe, geographically, culturally or ethnically (and thereby choosing to ignore, perhaps, not only the mixing of Inuit and Danish heritage over two centuries, but the mixing of Inuit and European blood), a distinctive Inuit ethnic identity was nurtured. For the first time, politicians talked of the idea of a unified Greenlandic community working together for the development of the country. At the time of Danish colonization, individuals and groups were referred to by geographical location, rather than by other characteristics. The naming of a group, usually comprising several related households, was suffixed with -*miut* (sing. -*mioq*), meaning 'people of', or 'inhabitants of'. These groups were highly localized with well-defined boundaries. But Greenlandic politicians now looked beyond this localized identity and sense of place towards a wider national identity. In this way, political rhetoric often emphasizes a homogeneous Greenlandic culture and points to Inuit as a people with a common origin, culture, history and future, rather than as diverse groups in space and time.

Ethnopolitical symbolism, such as the Greenlandic flag and national anthem, has also done much to strengthen the institutionalization of a Greenlandic national identity,[8] but the emerging diversity of occupational associations and the beginnings of structural differentiation complicate the discussion of contemporary Greenlandic identity and raise questions about how it can be studied and represented. It has been argued that Greenlandic identity has both a cultural and a structural dimension. The cultural dimension, espoused in particular by the Siumut party, is characterized by specific cultural and ethnic aspects such as language, occupation, genealogy and birthplace as defining components of Greenlandic identity. Identity as a Greenlander tends, therefore, to be regarded as an ethnic Inuit identity *vis-à-vis* Danes. A Greenlandic identity with a structural dimension, on the other hand, is broader, encompassing both Inuit and Danes living in the country. It also opposes Greenland Inuit to other Inuit in Siberia, Alaska and Canada.[9] But Greenlandic identity is also contextual in that people define their identity based on centres that have significance for themselves, such as kinship, locality, community or mode of occupation.

Economic development since Home Rule

The Home Rule Authorities inherited a post-colonial economy, which was characterized by a relatively high standard of living and housing compared to other parts of the Arctic. But this economy had been planned and developed by the Danes through the transfer of annual block-grants and had no sound internal basis to prove viable under a newly forged Greenlandic administration. The transition to Home Rule had to be a gradual one, and the difficulties of achieving autonomy are illustrated by the fact that Greenland remains dependent on Denmark for economic support and block transfer payments (indeed, some observers of the Greenland economy would say that this dependency is increasing, highlighting the differences between the economies of the two countries). Direct annual grants to the Greenland Home Rule Authorities often make up 40 per cent of the Home Rule government's total revenue.

As mentioned above, the Danes still retain control over defence and, until recently, retained control over many public institutions. In the areas of health and education there are still very few well-qualified Inuit, and large numbers of Danes still work as teachers and medical practitioners. Even at governmental level, the Home Rule Authorities rely on the political and economic expertise of Danish advisers. However, because of new educational establishments such as a university, more young Greenland Inuit are being trained to fill administrative positions previously held by Danes. Fishing, hunting and sheep farming are the main industries and provide the main means of employment for the majority of Greenlanders. Manufacturing depends on the fishing industry, and much employment is provided in the fish and prawn processing plants found in every major town and settlement.

Despite continued dependency on Denmark, Greenland has achieved an impressive degree of political autonomy. By the mid-1980s the Home Rule Authorities had taken control of a number of public institutions, most notably the KGH, which is now known as KNI (Kalaallit Niuerfiat, meaning Greenland Trade). This gives the Home Rule Authorities control over production and export in the fishing industry. Fishing (for Atlantic cod, northern prawn and Greenland halibut) currently accounts for 80 per cent of Greenland's total export earnings. On 1 January 1985 Greenland left the EC, but negotiated Overseas Countries and Territories Association status. This allows favourable access to European markets and a fishing agreement between Greenland and the EEC is renegotiated every five years. Withdrawal from membership of the Community meant that the Home Rule Authorities lost much-needed grants from the EC's development fund. However, the Home Rule Authorities currently receive an annual payment of 26.5m ECUs for allowing EC member countries fishing rights in Greenlandic waters.

The Home Rule Authorities aspire to greater political, financial and economic independence from Denmark, based on the exploitation of natural resources. Economic development since Home Rule has focused primarily on the shrimp and cod fishery. During the first few years, this proved profitable, but since the mid-1980s the fishing industry has been going through a severe crisis.[10] While this can be attributed in part to the recession currently experienced by most countries in Europe and North America, the causes also lie in policies of mismanagement within Greenland, uncontrolled growth of the fishing fleet and subsequent over-fishing. The last few years have seen bankruptcies in the fishing industry, in service industries and in the emerging private sector. Unemployment has also become a particularly acute problem in some areas.

The Home Rule Authorities are now looking to alternative industries, such as tourism and mining, and in the future oil and gas production. This marks a significant turnabout from government attitudes during the first few years of Home Rule. Then, the Home Rule Authorities regarded fishing, hunting and sheep farming (the latter is pursued in south Greenland only) as Greenland's main occupations, and did not look favourably on the exploitation of non-renewable resources. Concern was expressed, by both politicians and people living in local communities, that the development and transportation of oil, liquid gas and other minerals would be harmful to the environment and would pose a threat to traditional hunting and fishing activities. However, the political and economic realities of self-government and the need for increased revenues have forced the Home Rule Authorities to revise their policy towards non-renewable resource development. In 1991 the Greenland Parliament passed a new Mining Act to encourage mineral exploration and exploitation. This change in policy allows for favourable taxation and more lenient concession arrangements for foreign companies to mine minerals such as lead, zinc, coal and gold. It has been argued that if non-renewable resource development is managed effectively, the resulting revenues could strengthen the Greenlandic economy.[11]

The Home Rule Authorities see tourism as providing a lucrative source of revenue, and as something that can be developed into a viable industry in a diversified economy. Tourism is already quite well developed, albeit on a small scale. Greenland currently receives about 3,000 tourists annually, but the Home Rule Authorities wish to see this figure increase to some 35,000 by the beginning of the 21st Century. This will require some major infrastructural changes, for example in transportation and accommodation. At present, most visits are short-term, with tourists arriving on cruise ships or on guided excursions. Tourism also tends to be specialist in nature, with many tourists buying adventure holiday packages that have a particular interest, such as mountain walking, ornithology or wildlife. Although an increase in tourism would bring much-needed revenue to the country, it could also result in specific problems if allowed to go unchecked. Elsewhere in the world, the growth of adventure tourism has had a negative environmental, economic and cultural impact. Research into these possible impacts in Greenland is necessary and appropriate management structures and policies need to be adopted if tourism is to proceed in the best interests of local communities and the environment.

Language

Since Home Rule was introduced, West Greenlandic has been the official language. Greenlandic (*Kalaallisut*, lit. 'in the way of a Greenlander') is part of the family of Inuktitut languages spoken by Inuit from Siberia to East Greenland. The diversity of Inuit culture in Siberia, Alaska, Canada and Greenland is also reflected in language and many dialects are mutually unintelligible. Although the various Inuktitut dialects are all agglutinative and follow similar rules regarding the construction of words from roots and postbases, they differ in morpho-phonology (i.e. variations in the use of the same word, particularly in pronunciation) and in vocabulary.

Within Greenland alone there are considerable differences. West Greenlandic, as the official language, is spoken from Nanortalik in the south to Upernavik district in the northwest. People of Thule, and Tasiilaq and Ittoqqortoormiit on the east coast, distinguish themselves from West Greenland both linguistically and historically.[12] Even within West

Greenland variations in dialect make people aware of a separate identity. For example, in Upernavik district the dialect diverges from standard West Greenlandic and locally such differences are used and played upon in identity formation. Regional dialects are coming under pressure from the dominant official form, but also West Greenlandic itself is continually developing as a result of technological change and the accommodation of outside influence. As Greenland continues to carve an autonomous political niche, the Inuit language is responding to new challenges.

When Hans Egede arrived in Greenland in 1721, he encountered Inuit groups with no tradition of a written language. Myths, stories and legends were transmitted orally, and those that were collected during the early years of colonization provide important insight into a culture that had experienced little European influence.[13] Today the oral tradition persists in some areas such as the hunting districts and Upernavik and Thule. However, even there, this once central feature of community life is becoming a thing of the past. Storytelling has to compete with the widespread influence of video and television, as imported programmes and films now bring European, American and Japanese culture into the living room of the seal hunter.

The preservation of the indigenous language was a central feature of Danish policy in Greenland, and the establishment of a printing house in Nuuk during the 1850s was an important development for Greenlandic as a written language. From it the newspaper *Atuagagdliutit* was first published in 1861. Originally it came out monthly and its significance lay in providing a medium for cultural expression and being 'of the utmost importance for intellectual development in Greenland'.[14] Although it contained some world news, *Atuagagdliutit* focused on Inuit culture and life in many parts of Greenland. It provided a forum for the recording of oral histories, reminiscences, descriptions of hunting and the translation of European literature. *Atuagagdliutit* paved the way for the development of a Greenlandic literary tradition, facilitated by the creation of a standard orthography by the Moravian missionary Samuel Kleinschmidt in the mid-19th Century. This had the effect of unifying regional dialects along the west coast.

Most early publishing concentrated on translations of Danish and European classics and the first two Greenlandic novels appeared in 1914 and 1931.[15] The social changes and economic upheavals that have occurred since the 1950s provide considerable inspiration for much contemporary Inuit literature. By focusing on social problems, or by reaching into the past (whether into the hunting culture, or myth and legend), Greenlandic literature makes a strong contribution to both cultural identity and language.

When colonial status was abolished in 1953, the major social, economic and political developments that were to take place meant that Greenlanders needed a spoken and written understanding of Danish. However, at this time, few Greenlanders could speak Danish. As a result of greater demand for skilled and qualified workers in construction and administration, there was a tremendous increase in the number of Danes living and working in Greenland. In 1952 *Atuagagdliutit* merged with the Danish-language newspaper *Grønlandsposten*, giving more of a bilingual feel to Greenland as a developing country.

A clear example of Danish influence on Greenlandic is 'Copenhagen Greenlandic',[16] the language spoken by Greenlanders living in the Danish capital. Much of the vocabulary used in particular Greenlandic contexts, such as hunting and fishing, is lost. The rich terminology for different types of ice, weather and animals is unused, because it is not specific to Danish conditions. However, this is also the case within Greenland, especially in the larger towns. Even in the hunting districts many words are no longer used in everyday speech and young people are not familiar with elaborate hunting terminology. Just as successive generations are no longer inheriting specific aspects of Greenlandic culture, they are also disinherited from much of the language which is an effective medium for the transmission of that culture.

Within Greenland many Danish words have become Greenlandicized. For example, the word for midwife, *juumooq*, comes from the Danish *jormoder*. Similarly, the Danish word for motor oil, *olie*, has become *uulie* in Greenlandic. Technological developments have seen the introduction of many items that have been accommodated by the Greenlandic language as well as by Greenlandic culture. Examples include *motori*, *fyrnsyrni* (television), *batteri*, *fabrikki* (factory) and *banki*.

While Danish continues to be important, the influence of West Greenlandic on regional dialects is becoming a new issue. In Thule and on the east coast, West Greenlandic is taught in schools and is used in broadcasting, administration, church services, literature and newspapers. In Thule, West Greenlandic cultural and linguistic pressure has also come about as a result of people moving in from other parts of the country, in particular from Upernavik district.[17] In East Greenland, which has experienced a relatively shorter period of European contact, the dialect spoken there has changed in many ways. As a result of conversion to Christianity, the vocabulary associated with pre-contact Inuit cosmology, religious practices and shamanism has disappeared.

A major development for West Greenlandic was the introduction of a new orthography in 1973, which has made the written language more phonetic. As for the future, there is a need for the language to expand as Greenland enters the modern world. There are new challenges as regards the development of a political, social and technological vocabulary. It says something for the nature of Greenlandic as a flexible language that it has the ability to meet these challenges. One criticism of Inuit languages has been that they are unable to reflect abstract thought, and are therefore unsuitable for the modern world. This does not hold true for Greenlandic, amply testified by an extensive literature and the ability to express political aspirations and rhetoric.

Rather than using loan words, many imported items have been rendered intelligible in Greenlandic in descriptive terms. For example, in the past, this included words for sugar (*siorasat*, lit. 'looks like sand') and money (*aningaasat*, lit. 'looks like the moon'). More recent examples include the word for a general or municipal election, *qinersineq* ('the act or state of choosing', which is linked to *qinerpaa*, 'chooses him/her'). As regards changes in transportation, a motor boat is a *pujortuleeraq* 'makes a little smoke', while an aeroplane is *timmisartoq*, 'something that flies'.

Words which once had different meanings are now used in new senses. The word for factory or fish processing plant, *tunissasiorfik*, literally means 'a place where one gives or sells', and is related to *tunisivik*, 'an offering place' in the sense of a sacrifice or other religious offering. Similarly, a bank is known as *aningaaserivik*, literally 'a place to put money'. In the past, when seal, whale and fish fat (*orsoq*) was used for fuel and heating, the verb *orsersorpoq* had the meaning 'to fill the lamp with fat': today it means 'to fill up with fuel', usually kerosene and paraffin.

While English remains a direct threat to Inuktitut dialects in the Canadian North and Alaska, Greenlandic is no longer feared to be disappearing as it was in the 1950s. There is no doubt that Radio Greenland has helped in this respect. It broadcasts in Greenlandic and is run by Inuit, thereby promoting and safeguarding the Inuit language and culture. There is also some television broadcasting in Greenlandic and a vigorous and prolific publishing industry. Also, over half of all courses taught in schools are taught through the medium of Greenlandic, and new educational establishments, such as Ilisimatusarfik (the University of Greenland), use Greenlandic as the main language. However, as mentioned, certain aspects and dialects of the language are changing or disappearing, or are threatened in some way. And, for the future a more technical, economic and political vocabulary is evolving to cope with the demands of the modern world.

Education

Education in Greenland follows the Danish system. There are nine years of compulsory schooling between the ages of 6–15, followed by a further three optional years. There is a school in every settlement, a teacher training college in Nuuk, several vocational schools and, as mentioned above, a university. Greenlandic is the official language used in schools. This contrasts with the 1950s, 1960s and 1970s, when educational instruction was in Danish. Competence in the Danish language was also seen by many Inuit as a way of achieving social and economic equality with Danes. As instruction in Danish became more widespread in schools, owing in part to the large number of Danish teachers working in Greenland, more young Inuit had a bilingual education. The dominance of Danish in the education system, in both teaching and administration, was supported by a policy and prevailing attitude that Inuit should learn Danish as a prerequisite for the successful development of their country. A myth was perpetuated that, because of the complexities of an agglutinative language, it was impossible for Danes to learn Greenlandic. This was in stark contrast to the earlier attitudes of missionaries and colonial administrators who were highly motivated to learn the language of the Inuit.

In many parts of Greenland today, especially in the smaller settlements which are predominantly monolingual, people remain critical of those outsiders who spend several years in the country, yet make no attempt to learn Greenlandic. Now, in the schools in the larger towns at least, Greenlandic children are educated through the medium of their own language. There is still a problem, however, in that many Danish teachers do not speak Greenlandic.

Health problems

The arrival of whalers, traders and other outsiders in Greenland, which marked the beginning of extensive contact, had a deleterious effect on the health of Inuit communities. The introduction of new diseases and the severity of epidemics undermined the social and spiritual fabric of Inuit life and virtually wiped out the population of some areas. But, although the devastation of whole communities by infectious diseases such as influenza and tuberculosis may be a thing of the past, Greenland Inuit now suffer from a range of health problems which are especially disturbing. Of pressing concern are patterns of infant mortality, high rates of suicide, psychological disorders, various forms of cancer, changes in dietary habits, and the spread of HIV and AIDS.

The infant mortality rate, for example, is five times higher in Greenland than in Denmark, with causes attributed to meningitis, diarrhoea, measles, respiratory infections and congenital malformations,[18] while chronic bronchitis, ischaemic heart disease, lung cancer and cerebrovascular disease account for a large number of adult deaths.[19] Deaths as a result of accidents are also common, especially in the settlements where hunting and fishing are the main activities. Changes in dietary habits also account for health problems, and disorders ranging from heart disease to tooth caries can be attributed in part to an increased reliance on imported foodstuffs high in carbohydrates. In the traditional hunting communities, where people rely more on seal meat, whale meat and various kinds of fish and sea birds, there are lower rates of heart disease. This is probably due to the fact that the traditional Inuit diet is high in polyunsaturated fats.

As well as infectious illnesses and degenerative diseases, a variety of social and psychological health problems give cause for concern. Studies of substance abuse among children aged between 12–19, for example, have shown an extensive and increased use of alcohol, tobacco, marijuana, and a rising trend in the sniffing of glue and lighter-gas.[20] It has been argued that social and economic changes, such as demographic composition, urbanization, and changes in family life and socialization practices, have contributed to the rising trends in suicide, alcoholism and substance abuse.[21]

The modern health problems experienced by Greenlanders seem to correspond with those experienced elsewhere in industrialized and developing countries. Work on childrearing practices and kinship networks in traditional Inuit society suggests that suicide and psychological problems are more likely to occur in social contexts where individuals are isolated and alienated from kin and friends.[22] Recent studies of contemporary life in small hunting settlements in Greenland have also demonstrated that when the person is integrated in a wide and supportive network of interpersonal relationships, there is a lower incidence of social and psychological problems.[23] The same studies argue that modernization in Greenland has had severe implications for kinship patterns and that changes in social structure have resulted in changing personal identities.

Before the days of Home Rule, the Danish government was responsible for the administration of the Greenland Health Service, which was supervised by the Chief Medical Officer. Part of the responsibility of the Chief Medical Oficer was to monitor diseases and health conditions, and to oversee programmes of prevention of infectious diseases. The administrative centre in each district was equipped with a small hospital that could provide primary health care, and the outlying settlements were visited several times a year by the district doctor. Doctors and most medical staff came from Denmark. The hospital in Nuuk functioned as a referral hospital and patients who could not be treated in Greenland were sent to hospital in Copenhagen. As of 1 January 1992, the Home Rule Authorities have administered the Health Service. All hospital treatment and the prescription of drugs and medicines are free. In the future, it is hoped that greater medical specialization will be available in Nuuk, with the result that fewer people will have to be flown to Copenhagen for treatment. At present, the lack of available health care for serious illnesses in remoter areas often means that, when a patient has to be flown to Nuuk or Copenhagen, it is harder for the patient's family to be kept informed of their situation and progress. Telephone communication is often poor and the high cost of air travel both within Greenland and to Denmark makes visiting prohibitive.[24]

The spread of AIDS is one of the most pressing contemporary concerns regarding the future health of Inuit communities. The first HIV cases were diagnosed in Greenland in 1984. Based on the latest figures available at the time of writing, there were 37 people diagnosed as HIV-positive and five known cases of AIDS.[25] These figures may seem relatively insignificant compared to statistics from other countries, but given that the total population of Greenland in 1991 was 55,533 this gives a ratio of one HIV-positive case to every 1,500 persons.[26]

There is a high incidence of other sexually transmitted diseases in Greenland and other circumpolar areas. Studies of Inuit sexual behaviour have shown that Inuit have their first sexual experiences in their early teens and have regular and different partners. Given this, the potential for rapid transmission of HIV and the possibility of an AIDS epidemic in the Arctic is worrying. This situation was discussed at the Circumpolar Meeting on AIDS Prevention, held in Greenland in the town of Ilulissat in September 1989, and organized by the International Union of Circumpolar Health and the World Health Organization.[27] Since 1986 the Greenland Health Service has run programmes on AIDS education and campaigns for AIDS prevention. Surveillance of other sexually transmitted diseases is of a high standard and, therefore, it is hoped the spread of HIV can be monitored and future trends predicted.

There is growing recognition that anthropological research is needed to supplement medical research in order to contribute to an awareness of the cultural factors and sexual norms that increase the risk of spreading HIV in Greenland, and indeed in other parts of the circumpolar north. One aspect of the spread of AIDS that has not been seri-ously addressed is the cultural impact it may have in Greenland. There is evidence from other parts of the world to suggest that people with AIDS-related illnesses have been victimized, perhaps because the wider society generally places the responsibility for the cause of AIDS on the individuals themselves.[28] This has the effect of social and economic discrimination, which leads invariably to the isolation and alienation of the individual. The Inuit have tended to be labelled as promiscuous by foreign medical practitioners and researchers, but such external per-ceptions of promiscuity tend to obscure cultural meanings regarding sexual behaviour.

While the threat from AIDS is not to be taken lightly, health offi-cials are aware that they should assess and consider the possible effects that moralistic AIDS discourse could have, and whether AIDS could result in social conflict and prejudice. Indeed, one of the recommenda-tions of the Circumpolar Meeting on AIDS Prevention was that AIDS-related policy in the various circumpolar countries should recog-nize human rights and avoid discrimination.[29] The spread of HIV and the development of AIDS in the circumpolar north illustrate how the recent past and certainly the future of Inuit and other indigenous peo-ples are inextricably bound up in a wider world context.

The cultural significance of subsistence hunting

Despite the development of capital-intensive fishing along the west coast, subsistence hunting continues to underpin the social economy of many communities in the districts of Uummannaq, Upernavik and Thule in the northwest of the country, and in Tasiilaq and Ittoqqor-toormiit on the east coast. In these areas hunting households remain primarily units of production and consumption and people rely on the harvesting of marine mammals, especially seals, as the sole or princi-pal occupation. In particular, non-migratory ringed seals (*Phoca hispida*), harp seals (*Pagophilus groenlandicus*), hooded seals (*Cystophora cristata*) and bearded seals (*Erignathus barbatus*) are hunted. In add-ition, beluga (*Delphinapterus leucas*), minke whales (*Balaenoptera acu-torostra*), narwhals (*Monodon monoceros*), walrus (*Odebenus rosmarus*) and certain species of small cetacea and seabirds are also harvested. The latter include guillemots (*Uria lomvia*), eider ducks (*Somateria mol-lisima*), little auks (*Plotus alle*), barnacle geese (*Branta leucopsis*) and kit-tiwakes (*Rissa tridactyla*). Subsistence fishing is also of importance and people fish most commonly for char (*Salvelinus alpinus*), Greenland halibut (*Rheinhardtius hippoglossoides*), Atlantic salmon (*Salmo salar*), capelin (*Mallotus villosus*), cod (*Gadus morrhua*), catfish (*Anarhichas minor*), scuplins (*Acanthocottus scorpius*), tomcod (*Boreogadus saida*) and Greenland shark (*Somniosus microcephalus*).

Apart from those districts where hunting remains the principal mode of occupation, subsistence activities are carried out by a significant number of people who live elsewhere in Greenland. While commercial fishing is dominant from Disko Bay in central West Greenland, down to the Nanortalik area in the far south, the hunting of seals and other sea mammals is important all along the west coast either as a full-time occupational activity or as a supplement to wage labour.

In the settlements of Disko Bay, for example, seal hunting is the main occupational activity for many people. The hunting of beluga whales is also of great economic and cultural importance, and takes place during two seasons of the year, in spring and autumn. As well as having nutritional and economic importance, people attribute ideological and symbolic value to the beluga hunt, and it remains vital for the cultural viability of communities.[30] But whaling is not only confined to the settlements of the west coast, it is also an activity in which people from the towns engage themselves. For example, in the town of Qerqertarsuaq on Disko Island, Inuit continue to hunt for minke whales;[31] narwhals and beluga are hunted from Sisimiut northwards; and small cetacea such as harbour porpoise are caught either in nets or from small boats in southwest Greenland.

The cultural significance of subsistence hunting extends to that part of the Inuit population that does not hunt, or lacks the means and ability to hunt. The procurement, sharing and consumption of *kalaalimernit* (Greenlandic food, i.e. hunting and fishing products) provide a fundamental grounding for the continuity of Inuit culture and identity throughout Greenland. The recent development of a commercial sale of Greenlandic hunting and fishing products, both individually and through the KNI (the Home Rule Authority trade company), allows people who do not hunt or fish easy access to *kalaalimernit*.

Occupational hunters in the large towns along the west coast, such as Nuuk, Qaqortoq, Ilulissat and Paamiut, who hunt primarily for cash sell their products either to the KNI or privately from open air stalls known as *kalaaliminerniarfiit*, or more commonly as the *kalaaliaraq*. The *kalaaliaraq* is usually found down at the harbour and consists of one or two stalls where, depending on the area and according to seasonal availability, one can purchase seal meat, caribou meat, seabirds such as guillemots and eider ducks, and fish such as salmon, halibut, catfish and char. While hunting products such as seal meat and seal blubber, frozen *mattak* (whale and narwhal skin), frozen whale meat and *nikkut* (dried whale meat) are available in KNI shops, many people prefer to buy fresh *kalaalimernit* direct from hunters and fishermen at the *kalaaliaraq*. What needs to be explored for the future is whether the *kalaaliaraq* can provide the basis for small-scale sustainable community development.

But subsistence hunting has not escaped international opposition. In the late 1970s, North American and European anti-sealing protests, which were originally directed towards the commercial harvesting of harp and hooded seal pups off Atlantic Canada, were extended to include Inuit sealing. Opposition from Greenpeace and other environmental groups led to an EC ban on the import of sealskins and other sealskin products into EC member countries from 1983, a ban which was extended indefinitely in 1989.[32] Although the ban does exempt the importing of sealskins from adult seals hunted in Greenland, the market has effectively collapsed and social problems in some parts of Greenland have intensified. As many hunting families in small settlements rely on the sale of sealskins for their only source of income in an increasingly cash-oriented economy, this has placed a severe strain on their ability to meet basic needs.

Although Greenpeace International have since withdrawn their opposition to Inuit sealing, there remain many other animal rights organizations who continue their campaigns. The Inuit response has been one that regards anti-hunting campaigns as part of an 'unceasing missionary drive at the heart of western civilization toward the rest of humanity'.[33] Because seal hunting has social, cosmological and ideological importance for the Inuit, the animal rights campaign is seen primarily as an attack, not on the subsistence economy, but on Inuit culture.

The sale of hunting products in Greenland has also brought criticism from anti-sealing and anti-whaling groups who claim that hunting has undergone a transition from a purely subsistence activity to something that has more of a commercial rationale. Animal rights groups have argued that cash and the use of modern technology have removed subsistence hunting from its traditional context and have radically altered the customary ideology of subsistence.[34] These criticisms are perhaps unjust, and demonstrate a profound misunderstanding of the way of life of Inuit in the modern world. In the hunting districts in Greenland today, as far as sealing is concerned, changes in technology have not altered the cultural, emotional and spiritual interplay between the human and animal worlds.[35] Although money is very much a part of the subsistence economy it is not necessarily inconsistent with it or harmful to traditional modes of subsistence. Indeed, money has been incorporated into an already flexible and variable range of subsistence techniques. Money is a supplement to, and indeed helps sustain, subsistence hunting in many small hunting settlements in Greenland, where it is also part of a symbolically constructed framework emphasizing social and economic continuity.

Those who argue that subsistence hunting, because of the trade and cash elements, now has more of a commercial nature do so from a perspective that regards money as previously having had no part to play in traditional hunting societies. The stereotype is of pristine hunter-gatherers living in isolation from other cultural groups. The revisionist perspective in hunter-gatherer studies has recently sought to address the issue of isolated hunting societies, by arguing that extensive trade, barter and contact with other peoples have been a characteristic feature of hunter-gatherer societies, for several centuries in some instances. Recent research has demonstrated that many hunter-gatherer societies have a cash economy that is central to, and is important for supplementing, their subsistence activities.[36]

In small Greenland Inuit hunting settlements, meat from seals and other marine mammals is not regarded as a commodity but as something which is inalienable, containing an element of the giver when it is shared or given away as a gift. When meat from the hunt is shared it expresses the relationships people share with each other and cements bonds of kinship and close social association. Identity is founded upon, and derives meaning from, a complex network of shared relations, not only between persons, but between persons and animals.

The environment and Inuit resource management

In traditional Inuit society unwritten rules and regulations underpinned the subsistence economy, informing hunters how to act in relation to animals and the environment. With no tradition of formal or institutionalized leadership rules in small communities, those who were responsible for passing down knowledge about hunting were known as *piniartorssuit* ('great hunters'), people recognized as having skill and prowess in hunting, together with a deep understanding of animals, the weather and the environment. While subsistence in the hunting districts is still guided and informed by traditional unwritten regulations, these are becoming formalized by the municipal authorities in each district.

However, subsistence hunting is under increased regulation from the Home Rule Authorities, who have been placing greater emphasis on environmental protection strategies in recent years. The Home Rule Authorities regard this as necessary if the human use of renewable resources in Greenland is to be sustainable and thus possible for future generations. The legal right to hunt is dependent on the individual holding a hunting licence allocated by the municipal authorities. *Green* licences are required by those people who are defined by the Home Rule Authorities as occupational hunters, i.e. their sole or principal occupation is hunting. *Red* hunting licences are issued to people who wish to hunt and fish part-time. These are people who live mainly in the towns, rather than the smaller settlements, and who do most of their hunting and fishing at weekends or during holidays. Danes living in Greenland can also obtain this kind of licence. As regards other legislation, the Home Rule Authorities decide on the percentage of Greenlanders employed on all trawlers fishing in Greenlandic waters, the allocation of shrimp quotas in all districts and the regulation of the caribou hunting season, and, in collaboration with the International Whaling Commission, they play a role in the regulation of fin and minke whale hunting.

Because of concern over possible global warming, increased atmospheric pollution and ozone depletion, the Arctic is regarded as a critical zone for global environmental change not only by scientists, but by Inuit themselves. Environmental agencies have stressed the need to design appropriate resource management systems and environmental protection strategies. Yet, science-based resource management systems designed to safeguard wildlife and the environment in the Arctic often ignore the perspectives of those Inuit communities that depend on hunting and fishing.

In order to safeguard the future of Inuit resource use, the Home Rule Authorities have begun to outline and put into practice their own environmental strategies and policies. From an Inuit perspective, threats to wildlife and the environment do not come from hunting, but from airborne and seaborne pollutants, such as cesium isotopes, sulphuric acid, lead and mercury, entering the Arctic biosphere from industrial centres far to the south. Threats to the Greenland environment also come from the impact of non-renewable resource extraction, such as hydrocarbon development. In setting out to counteract such threats, the Greenland Inuit have claimed the right for international recognition as resource conservationists, and have begun to use indigenous knowledge as political action.

Full jurisdiction over environmental issues had been transferred from Denmark to the Home Rule Authorities by January 1989, and in 1991 the environment, which had previously been the responsibility of the Department of Fisheries and Industry, became the concern of the new Department of Health and the Environment. The Greenlandic Parliament passed the country's first Environmental Protection Act in

1988, and this became effective in January 1989. As a result there has been much recent environmental legislation, together with research on the human use of renewable and non-renewable resources by Inuit themselves. This marks a significant turn-about from the days when this kind of research was carried out exclusively by Danish and other foreign institutions. The Home Rule Authorities regard environmental issues as the concern of the indigenous Inuit and consider it essential that local knowledge guides and informs the directing of research on natural resources.

Regulation, such as the working out of quotas and seasonal limits, is considered important for sustainable use, and in 1988 the Greenland Parliament also passed legislation concerned with the protection of wildlife most commonly harvested by local communities. In particular, protected seasons for birds such as common eiders, Brunnich's guillemot and white-fronted geese have been imposed. Caribou reserves have been designated along parts of the west coast, while outside of these reserves there is an open caribou hunting season from the beginning of August until the end of September. Similarly, the hunting of musk-ox is confined to the same period (and to four weeks during early winter). The hunting of polar bears is strictly regulated and confined to subsistence purposes only, but there is an open season from the beginning of September until the end of June.

While the hunting of seals and small cetaceans is not regulated, whaling is under increased scrutiny from the International Whaling Commission (IWC). While acknowledging the importance of subsistence whaling for Inuit, the IWC has not allowed it to continue unregulated. In recent years, the IWC has not only focused its attention on regulating commercial whaling carried out by nations such as Japan, Norway and Iceland, but has been concerned with the exploitation of the humpback whale by Greenland Inuit, the Beaufort Sea bowhead whale by Alaskan Inupiat and Yup'ik Eskimos, and the Eastern Pacific grey whale hunted by Siberian Inuit. Since 1985 the IWC has not allocated any quota for humpback whaling in Greenland, but the hunting of both minke and fin whales by Greenland Inuit is subject to a quota system. The hunting of beluga whales and narwhals, which takes place mainly in Greenland and the Canadian East Arctic, is not currently regulated, but a real possibility exists that a quota system may be imposed in the future.

The IWC quota system for the hunting of minke and fin whales in Greenland is monitored closely by the Home Rule Authorities who distribute the IWC quotas after consultation with KNAPK (Kalaallit Nunaat Aalisartut Piniartullu Kattufiat: the Greenland Association of

Fishermen and Hunters), an organization which represents the interests of all those dependent on hunting and fishing for a living. The municipal authorities are then responsible for distributing their share of the quota to individual whaling vessels. It is incumbent on the municipal authorities to inform the Home Rule Authorities about the numbers of whales caught as well as struck but not killed, and about any infringements of the whaling regulations. In turn, the Home Rule Authorities are responsible for providing the IWC with an annual report on all whaling activities in Greenland, and this forms the basis for the working out of the quota for the following year.[37]

KNAPK is able to present the case for the continuity of subsistence whaling in Greenland at the annual meetings of the IWC. KNAPK challenges the scientific knowledge that the IWC uses to work out its regulatory policies as inaccurate, and carries out its own whale counts, as well as participating with scientists from the IWC. Both the IWC and the Inuit agree that sound management programmes cannot be implemented without sufficient knowledge about the size and distribution of whale populations, together with a greater understanding of their exploitation. To ensure an adequate participatory approach to the management of subsistence whaling, and that any decisions made by the IWC ultimately take into account the subsistence, nutritional and cultural needs of local communities in Greenland, Inuit organizations stress the importance of undertaking more use-based research. Much work needs to be done and the Home Rule Authorities have outlined their own research strategies which give priority to understanding all aspects of contemporary subsistence hunting in Greenland. Research programmes that aim to gather as much information as possible on the Inuit use of natural resources are already under way, with Greenlandic and foreign anthropologists, biologists and other scientists working in close collaboration with local people.

Prospects for the future

In the immediate future, it seems that threats to Inuit cultural survival in Greenland will centre on the exploitation of marine mammals and the importance of hunting for Arctic coastal communities. The animal rights campaign, for example, shows no sign of relenting and there are real fears that that it will continue to undermine the subsistence economy.[38] Furthermore, the International Whaling Commission has been accused of moving away from its original role as a regulatory body towards an anti-whaling stance.[39] Subsistence whaling faces increased regulation as a result, placing Greenland Inuit under even more pressure to defend subsistence hunting. This defence relies on an ability to increase international awareness of indigenous rights and to impress upon international environmental agencies that a participatory appr-oach to environmental management is the only way forward. The Greenland Inuit are therefore challenging the assumed right of inter-national organizations to determine what Inuit can and cannot hunt.

This is made possible partly by and with the support of the Inuit Circumpolar Conference (ICC). The ICC is a pan-Arctic organization that represents the interests of Inuit in Greenland, Canada, Alaska and Siberia. Formed in Alaska in 1977, in response to increased oil and gas-based development in the Arctic, the ICC has had non-governmental status at the United Nations since 1983. Challenging the policies of governments, multinational corporations and environ-mental movements, the ICC has argued that the protection of the Arc-tic environment and its resources should recognize indigenous rights and be in accordance with Inuit tradition and cultural values.

In 1985 the ICC set up its own Environmental Commission (ICCEC) which formulated the Inuit Regional Conservation Strategy. This out-lined how best to design and implement sustainable resource manage-ment programmes that take into account the subsistence and cultural needs of Inuit communities. Basically, the Inuit Regional Conservation strategy aims to secure for the Inuit the rights to hunt and fish in tra-ditional areas, and to preserve and protect living resources and so ensure the subsistence needs of future generations. Such a conserva-tion strategy can only be effective, however, if there is adequate knowledge of resources and their use, and of Inuit environmental val-ues. Recognizing this, the ICC gives priority to the collection of infor-mation from scientific sources and from local hunters and fishermen, and has established a database on renewable resources. This requires the participation of Inuit communities and organizations throughout the Arctic.

The picture regarding the Greenland Inuit, then, is as follows. Despite several centuries of contact and colonial rule, Inuit in Greenland have shown resilience in lifestyle and identity. Much of this has been in the face of applied government policy. The Greenland Inuit have emerged in a position of self-determination which has allowed them a greater role in shaping their own social and economic development. In estab-lishing relations with the wider world, Greenland has chosen to focus on the issue of environmental protection and indigenous rights. Green-land has not only set a precedent for indigenous self-determination, the Inuit population also has a greater degree of decision-making power concerning environmental management than any other aboriginal people. As land rights and questions of access to resources are often at the very centre of self-determination movements, the Greenland Inuit can perhaps make claims to be in the vanguard of indigenous rights.

However, the Greenland economy is weak and in order to develop and survive in the future, the Home Rule Authorities will probably have to defer to increased domestic and international pressure to exploit the country's resource base. This will present the Home Rule Authorities with a dilemma: how best to reconcile the interests of the Inuit population with the need for increased revenue from resource development and the further social and economic changes this will entail?

2

NATIVE PEOPLES OF THE RUSSIAN FAR NORTH

by Nikolai Vakhtin

Introduction

The 'Northern Minorities' is an official term used to describe the 26 peoples who live in a vast territory covering about 45 per cent of the former USSR and 58 per cent of the new Russian state. This land encompasses almost all of Siberia and stretches along the coastline of the Arctic Ocean from the White Sea in the west to the Bering Strait in the east, including Kamchatka and the island of Sakhalin. Thus 'the North', according to most definitions, measures about 11.1 million sq. km. and is, by comparison, substantially larger than the United States including Alaska.

The environment

The lands of the Northern Minorities are crossed by several great rivers including the Ob', Enisey, Lena, Kolyma and Amur, and are divided into three separate climatic zones: tundra (Arctic plain, where the subsoil is frozen), forest-tundra and taiga (coniferous forest). The forested region contains elk, bears, squirrels, hares, foxes, martens, ermine and a variety of birds but, further northwards, the forest gives way to tundra between latitude 66° and 70°N. The latter has relatively few species of fauna: reindeer, Arctic foxes, lemmings, snowy owls, ptarmigan, various ducks and geese, several species of salmon as well as fishes similar to those of the forest area.

Summers are short and cool, while winters are long, dark and sometimes extremely cold, especially away from the sea. Winter temperatures of the eastern coast (in Chukotka and Kamchatka) as well as those of the westernmost part (close to the Norwegian border) are

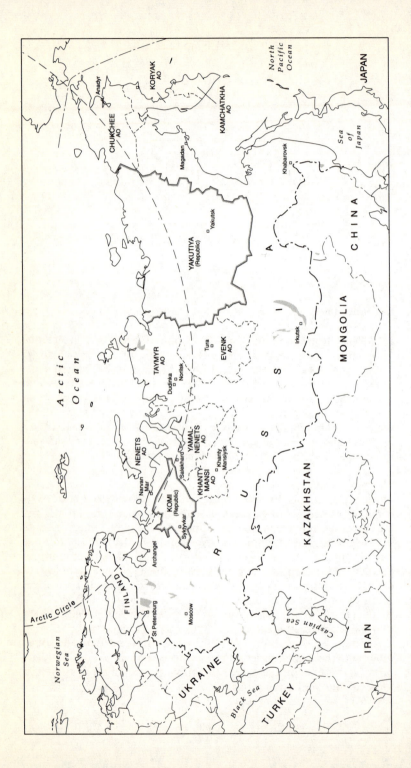

relatively mild. Yet deeper into the land mass (in continental Chukotka and Yakutiya) the mean January temperatures often reach -50°C,
with a maximum of -70°C recorded in Verkhoyansk and Oymyakon.
Summer temperatures of +30°C are common.[1]

The people

The phrase 'Northern Minorities' is more of a metaphor than a scholarly term and was first introduced into Soviet legislation by two
decrees of the Central Executive Committee and the Council of People's Commissars of the USSR in 1925 and 1926. Yet, like 'American
Indians' or 'Africans', it covers very different ethnic groups which
archaeological sources prove have been living in this area for thousands of years and which, in the past, had different subsistence strategies, cultures, mythologies and languages.

Traditionally, there were two main types of economy: reindeer herding, mostly in the tundra; and fishing and hunting in the forest, tundra and the sea. Reindeer herders were nomadic, while hunters and
fishers either were permanent settlers or wandered within a limited
territory on a seasonal basis. Although culturally very diverse, in the
past the Northern Minorities adapted to the climate and seasons so
that a Chukchee herder obtained everything he needed from his
reindeer, an Eskimo sea-hunter extracted as much from the sea, a
Nivkh fisherman managed to find all that was necessary from fishing
and hunting.

The houses of the nomads were movable and made of deerskins while
the fishermen and sea-hunters lived either in tents made of tree bark, or
in semi-subterranean huts covered by skins, or earth and moss. All the
peoples used animal skins (deer, fox, wolf, seal, etc.) to make their
clothes, and these differed very much in style and design. Transport was
by deer- or dog-sledge although some would also ride on deer back.

The languages spoken belong to different language families: Tungus-
Manchu, Finno-Ugric, Turkic and Paleo-Siberian. Many of these
languages are linguistic isolates (having no known genetic relations)
and none of them are related to Russian in any way.

Today

This chapter, in spite of its brevity, attempts to cover all the 26 Northern Minorities, each with their own history, problems and characteristics. All the Northern peoples share one common feature that makes
writing a general account of them a necessity: today, in the 1990s,
they live in a situation that can best be described as an 'ethnic
catastrophe'.

Contact with an industrial state has caused this disaster (and has been responsible for similar extreme problems all over the circumpolar north) but, in the case of the Northern Minorities, the consequences were increased tenfold by the incompetent, unthinking and often even criminal policy of the totalitarian state which held complete control over the situation for 70 years.

The Northern Minorities, of course, were not the only people to suffer from this policy for it affected the whole country, every man and woman, every social and ethnic group. Indeed, some groups may have suffered more than others, if it is possible to compare sufferings at all, but the problem of the Northern Minorities was that they were, and still are, extremely vulnerable because of their fragile environment and small numbers and because of certain cultural characteristics they possessed. This is why, although they were never an object of deliberate suppression, the situation they find themselves in today is so desperate.

In spite of this very difficult situation, the Northern Minorities still exist. They continue to live in their traditional territories; they still retain close bonds with their land; they still keep, at least in some places, their traditional cultures and languages and they still retain a right to be called human beings and to have human rights.

However, this chapter argues that individual human rights are insufficient in their case. They need group rights, special attention, special protection and very strong affirmative action policies.

Names and numbers
Different sources give different lists of names for the Northern Minority groups. This unstable terminology reflects changes in knowledge so that, for example, during the 19th and early 20th Centuries, different 'external' names, chance names and nicknames were widely in use instead of the self-appellations which are now commonly, although not consistently, used. (See Table 1.)

Officially, 26 Northern Minorities are recognized but it is difficult to be exact since there are no reliable criteria to distinguish between a 'people', a 'tribe', an 'ethnos' and an 'ethnic group'. Linguistic criteria do not help either: it is impossible to distinguish between a language and a dialect when discussing a language with no written form.

Today, the accepted official nomenclature of the Northern Minorities, and of their languages, no longer matches the level of our knowledge. Groups that are described as one 'people' often live thousands of kilometres away from each other in completely different environments and, moreover, may not even know of each other's existence (Yukagirs

TABLE 1

Official names and self-appellations

Official names, variants of names and self-appellations[1]

Aleuts,[2] Unangans
Chukchee, Luoravetlans, Oravedlans, Chawchuwats
Chuvans
Dolgans, Sakhas
Entsy,[3] Enneche, Yenisey Samoyeds, Madu
Eskimos,[4] Yupigyts, Yuits
Evenks, Orochons, Tungus
Evens,[5] Lamuts
Itel'mens, Kamchadals
Kets, Yenisey Ostyaks
Khants,[6] Khante, Ostyaks
Koryaks,[7] Nymylans, Chavchuvens
Mansi, Voguls
Nanais, Nani, Gol'ds
Negidals, El'kan Beyenin, Elkembeys
Nenets,[8] Hasava, Yuraks, Samoyeds
Nganasans, Nya, Tavgiyan Samoyeds, Tavgiyans
Nivkhi,[9] Gilyaks
Orochi, Orochili, Nani
Oroks, Ul'ta, Ul'cha
Saami, Lopars
Sel'kups,[10] Ostyak-Samoyeds
Tofalars, Tofa, Tokha, Tufa, Karagas
Udege, Udekhe, Ude
Ul'chi, Nani, Nanei
Yukagirs,[11] Oduls, Vaduls

FROM: *Indigenous Peoples of the Soviet North*, IWGIA, Document 67, Copenhagen, 1990, p. 13; *Etnicheskoye razvitiye narodnostey Severa v Sovetskiy period*, Nauka Publishers, Moscow, 1987, pp. 67, 101.

NOTES

1 The list sometimes includes Shors but excludes the Yakuts and Komi.
2 Actually two groups and two languages.
3 Several subgroups and dialects.
4 Three groups and three languages (one nearly extinct).
5 Several subgroups and dialects.
6 Two groups and two groups of dialects.
7 Several subgroups, speaking closely related languages (Alyutor, Karagin, etc.).
8 Several subgroups, speaking different dialects.
9 Several subgroups, speaking languages that are not mutually understood.
10 Several subgroups and several languages.
11 Two groups and two languages.

TABLE 2
**Numbers of Northern Minorities according to
the censuses of 1926, 1959, 1989**

	1926	1959	1989
Aleuts	3,534	421	702
Chukchee	12,332	11,727	15,184
Chuvans	705	–	1,511
Dolgans	656	3,934	6,932
Entsy	482	–	209
Eskimos	1,293	1,118	1,719
Evenks	38,805	24,710	30,163
Evens	2,044	8,121	17,199
Itel'mens	859	1,109	2,481
Kets	1,428	1,019	1,113
Khants	17,334	19,410	22,521
Koryaks	7,439	6,287	9,242
Mansi	6,095	6,449	8,461
Nanais	5,860	8,026	12,023
Negidals	683	350	622
Nenets	16,217	23,007	34,665
Nganasans	867	748	1,278
Nivkhi	4,076	3,717	4,673
Orochi	647	782	915
Oroks	162	–	190
Saami	1,720	1,792	1,890
Sel'kups	1,630	3,768	3,621
Tofalars	415	–	–
Udege	1,357	1,444	2,011
Ul'chi	723	2,055	3,233
Yukagirs	443	442	1,142

FROM: *Indigenous Peoples of the Soviet North*, IWGIA, 1990: p.13; *Etnicheskoye razvitiye*,
1987, pp.67, 101.

are the most striking example). Also, they often speak languages that are not mutually understood. On the other hand, common self-appellations often help different groups to keep a common identity: this is true for the Evenks of southeast Yakutiya and for different groups of Nenets.

Two other indigenous groups should be mentioned. The Yakuts and Komi are usually excluded from the list of Northern Minorities because they are much larger than the others, and also because they possess their own autonomous republics within Russia. However, they do share some characteristics with the 26 smaller groups.

As with the names of the different Northern Minorities, 19th Century data about numerical strength is reliable for very few tribes and should be referred to with caution. However, statistical sources, beginning with Patkanov's work in 1911 and using the very detailed analyses by anthropologists working at the Siberian Department of the Institute of Ethnography in Moscow,[2] do allow for a fairly accurate picture of the population dynamic during this period.

It was not until the census of 1926 that relatively sound statistical information could be found on the Northern Minorities. According to this document, the total 'Northern' population (those living in a vast area of over seven million sq. km.) was 124,625.[3]

By the 1959 census, the size of the Northern Minorities was 131,436 (about 0.1 per cent of the population of the ex-USSR). The 1989 census gives the total strength as 183,700 (0.06 per cent of the total population of the ex-USSR). (See Table 2.)

The coming of the Russians

'Siberia is sometimes regarded as a country originally peopled by political exiles and criminals.'

M. Czaplicka, 1914

There are few serious Soviet historical studies of the peoples classified as 'Northern Minorities', or of the area they inhabit. The material that does exist is largely pseudo-scholarly speculation outlining their supposed rapid and consistent development which allegedly began immediately after the October Revolution of 1917 and quickly brought them from a stone age environment to a technologically advanced and flourishing economic, social and cultural condition, in line with the rest of the country.

This perspective arbitrarily splits the history of the Northern Minorities into the same periods as Soviet history: the Revolution of 1917; the Collectivization of 1929–33; the Patriotic War of 1941–5 and so on.[4] However, in order to understand the contemporary situation of the native peoples of the North it is necessary to go much further back in time than 1917, and also to use very different criteria to outline the changes in their experience.

Without this longer historical viewpoint, it is not possible to see how they came to be in the catastrophic situation they are facing today, nor is it possible to explore constructive solutions which might enable them to find a new and more positive role.

Russian colonization

Before the 16th Century, the native peoples of the far North had no contact with Europeans. It was only around the 1550s that the first fur traders and cossacks penetrated the area east of the Ural mountains, which form a natural borderline between Europe and Asia. Russians, and others in the service of Russia, made a spectacular advance across Siberia from the Urals to the Pacific between 1580 and 1640 – a distance of 5,000 km. in 60 years. This conquest of north Asia was accomplished more by a process of infiltration than by military action[5] but nevertheless the whole process had great impact on the life and fate of the indigenous population.

By the 17th Century, the Russians knew, under various names, the ancestors of all the ethnic groups now living in the far North; by the end of the 18th Century, settlements of Russian peasants, hunters, sailors and merchants, located mostly along large rivers, were covering the vast territory, including the coast of Alaska.

The Russian annexations of the first 200 years did not lead to any noticeable decrease in the numbers of native peoples. The main goal of the central government, as well as of the local authorities and private merchants, was not to wipe out the tribespeople but to turn them into reliable suppliers of tribute, mostly in the form of furs. Trade with the Russians, however, greatly affected some traditional economies. From reindeer breeding, hunting and fishing many of the native peoples shifted gradually to fur hunting and trapping in order to exchange the furs for industrial goods at the trading stations. Others developed a much larger-scale reindeer-breeding economy which had not previously existed. (Reindeer were bred for meat, skins, fat and transport. Their skins were used for clothes and tents and their fat for heating, fuel for lamps and food.)[6]

In its encroachment on native peoples and their land, Russian colonialism therefore showed similarities to that in other parts of the world. Some native groups willingly became subjects of the Russian Empire, seeking from Russian military forces protection against their neighbours, while others opposed the intruders, either by abandoning their territories and moving away, or by armed resistance. Contrary to commonly accepted opinion within Russia, however, the Russians demonstrated racial prejudice and treated their subject peoples no more kindly than did other colonial powers.

Traditional tribal organization underwent deep changes during this period and many ancient social institutions were changed. In the 17th and 18th Centuries there were migrations and population shifts both within single ethnic groups and between several of them[7] but, as a rule, these migrations were not accompanied by military clashes.

The ethnographic map of Siberia therefore changed and became much more complex in the 400 years from the early period of Russian contact to the beginning of the 20th Century. Those areas occupied by tundra Nenets, Chukchee, Evenks and Evens grew noticeably, while Entsy, Yukagirs, Koryaks, Itel'mens and Eskimos lost much of their territory. In general, the groups who lived on fishing and hunting lost land, while nomadic reindeer breeders gained it.[8]

19th Century administration

From the 17th to the 19th Centuries, administration of the native peoples was carried out by a system of governors, through local chiefs and elders. The responsibility of the elders included judicial, policing and fiscal functions, as well as collecting the fur tribute. In practice, the tribes were thrown upon the mercy of the Siberian administration which, even compared to that of European Russia, was notorious for its embezzlement of state property and for violence.[9]

During 1819–20, Mikhail Speransky, the closest adviser at that time to Emperor Alexander I and the author of the first liberal reform plan for Russia, devised the 'Code of Indigenous Administration'. The code, which became law in 1822, was, by the standards of its time, an exceptional legal document in which an attempt was made to protect by law the native population of the land that was being colonized and to give those who were settled the same rights as Russian peasants. It also showed a sincere desire to preserve the native economy against Russian capitalism and to protect the original culture.

During the course of the 19th Century, numerous amendments were made to the code in attempts to improve it. Finally, in 1892, all these were amalgamated into the 'Statute of the Indigenous Peoples'[10], which remained in effect until the 1917 Revolution.

Unfortunately, though, the implementation of the law lagged far behind its adoption. In particular, the government failed to limit the wave of Russian colonization by legal boundaries and Russians penetrated deeper and deeper into native territories, violating indigenous rights. Governmental officials had only limited knowledge of local conditions in the North and their honesty left much to be desired. Gradually, especially after Speransky retired, the protective measures receded and the administration took the side of the colonialists completely. Expropriations of indigenous land followed, often accompanied by violence and military clashes.

The law also failed to protect the minorities from exploitation by traders. For example, the fur merchants, who had real power in Siberia, often bartered with vodka for the goods offered by the indigenous peoples, and it was not long before the natives became addicted to alcohol and their impoverishment reached new depths.[11]

By the early 20th Century the situation in the North was relatively stable and the living conditions of most of the native peoples were generally hard. Although in theory they possessed various rights and privileges, in practice their actual rights were almost nil. Many therefore tried to preserve their way of life by escaping further to the north or east where there were no Russians: they would come out to the trading stations once or twice a year to exchange fur for powder, bullets, rifles, flour, salt, cloth, instruments, and then disappear again into remote tundra and taiga.

The poor conditions and general situation of the native peoples did, however, concern some of the Siberian intelligentsia who developed a school of thought called *Oblastnichestvo* ('Regionalism'), a political movement very popular in Siberia in the early 20th Century. The Regionalists supported Siberian self-government and the establishment of a Siberian regional parliament, arguing that it was impossible to implement a working system of representatives from the minorities in the state Parliament in Petersburg, at that time the capital of the Russian Empire. They therefore proposed the establishment of 'special territories', after the model of North American Indian or Australian Aboriginal reserves, where non-native settlements would be forbidden.[12] However, these ideas were not implemented.

Northern Minorities: 1917–1930

The first decade after the Bolshevik Revolution was an important one for the Northern Minorities. They were still subject to the laws of a foreign government and a foreign ideology but while some scholars and officials attempted to protect them, others saw them as ignorant and inferior and their lands as rich resources for the state. Several of the ideas and plans formed on their behalf during this period are still relevant today.

The Bolshevik Revolution of 1917

Many new laws were passed after the 1917 October Revolution when the Bolshevik Party, under Lenin's leadership, seized power. Some of these concerned the Northern Minorities and the most important of all from their point of view was passed in November 1917. Called the 'Declaration of Rights of the Peoples of Russia', it proclaimed the inalienable right for the 'free development of ethnic minorities and ethnographic groups that live within the territory of Russia'.[13] The 1918 Constitution also guaranteed 'equal rights to all the citizens, irrespective of their racial or ethnic affiliation'.[14]

During the Civil War (1918–23), Soviet power in the North was consolidated although the new government paid little attention to the native peoples. 'Soviets' (councils) were formed but in many areas the native population did not understand their function and, not without reason, saw them as a threat to their welfare.

By 1923, the dominance of the Soviet authorities was complete in most parts of the North. The former native administrative structures, together with all the organs of the former Tsarist administration, had been dismissed and the 'Statute of the Indigenous Peoples' had been abrogated.

The Committee of the North

After the 1917 Revolution, a special ministry called 'Narkomnatz' (People's Commissariat of Nationalities) was formed which was responsible for national affairs. Until 1924, Narkomnatz functioned as an administrative body ostensibly responsible for Northern affairs but it had no local structures of its own and hence no real authority. This was eloquently expressed in a report by the Yenisey Soviet in 1923:

> *'The natives live by exploiting the zoological resources, while the Russians live by exploiting the natives...The native people of the North live beyond the Constitution of the Russian Republic.'*[15]

In April 1923, mainly as a result of the persistent and patient efforts of Professor Vladimir Bogoraz, a distinguished anthropologist who had spent a decade in exile among the Northern Minorities, Narkomnatz recommended that a new body be established with the primary aim of helping the indigenous peoples towards equal rights. Thus, on 20 June 1924, the Presidium of the Central Executive Committee (the supreme governmental body of the USSR before 1936) voted to establish the 'Committee for Assisting the Peoples of the Far North', better known as the 'Committee of the North'. Its purpose was to 'define and to reserve the territories necessary for the life and cultural development of each ethnic group'.

The Committee of the North consisted of high-ranking government officials and scholars with the following organizational, planning and research functions:

- To investigate, develop and implement the measures necessary for economic progress in the region.
- To study the history, culture and everyday life of the Northern Minorities and to collect information about their needs.
- To investigate measures necessary to guard them against exploitation.
- To define the basic principles of an administrative and judicial system in the area.

In practice, the achievements of the Committee of the North were more modest because of insufficient funding and its work was eventually curtailed because of the growing power of totalitarian Communism. Nevertheless, it was made up of exceptionally knowledgeable and enthusiastic scholars who had an enormous influence on every aspect of the economic, cultural and social life in the North. Its journal, *Severnaya Asia*, contained brilliant studies of the lifestyle of the Northern Minorities.

Conservatives and Radicals

For the first ten years after the formation of the Committee of the North, all discussions about the social and legal status of the indigenous peoples concentrated, at first covertly and later quite openly, around the struggle between two main schools of thought which can be designated 'Conservative' and 'Radical'.[16]

The Conservatives had as their basic aim to protect the culture and way of life of the Northern Minorities from outside interference. This position was the essentially ethnographic and philanthropic view of many members of the Committee. However, the Radicals put class above nationality and had as their ultimate aim the elimination of ethnic distinctions and eventually the merging of all the ethnic groups in one 'Soviet people'. This was the official view of the ruling Communist Party.[17]

The main issue of controversy was the status of the territories populated by the Northern Minorities. Since the Conservative position was based primarily on a humanistic and respectful attitude towards the peoples and cultures of the Northern Minorities, it advocated their slow and gradual inclusion into the economic and social life of the rest of the country.

To achieve this, the Conservatives put forward a plan (similar to that of the Regionalists) that certain 'reserved' lands should be established on the same principle as the American Indian reserves.[18] These would be controlled by the central government but the traditional life of the Northern Minorities would be able to be sustained. At the same time, there was to be a ban on new settlers, both Russian and those belonging to other indigenous tribes, since the merging of the Russian and aboriginal population 'means death for the indigenous people'.[19] The territories were to be protected by special laws, such as a prohibition on sales of alcohol, restrictions on private trade, the organization of schools and medical services and allowances in the form of clothing and food. Education was to link closely to traditional life and activities. 'Nomadic' schools were proposed and teachers were to be recruited and trained from the tribes themselves.[20]

The Radicals, on the other hand, claimed that the supposed differences between the Northern Minorities and the majority population were not factually based and so their road to social progress should be similar to that of the country as a whole. Generally, the main objective of their 'Northern offensive' was to discover and exploit the natural and mineral resources of the area: timber, gold and, later, oil and gas. The aboriginal population was seen only as a means to this end and in fact were often considered to be 'savages', culturally inferior to the Russians. At the same time, the Radicals recognized that it was necessary to supply food to the minority peoples since they would not otherwise service, nor be able to help, the Russians to colonize the region. This position was formulated quite bluntly and explicitly in an article in 1925: 'all other problems of Northern Asia are inevitably subordinate, in some way or other, to the possibility of future industrial development'.[21]

At the beginning of its existence, the Committee of the North followed the Conservative position. This was only possible while the new Communist power was still weak and while it reluctantly tolerated those who advocated a cautious and gradual development policy for the North. However, in line with changes elsewhere in the USSR, the position of the Radicals had become stronger by the end of the 1920s. They urged an end to 'fussing over' the Northern Minorities, denied the necessity for 'special conditions' for their development and demanded immediate collectivization as well as a ruthless campaign against the *kulaks* (rich peasants) and shamans.

The Conservatives quickly retreated. They became resigned to the 'necessity' of Northern industrial development, mainly through imported labour from elsewhere in the USSR, but they still called for a parallel traditional economy for the indigenous peoples. They also advocated special protective measures and controls over the incoming stream of settlers in order to help the native population to 'reach the cultural level of the Russian population'.[22]

By 1929, the Conservatives had lost their previous influence on the Committee of the North. This was reflected in the change of tone of the articles in *Severnaya Asia* which became more like party slogans and less like academic research. They dealt almost exclusively with economic problems and the Northern Minorities were not mentioned. After 1931, *Severnaya Asia* ceased to exist.

Formation of Tribal Soviets

Constantly increasing pressure from the Communist Party leadership forced legislators to make desperate attempts to reconcile those models of land-tenure, administration and economy which they thought proper for the Northern Minority areas with party directives, Stalin's orders, party congress decisions and instructions from the ministries. It became ever more apparent that the ideals of the Conservatives and Radicals not only contradicted each other but were irreconcilable in principle: self-administration by small ethnic groups on the basis of common law and traditional culture could not coexist with a centralized totalitarian system of power. Thus, laws concerning administration in the Northern Minority areas became more ambiguous and compromising.

The 'Temporary Statute of Native Administration in the North of the USSR' and the 'Temporary Statute of Organization of the Court System in the North of the USSR' are examples of such laws.[23] According to their authors, the primary goal of these statutes was to allot rights of ownership and administration over a given area to the tribe(s) which had traditionally occupied it and, consequently, to secure the borders and solve territorial disputes both between tribes and, more importantly, between the indigenous population and the incoming settlers.

Administrative functions were handed over to organs of native administration:

1 The **Tribal Assembly** comprised all the adult members of the tribe who lived together in a given area. It met at least once a year with functions including elections to higher bodies and decision-making on issues of land usage, taxation and tribute, food supplies and so on.

2 The **Tribal Soviet**, the local administrative body, was elected for one year and consisted of three people. It had executive power over the tribal territory and judicial rights over the court cases

within the tribe and with neighbouring tribes. These cases dealt with such issues as marriage and family, inheritance, property and land usage issues.

3 The **Raion Congress** was a territory's supreme administrative body and consisted of from 10 to 30 members depending on the number of Soviets contributing delegates. It approved and distributed the regional budget and other issues and was elected by several tribes living in a designated area.

4 The **Raion Aboriginal Executive Committee** consisted of three people. It had executive power within the region and also the right to handle most criminal cases.

These administrative bodies were to maintain the traditions and customs of the tribe as long as they did not overtly contradict the laws of the country. However, the higher (third grade) court (the People's Court of the Russian Federation) was the same as that for the whole population. At the same time, a class qualification which obviously conflicted with traditional models of administration was also introduced by statute so that rich reindeer owners, trade middlemen and shamans could not be elected.[24]

The number of Soviets in the North grew rapidly. In 1925–6 there were 201, in 1927–8, 352 and in 1929–30, 455. In many areas the local administration, unable to find 'tribes' within their territory, hastily created them. For example, Penzhinsky Raion Executive Committee created a Mikin Koryak tribe that had not previously existed, while five Koryak and two Even 'tribes' were created by a decision of Kamchatka Revolutionary Committee.[25]

However, the drawbacks of the Tribal Soviet system were already clear by 1927. The main issue was that in many areas there was no connection whatever between blood relations and territory. Members of one tribe travelled with deer in different regions; members of different tribes and often different minorities lived together in the same villages. In practice, the Tribal Soviets were formed in accordance with the territorial principle but in many ways it was difficult to tell the difference between this system and the traditional structures of aboriginal self-administration that had functioned before 1917 under the 1892 Statute of the Indigenous Peoples.[26]

In many areas, the Tribal Soviets existed only in administrative theory. A representative of the Committee of the North reported in 1925 from Turukhan Krai: 'I have seen no work done by the Soviets. The Soviets are completely passive.' From Kamchatka, at the other end of the vast Northern territories, the reports were similar: 'The Tribal Soviets exist only on paper and do nothing because of their illiteracy and backwardness.'[27]

As a rule, the Northern Minorities did not oppose the establishment of Tribal Soviets; most were generally indifferent to them. In some places, though, the native population was suspicious of all that originated from the Russians: Soviet power was seen as Russian power. The Synya Khants, for example, expressed their opposition to a Tribal Soviet thus:

'If there is a Tribal Soviet in the Synya river area, we, the natives, will have nowhere to live. Schools and medical institutions will grow gradually around the Executive Committee, the natives will be taught, drafted to the army; trading stations will be established. Russians will come to the Synya river and settle down, steamboats will come into the river. We don't like this, and we don't want this.'[28]

The Northern economy

During the 1917 Revolution and the Civil War, the old economic ties were broken and the traditional supply routes to the region were blocked. By 1922, tribespeople found themselves in a perilous situation: imports (guns, powder, instruments, food, cloth) were non-existent, the yearly fairs were no longer organized, trade between the reindeer breeders and the settlers ceased. In many areas, hunting rifles were confiscated by the new administration for fear of 'aboriginal riots'.[29]

In 1919–20, a massive loss of deer occurred. In their revolutionary zeal, the new rulers often confiscated furs and riding deer from those whom they considered 'too rich'. The allotted number of deer was calculated by the same standards as those used for horses and cows in a European Russian household, where four animals were considered excessive, while a Nenets household, for example, had to possess at least 250 deer in order to avoid starvation. As a result, in the rich Turukhan tundra the indigenous peoples began to starve.[30]

The economic situation eased somewhat in the early 1920s when both private and state trade resumed supplies to the North. Flour, dried bread, salt, powder and textiles were imported in exchange for furs, fish and meat. The government raised the price of furs while the price of state-imported goods was lowered: this process was used as the main instrument for development of the Northern market. Between 1924 and 1929, furs, together with grain and oil, headed Soviet exports. The government used the resulting foreign currency receipts to buy equipment for heavy industry, hence it had a vested interest in the Northern Minorities keeping their traditional occupation.[31]

At first, private trade was licensed in areas where there was no State or cooperative trade but, by 1929, it was completely banned. In 1924, a law was passed according to which the state took the responsibility to allocate special funds for supplying goods to the Northern areas. In 1927–8, this budget totalled 16.8 million roubles, in 1929–30, 27.5 million roubles.[32]

The first consumer cooperatives and hunting and fishing cooperatives were organized in the early 1920s. In 1927, integrated cooperation was introduced which combined production, consumption, supplies, marketing, credit and trade. This economic form was popular and profitable and had tax privileges. By 1930, integrated cooperation already covered up to 35 per cent of the economically active population of the North.

In 1925, the Central Executive Committee released the Northern Minorities from all taxes. In 1929, the Council of Ministers released them from military service, and this directive was maintained until 1936.

Education and language

The Committee of the North promoted a three-pronged education initiative. The first strand was the so-called Northern 'culture bases', complex institutions which combined economic, educational, medical, veterinary and research activities, and which were established in 1925.[33] By 1931, eight culture bases had been founded: East (First), Second and Third Tungusic; Nenets; Chukotkan; Sakhalin; Ostyak; Koryak.[34]

The second strand was the school system. In 1925, there were already 41 schools in the Kamchatkan area (which then included the present territories of Kamchatka and Chukotka) with around 2,000 students. By 1930–1 there were 123 schools, including 62 boarding schools, which housed about 3,000 students, or 20 per cent of all Northern children of school age.[35]

The first teachers were Russian so they had to learn the basics of the minority languages before they could start teaching. Russian, reading, writing and simple arithmetic were the first subjects. Given the high illiteracy rate and lack of knowledge of Russian, teacher training was a major priority. From 1926 onwards, teachers for the Northern schools were trained in institutes in several cities: Tobolsk, Khabarovsk, Archangel, Tomsk and Leningrad (in 1930, the latter was reorganized into the famous Institute of the Peoples of the North).[36]

The third strand was the development and alphabetization of

Northern Minority languages. In 1930, a group of scholars who organized the Scholarly Association of Northern Research in Leningrad developed the Unified Northern Alphabet, based on the Roman alphabet, and work began on developing writing systems for the Northern Minority languages. By 1931, 13 peoples had received alphabets and three primers had been published.

It was a difficult task to create writing systems for all 26 languages and, in an attempt to work quickly, the languages were grouped into clusters. One basic language was chosen in each according to the number of speakers, linguistic features and its economic importance. Then writing systems were created for these basic languages.

Related groups of people could either adapt the basic language writing systems to meet the needs of their own language, or else switch gradually to the basic language in its pure form. For example, in the far east, the number of writing systems was reduced to five basic languages (Evenk, Nanai, Ul'chi, Nivkh, Chukchee) and four isolates (Eskimo, Itel'men, Aleut and Ainu), ignoring Even, Orok, Orochi, Koryak and others.[37]

Although it was difficult to avoid at the time, the language groupings had an adverse effect on the development of literacy. For instance, Yukagir and Ket were not on the list at all and even today do not have standard writing systems. More importantly, within each group, and even within some of the 'isolates', there are several languages, of which some differ too greatly to use the same writing system.

Recommendations made by the Committee of the North for the school curriculum were discussed and adopted in 1925. The central principle was that the Northern Minorities should stay within their traditional territories, following their traditional trades and way of life. The school timetable was to run in accordance with local customs and seasonal economic activity.

The first grade (aged 10–14) included primary school courses to be taught first in the students' mother tongue and later in Russian. The second grade (aged 13–17) was designed to give the gifted an opportunity for further education. The most talented could then continue their education at the same school after the age of 17 in order to be trained as teachers, veterinaries or doctors' assistants.

In spite of difficult living and working conditions, the first teachers accomplished a great deal. For example, in 1928, there were no literate people in the Eskimo village of Sireniki in southern Chukotka but, by the spring of 1930, about 20 adults could read and write and 42 schoolchildren attended classes.

At the same time, the first modest attempts were made to teach

native languages at local schools. In Leningrad, the educational publishing house, Uchpedgiz, published primers and readers. However,
given that only a few Russian scholars had even a moderate knowledge
of Siberian languages, it was difficult to sustain publications on a regular basis.

In 1937, a new alphabet based on Cyrillic was introduced 'to facilitate learning'. This was done for political reasons by government
decree but without any consultation with scholars or others with practical experience. Many scholars who worked on the Northern alphabet
in 1930 were arrested as 'enemies of the people' and were reviled by
the government media.[39]

Industrialization and collectivization, 1930–1941

*'Even a cursory glance at history should convince one that individual
crimes committed for selfish motives play a quite insignificant role in
the human tragedy compared with the numbers massacred in unselfish
love of one's tribe, nation, dynasty, church or ideology.'*

Arthur Koestler, 'The Urge to Self-Destruction'

During the 1930s the Northern Minorities shared the tragic fate of the
rest of the country but the consequences of Communist rule were
much worse for them than for most of the population of the USSR. As
small societies living in a fragile environment, they had evolved a
lifestyle in keeping with their hostile surroundings. Yet, in only ten
years, the way of life and balanced economy which they had developed over centuries were largely destroyed.

National Okrugs
National Okrugs were autonomous administrative and territorial units
set up along ethnic lines by the Soviets according to a plan put forward by the Committee of the North. They can be interpreted as the
Committee's last attempt to find a compromise between the need to
protect the indigenous peoples and the inevitable offensive of industrial development in the North, and their aim was 'to establish new and
rational economic boundaries that would not contradict the
ethnic boundaries'.[40]

The Committee of the North suggested two alternative models:
National Raions and National Okrugs. National Raions, which were
already in existence, implied a more direct line of subordination to the
regional authority (the Oblast). Thus, the line of control began at the
level of the local Soviet, then moved up to the Raion and then up to

the Oblast, which was the largest administrative unit within a Republic. A National Okrug, on the other hand, could be positioned between a Raion and an Oblast and allow a supposedly greater level of autonomy for those under its jurisdiction. Eventually, a combination of the two was accepted: in some areas Raions were directly subordinate to Oblasts while in others Okrugs were set up between them.

In 1929 the Nenets National Okrug was the first to be established. In 1930 the majority were formed, namely, in eastern Siberia five National Okrugs and one National Raion; in the far northeast, three National Okrugs and two National Raions; in Yakutiya, five National Raions. By 1932 a further nine National Okrugs had been formed, covering 38 Raions, along with 20 National Raions in other areas.[41]

In December 1930, the Committee of the North proclaimed that, with the formation of National Okrugs, the content of its work should change so that instead of representing the Northern Minorities in non-native administrative units, its primary objective should now be to represent the whole catchment area of National Okrugs and National Raions irrespective of their ethnic affiliation.[42] Unfortunately, under highly centralized Communist Party rule, these good intentions could not be realized because contradictions between the social organization, customs and traditions of the indigenous population and the Communist theories and slogans of 'class struggle' were too deep, the strengths of the Conservatives and Radicals too unequal. The gap between the interests of the minorities and of large-scale industry proved irreconcilable in a totalitarian state.

The result was that government decrees that local aboriginal administrations should be funded on an equal basis with the local Russian Soviets were ignored, as were orders to allocate funds to local representatives of the Committee of the North for educational and medical development, to complete the building of cultural bases, and so on.[43] Contrary to government orders, local administrations taxed the Northern Minorities in the same way as the rest of the population[44] and there were continuous reports of multiple violations of the law, both by unauthorized Russian settlers and by state institutions and enterprises.

Industrial development
The 1930s marked the beginning of an enormous industrialization programme throughout the USSR and, in particular, in the North. Not only were the Northern Minorities not given back land appropriated before the Revolution, as the law prescribed, but new land was forcefully taken away from them by state-run industries which moved on to native land and ousted native peoples all over the North.

In many cases, the industrial enterprises behaved like a victorious army in an occupied town. For example, the entire Obdor Raion (in Tobolsk Oblast) was allotted monopoly rights to a fishing trust and, as a result, members of the local fishing cooperatives were forced to sign a contract which reduced their function of supplying labour to the trust.

It was logical that those state industries which supplied their workers with food preferred to rely mainly on their own agricultural state farms and imported labour. These state farms heavily exploited the natural resources which formed the basis of the traditional native economy so that the state deer-breeding farms arbitrarily used any pastures they wished without the slightest hesitation. The state fishing farms blocked rivers with fishing nets, breaking all the rules and violating the seasonal fishing periods, thus depriving the indigenous people of their traditional food.[45]

The Northern Minorities were not involved with the modern industrial sector since the latter relied largely on imported labour. At the same time, Russian settlers, who occupied the same territory as the indigenous peoples, were beyond the jurisdiction of the native courts.[46]

Since government supplies were insufficient and inappropriate, native hunters could not find what they needed at the trading stations and so often refused to sell their furs. Several cases were reported where the Fur Syndicate was unable to collect enough furs and so it alerted the Ministry of Foreign Trade. The latter then ordered alcohol to be set out for sale in the areas populated by the Northern Minorities. This was contrary both to many attempts of the Supreme Executive Committee in Moscow to outlaw alcohol in the North (for example in 1929 and 1930) and to those of the Committee of the North, which was neither informed nor even consulted.[47]

In this way, throughout the 1930s, real power in the North started to leak away from the local administration and the Committee of the North to the mighty, central, industrial ministries, to giants like 'Glavsevmorput' (Central Agency for the Northern Passage) and later to 'Dal'stroy' (Chief Administration for the Development of the Far North). The latter had a whole GULAG system under its jurisdiction and was using labour-camp prisoners as manpower.

In 1938, Dal'stroy was placed under the command of the NKVD (People's Commissariat of Internal Affairs) and began extensive timber exploitation and gold mining, first in the Upper Kolyma area and later all over the Magadan Oblast and Yakutiya. Dal'stroy activities greatly affected the Northern Minorities, particularly the western Chukchees and the Evens who, after collectivization, were turned into mere food and transport suppliers for Dal'stroy. Many groups of Chukchee and

Even fled into inaccessible parts of the tundra and taiga in order to escape from Dal'stroy and from collectivization and, in this way, some managed to avoid collectivization until the mid-1950s.[48]

Collectivization

Forced collectivization in the USSR began in 1929 with the 'intensification of the rural class struggle'. Mass purges of those peasants who owned at least modest private farms followed. Land, animals and buildings were all seized from their owners and 'collectivized' (became the property of the state). Collectivization led to a rapid impoverishment of the country and, in many areas, mass opposition and repression.

Before 1930, despite the efforts of the Communist administration, no 'class struggle' could be organized in the North because the native population simply could not understand the meaning of the term.[49] For example, when a group of shamans and rich deer owners in a village in Kazym Raion were not allowed to attend the village assembly by the party commissars, the whole assembly simply left.[50]

In spite of the numerous attempts of the Committee of the North, first to oppose collectivization and later to delay it and soften its impact, the campaign did finally reach the Northern regions.[51] At first, though, the rate of collectivization was much lower than in the country as a whole, probably because of the remoteness of the region but possibly also because of the resistance of the Committee of the North. By 1931, for example, only 12 per cent of the natives were members of the *kolkhozy* (collective farms).

However, this state of affairs was not satisfactory to Communist Party officials and in 1934 collectivization was accelerated. At the beginning of that year about 12 per cent of deer herds were in collective ownership. By 1936, the figure had risen to 50 per cent and, by 1943, to 89.2 per cent.[52]

It was impossible to oppose the process; suicidal to protest. For example, in 1930–2 a wave of armed uprisings, in effect small civil wars against forced collectivization, swept the Samoyed North and Taymyr Peninsula but the rebels were ruthlessly suppressed and purged.

Population movements

Between 1917 and 1926, the incomer population of the North grew between 5 per cent and 8 per cent per annum but between 1926 and 1935 the growth was 15–20 per cent. The proportion of the native population in National Okrugs decreased from 56 per cent in 1926 to 35 per cent in 1935.[53] In 1926, the Northern Minorities constituted 20 per cent of the total Northern population; by 1937 their proportion was estimated at a mere 7 per cent.

The actual effects of this increase in the non-native population can be seen by looking at specific population groups. For example, in 1926 the total population of the Chukotka National Okrug was 14,931, of which 13,946 were native (93.4 per cent). By 1937, the total population had reached 35,000, of which the native population was 16,500 (47 per cent). This, however, was modest compared to Kamchatka Oblast where in 1926 the total population was 9,684, with a native population of 1,456 (15 per cent). By 1937, the total population had increased to 75,000 with a native population of only 1,800 (2.4 per cent).

In 1931, the Committee of the North had decided that 'alienation of the land of working land-users is possible only in special cases of great state necessity, and only then after special permission has been granted by the Oblast Executive Committee, with full compensation'.[54] Yet there was no consultation and no compensation. Even the massive forced relocation of the wealthy peasants from European Russia to Siberia, which was carried out as part of Stalin's collectivization campaign in 1929–32, was done without consultations with the local administrations.

One of the consequences of this large-scale influx of people was differential treatment between the native population and the incomers, expressed in a 1932 law. This latter divided the whole Northern population into two categories. The first category comprised professionals (higher and middle administration officers, highly qualified specialists, judges, attorneys, police inspectors, solicitors) who received a 10 per cent yearly increase of salary, a 50 per cent reduction in taxes, privileges in allocation of apartments, university entrance and so on. Those of the Northern Minorities who belonged to this category also received these benefits but they were very few in number.

The remainder of the population fell into the second category. This group could enjoy these privileges only if they came as workers to the North from other areas of the USSR, which automatically excluded the vast majority of the native population and created two categories of payment for the same work. For example, two carpenters, a Russian and a Chukchee, who worked together in the same team, would receive different payments. This was the germ of the ugly situation that still exists today throughout the North: the difference in wages for the same work can reach three times and more.

The end of opposition

In 1934, four years after *Severnaya Asia* was closed, its successor *Sovetskiy Sever* also ceased to exist. In the replacement journal, *Sovetskaya Arktika*, the tone of publications differed drastically. From 1937

51

onwards, *Sovetskaya Arktika* did not publish a single serious article on the economic, political or cultural situation of the Northern Minorities, nor make any references to the rights they might possess. Instead, it was an organ of Communist Party propaganda, filled with statements about the 'backwardness of nomadic tribes' and the need for 'radical socialistic reformation'.

Although the opposition could not publish their views, nevertheless there were brave people who openly protested, such as B.V. Lavrov, the former chairman of the Northern Passage Committee, whose speech in May 1937 sharply criticized the activities of the newly formed Glavsevmorput.

Not only individuals but also the Soviet government itself was not able effectively to oppose the Communist Party apparatus embodied in the industrial trusts and their party committees. The Supreme Executive Committee and the Council of Ministers in Moscow passed an act in August 1933 called 'On Nomadic Soviets in National Okrugs and Northern Areas of Russian Federation'. Next, in October 1933, a similar act was passed that regulated the work of the courts. The intention was, on the one hand, to provide protection for the Northern Minorities against industrial expansion, thus giving them at least some independence from the economic administration, and, on the other, to speed the collectivization process. However, while the second goal was achieved, the act proved ineffective against the industrial giants.

Finally, in 1935, the Committee of the North was itself abolished. For years its ethnographers, linguists and administrators had been fighting a losing battle on behalf of the Northern Minorities. Now, as the whole country slid into massive political and cultural repression and economic upheaval, their opposition was no longer possible.

The dark years: 1941–1985

'And then someone obedient and timid
settled down in our souls,
someone who got accustomed
to being shouted at,
someone who would just humbly beg.'

Vyachslav Ankhaki, a Kamchatkan native

The greatest pressures on the Northern Minorities came between 1950 and the mid-1980s. Soviet influence on them was institutionalized and became inescapable; they could only watch helplessly at the heartless amalgamation of their communities and the multitude of social problems which resulted. Given the power of the state, protest was virtually impossible.

Russification

During the Second World War, the Northern Minorities were protected from military conscription by a special act. Nevertheless, many of them volunteered and went to the front lines where many were killed and several decorated as military heroes. The country suffered heavy losses and severe damage during the war and, for the following five years, the government in Moscow could give little thought to the Northern Minorities. By 1950, however, it once again turned its attention to the North.

By this time, a general ideological shift was under way. While in the 1920s–30s the official Communist ideology embraced the concept of 'class struggle' and regarded national and ethnic identification as obsolete, by 1945 Stalin's political course had changed sharply. Russian superiority in the sciences, industry and the arts was proclaimed by official propaganda. Arrests and purges which two decades previously had been carried out under the banner of the 'class struggle' were once again effected, but this time against the 'loss of national pride', 'cringing to the West' and 'cosmopolitanism'.[56]

Russia was proclaimed first among the 128 'equal' nations of the USSR while its 'junior brothers' (Ukraine, Byelorussia, Kazakhstan, Georgia and the other nations and ethnic groups) were supposed to live in peace with Russia and emulate it. On the other hand, the 'criminal peoples' (Ingush, Crimean Tatars, Chechens and so on) were to be punished by the state for 'treachery' or 'bad behaviour'.

This new governmental ethnic policy was based on the concept (although not yet the term) of the 'new historic unity, the Soviet people', a monolithic unity which was to form very quickly around the central core of the Russians. The 'international language of the Soviet people' was declared to be Russian and given top priority in all school timetables. The population of the USSR was supposed to suppress all its ethnic, linguistic and cultural differences and merge into a homogeneous mass of the Soviet people.

The Russification policy was supported by the dramatic changes in the legal code in the pre-war years. In 1936, soon after the Committee of the North was abolished, the system of integral cooperation in the North was dismantled. In the new Constitution of that year there was no concept of National Raions; these were gradually dissolved over the following three decades. Some National Okrugs were also eliminated and, in 1938, the whole Arctic region was divided between the central ministries so that no central body existed to control the colonization of the North. Thus, the Northern Minorities lost all control over their own existence.[57]

Chauvinism

A campaign called 'Nativization' was pursued for several years in which lower- and middle-grade positions in the local Communist Party and the Soviet administration were given only to members of the Northern Minorities. However, since they were appointed because of their ethnic background and not for their professional skills, many of them proved unable to fulfil the requirements of the administrative posts. So the pendulum swung to the other extreme and the natives were declared incapable of doing responsible work, thus fuelling outbursts of Russian chauvinism against the indigenous peoples which are still common in the North today. (In this context, and in many others, the word 'Russian' is used to designate any incomer irrespective of his or her real ethnic identity. About 20 per cent of the incoming population of the North are, in fact, Ukrainians, Armenians, Tatars and other peoples.)

Parallel to Russian chauvinism are similar outbursts by Yakut, Komi and Buryat people towards the smaller Northern Minorities. For example, motiveless beatings of the natives by the Russian incomers took place in Dudinka in the mid-1980s.[58] A Yukagir student told the author in 1987 that she had had to leave Yakutsk University because of constant insults from Yakut students, who felt that only the Yakuts should study there.

Multiple cases were reported in many Raion registry offices where the clerks refused to register new-born children under a native name on the grounds that 'such a name doesn't exist, it isn't a human name'. The remarks of a Russian librarian who had lived for several years in a Chukotkan village are typical:

> '*The Chukchees and the Eskimos? They live in the stone age!...They are all idlers! All they can do is have children, but they can't even take care of them. The state has to do that...Nurseries, kindergartens, boarding-schools, even the university...Everything free, of course...Hunting? They don't need it: they can buy everything they need in the village... Money? So long as they have enough to buy alcohol they are happy...*'[59]

At the same time, those Russians who were born in the North or have lived there for 20 years or more, generally behave towards the natives with more respect and tolerance. For example, permanent Russian settlers in the Kolyma region are likely to speak Yakut and understand Even and Yukagir. Mixed marriages are not uncommon, and generally a person's ethnic identity is considered his own affair.

Yet, for the native peoples, bitterness runs deep. One Khant woman expressed her feelings:[60]

> *'I wish I was dead, to avoid this earthly hell. What have I had children for – for this torture and disgrace? Let Russians be everywhere, then there will probably be Paradise. They will have nobody to destroy and ruin. They will have everything, they will raze to the ground the graves of our ancestors and our own, and that's it. Nobody will ever remember that there were once Khants, Mansi, and other useless nations.'*

Russian language policy

By 1950, the new settlers constituted about half of the total population of the National Okrugs. At this time, practically all the Northern Minority population could speak, or at least understand, Russian. In many ways, its acquisition as a second language was a positive development, as it allowed access to information via books, newspapers, radio and, later, television. However, Russification, and not bilingualism, was the real aim of the government's policies.

In the Northern schools, the number of hours for native language teaching was reduced. In the areas where there were problems in teaching Northern Minority languages, such as in those with rich dialectal variety (Khant, Koryak, Nivkh), or those with an absence of alphabets (Yukagir, Ket, Naukan Eskimo, Aleut) or when the size of the group was small, all education in native languages ceased. Everywhere, Northern Minority languages became at best a subject of study instead of being the primary medium of instruction.

Around 1957, school teachers throughout the North began to exert pressure on the children with regard to their native languages. They were punished if they were heard to speak anything but Russian at school, and parents were requested not to speak their native language to their children at home. The usual explanation was that it would be better for the children to study only Russian at school since their education and understanding of the future mono-ethnic 'Soviet' state would be made easier.

This Russian language policy was never officially announced or published. However, it is interesting that Moscow's policies towards the Northern schools were very similar to those of the US Federal Administration towards Alaskan schools several decades earlier. Yet the difference is that the instructions of the Federal Administration were published and available for open discussion and criticism.

By 1970, out of the 26 languages in the North, only Nenets was used at school as a medium of instruction and, even there, only in primary schools. Chukchee, Eskimo, Khant, Mansi, Even and Evenk were taught as a subject of study; Sel'kup, Nivkh, Koryak and Nanai were no longer on the school timetable.[61]

The 'broken generation'

The degree of language competence of an individual and/or a community is closely correlated to the age of the speakers. The older generation is the bearer of linguistic and cultural tradition, a conservative group; the younger generation tends to switch to a language of a larger ethnos, in this case mainly Russian but sometimes other Siberian languages such as Yakut, Buryat or Komi.[62]

In many communities, a third group is present between the older and the younger generation. This group, usually between 30 and 50 years of age, is the 'broken generation'. It is characterized by 'group semi-lingualism' (where part of the group prefers Russian even though it does not yet have proficiency in it, while the other still prefers its native tongue, although it may have already lost proficiency). Normal communication within the group, as well as between the group and other generations, is therefore blocked.

From the cultural point of view, the 'broken generation' is also a hybrid: it has lost most of its traditional customs and values but has not yet acquired new ones; normal transmission of cultural values is also blocked.

If the transition takes several generations to complete, and is supported by a sound language and social policy, the group may even feel little frustration: after all, for a generation that speaks, as their mothers and grandmothers did, two languages, the loss of one of those may be a problem, but hardly a tragedy. However, in the North there has been a rapid ousting of Northern Minority languages by Russian, as well as the loss of bilingualism even before it was established. The children of the 1950s, who began or continued their education at the time when the Russification policy was launched, were particularly affected. This generation lost its language, its culture and sometimes also its identity, without receiving any viable substitute.

Forced relocation

In the 1950s and 1960s another widespread campaign was launched in the North which was carried out with all the ruthlessness and incompetence of a totalitarian system and which had a catastrophic effect on the Northern Minorities. The campaign, of which the Russification process was only a forerunner, was based on the utopian ideal to bring the Northern region, and the Northern Minorities in particular, to 'modern socialist civilization' as quickly as possible.

In March 1957, the Communist Party Central Committee issued a resolution, 'On the Measures for Further Economic and Cultural Development of the Peoples of the North'. The core of this was Article 5 which instructed the Oblast, Okrug and Raion administration: 'to study the urgent problems of the further improvement of the economic and administrative territorial organization of National Raions and Okrugs...to consider the question of simplifying the structure and improving the work of the economic, Soviet and party administration in the North'.[63]

Improving and simplifying were understood by the local administrations as a call to bring the Northern areas into line with the administrative structure of the rest of the USSR but what followed in practice was the shutting down of state and collective farms in smaller villages, together with the dismantling of local administrative bodies. At the same time, smaller villages were amalgamated into larger ones and the population was forcibly relocated.

Nomadic people were made to settle. Even the Khants, who were never really nomadic but migrated on a seasonal basis within a limited territory, had a regular war waged against them by the local administration. The state and collective farms were closed in their villages, leaving the population jobless; schools, hospitals and shops were shut; some villages were closed completely and the population moved to larger settlements.

An area with fewer villages and a unified economy is, of course, easier to administer but this form of organization was in direct contravention to the way of life of most of the Northern Minorities. For example, the traditional seasonal migrations of the Khants were economically suitable for a territory that could support only a limited number of hunters. Since the new settlements were chosen purely for their convenience for transportation, administration and centralized supplies, the native Khant population soon found itself with no means of support.[64]

In the settled areas, the local administration, pleading various reasons (supply routes, need for new roads and houses, the 'unprofitability' of small villages, military necessity), did their best to force the abandonment of small traditional villages of 30–50 inhabitants and move to new standard settlements of 600–800 people which had been built closer to Raion centres. The sites for these new settlements were chosen according to European standards of convenience: close to a large river or safe bay, the lie of the land, ease of roadbuilding and so on. Convenience for traditional occupations, such as hunting, fishing and others, was not considered at all.

A good example is the amalgamation of Eskimo and Chukchee villages. Naukan lay on a steep slope south of the Bering Strait and was an ancient settlement where a branch of the Eskimo tribe had lived for centuries. In 1958, it was declared 'unprofitable' and the dwellers forced to move to the neighbouring villages of Nunyamo and Pinakul. The methods were simple: at first the local administration tried to persuade the inhabitants that they would be better off in the new villages but, when they did not succeed, the village school and the shop were shut down and, finally, the collective farm was liquidated, leaving the people unemployed. The Naukan Eskimos had no choice but to move.

After 19 years, Pinakul and Nunyamo were themselves amalgamated and the people transferred to the Chukchee villages of Lorino, Lavrentiya and Uelen where they formed only a small percentage of the population. Here, the Eskimo population decreased by 6 per cent; the Chukchee increased by 7 per cent, while the incoming (mainly Russian) population jumped by 116 per cent.[65]

Similarly, the Eskimos of southeastern Chukotka who lived in the small villages of Unazik, Kivak, Avan, Siklyuk and others were transferred in 1958–9 to a new, large settlement, Novo-Chaplino, which had been built inside a deep bay. The traditional small villages were abandoned and soon ceased to exist. The new location made traditional sea-mammal hunting much more difficult since the settlement was built far away from the whale, walrus and seal migration routes. Thus, the traditional way of life and subsistence of these Eskimos changed completely within the lifetime of one generation and, in the new settlement, they constituted less than half of the population, the remainder being Chukchee and Russian.

The social and economic results of the Eskimos' enforced relocation were immediately evident: 'loss of meaning' was in turn followed by such social problems as unemployment, alcoholism and high suicide rates. In 1989 in Novo-Chaplino, there were 98 fully or partly unemployed men and women out of the total population of 534.[66]

During the 1950s and 1960s, there were six Saami villages in Lovozero Raion. In accordance with the relocation policy, they were amalgamated into one settlement but the process was slapdash and unprepared. The relocation was described by an onlooker:

'I personally witnessed the relocation of the people from the village of Varzino. No houses had been prepared for them. People were put either into the houses of their relatives, or into slums no one needed. Three

families of relatives, 11 people, moved into one small house. Imagine a
two-room house with a kitchen where 16 people lived, not for one year,
but for six years! And now they ask hypocritically why there is such a
high crime rate among the Saami, why they drink so much![67]

In 1960, the collective farms in Gornaya Shoria were closed down as
unprofitable by a special decree of the Council of Ministers of the
Russian Federation. This completely destroyed all organized economic
activity in this rural area; the Shors became unemployed, since nothing was set up to take the place of the collective farms. Funding for
house building also ceased. The Shor population had to abandon over
40 villages. Over two-thirds of the active population had to move to
larger settlements and towns in search of jobs.[68]

In the 1960s and 1970s, the forced concentration of the Nivkh population took place on Sakhalin with such ruthlessness and incompetence that the tragic results are almost unprecedented in the North.[69]
The natives were moved to two large settlements, Nogliki and
Nekrasovka, which were located in places where traditional activity
was out of the question. This soon caused unemployment, alcoholism
and other related social problems.

The relocation and amalgamation policies were accompanied by
pressures to end the traditional livelihood of the Northern Minorities.
For example, for 15 years before 1987, the Eskimos of Chukotka frequently had difficulties in getting permission to hunt sea-mammals.
The ban was supposed to be for reasons of state security (the international border was 19 kilometres away) and also, with unbelievable cyn-
icism, out of apparent 'concern for the life and health of the hunters'.
In the 1970s, the author witnessed pitiful scenes: the Eskimo
sea-hunters, excellent sailors, consummate masters of whale and walrus hunt, had to ask the Soviet border-guards for a licence to put out to
sea for a couple of hours. Frequently, permission was refused.

In Tyumen Oblast in 1986–7, the Executive Committee banned all
hunting except state commercial hunting, 'in order to oppose poaching'. This meant that the Khants could not carry on the activities
which had always been the core of their culture. Anti-poaching laws
were passed in many regions with no regard for the traditional ways of
life of Northern Minorities. As a result, the natives could not hunt for
the food they were accustomed to, which led to a drastic change in
their diet and, consequently, to medical problems.[70]

Statistics

Even the published statistics prove beyond doubt that the Northern Minorities suffer from far worse conditions than the population of the USSR as a whole, or, for example, the native Indian population of North America. The average mortality rate in the Russian Federation in 1978–9 was 10.6 per 1,000, but in Magadan Oblast it was 12.7 per 1,000. Between 1979 and 1990 life expectancy in Magadan Oblast decreased by three years for men and two years for women, and is now respectively 42.5 and 50 years.[71] The average life expectancy of members of the Northern Minorities is between 40 and 45 years, about 16–18 years less than the average in the Russian Federation.

The suicide rate in the North is 80–90 per 100,000.[72] The incidence of tuberculosis is 42 per 100,000 for the former USSR, 225 per 100,000 in Chukotka.[73] The percentage of children born outside marriage is also extremely high. For example, according to a survey conducted in 1979, out of 24 children born in Sireniki in 1975–9 to Eskimo mothers under the age of 30, two-thirds were to unmarried mothers (for mothers under 24, the proportion was three-quarters). The proportion of single women between 21 and 30 was 76 per cent, of unmarried men, 53 per cent.[74] (The high proportion of young unmarried mothers can partly be explained by traditionally more liberal sexual morals. However, to a large extent this is now due to the disintegration of traditional family and social structures and to the fact that a high proportion of the incoming population are unattached males.)

Independent and reliable statistics were (and still are) hard to obtain. Scholars who tried to do field research involving statistics immediately got into trouble with the local KGB. Where such figures are available, the official statistics give a more optimistic picture than the reality. For example, the average life expectancy calculated by M. Volfson for the Northern Minorities in Chukotka was 44–5 years in the 1960s, and 40 years in the 1970s.[75] The published figures, however, gave 62 years as the average life expectancy of all the Northern Minorities in the 1960s.[76]

The Boarding-School System

Originally, boarding schools were designed to give children of nomadic groups an opportunity to obtain a systematic education. In the larger villages, special buildings were erected, equipment was imported, teachers were trained and the children of reindeer breeders and hunters began staying there nine months a year, thus having an opportunity to reach a similar standard of education to that of the non-nomadic peoples.

However, as part of the Russification policy, the system was later extended, firstly to cover the nomadic children of kindergarten and nursery age, and later to include children of the settled population. It soon became the only possible way to obtain school education and was made compulsory for all the children. This created an ugly situation whereby the parents had to 'turn in' their children at the age of one year, first to the nursery, then to kindergarten, then to boarding school for six days a week 24 hours a day, while themselves living in the same village.

As a result of the boarding-school system, children became fully state-dependent in many places and deprived of a family upbringing. They also lost their native mother tongues. At the age of 15 or 17, they returned to their families as complete strangers, with no knowledge of traditional native culture or of home life. Parents also suffered since, in many cases, they lost all their feeling of responsibility towards their children and delegated it all to the state.

Eventually, the boarding-school policy led to dramatic changes in traditional social and family structure and contributed to the formation of the above-mentioned 'broken generation'. It led (and in many areas still leads) to the situation where the majority of the Northern boarding-school graduates completely lack the necessary living skills, and often emerge without initiative and energy. The dominant psychological characteristic for many of them is apathy combined with aggression; they experience enormous stress when they begin their adult life.

The boarding schools are normally located in larger settlements and towns, with children coming there from ethnically different villages. Most often, the only common language they have is Russian. The schools are thus a very effective means of destroying the Northern Minority languages: after eight or ten years of round-the-clock school training, the children cannot speak any language but Russian.

Two or three generations of Northern Minorities have already been taken through the boarding-school system and very few of them have been able to escape its destructive effects. In the last few years, however, the boarding schools have been gradually turned into ordinary day schools and the system is now being reconsidered. This is a positive development but, it will hardly repair the damage already caused.

The Autonomous Okrug law
State policies concerning the Northern Minorities received a legal foundation in 1980 when the law on Autonomous Okrugs was passed.[77] Autonomous Okrugs replaced National Okrugs, while National Raions were officially liquidated, although the latter had in fact been dwindling in numbers since the 1930s. All references to the

Northern Minorities were removed from the text of the law and a more neutral term, 'autonomous', replaced the word 'national'.

Another change was that the Autonomous Okrug (as supreme administrative body) was elected by equal suffrage which meant the native peoples, who were by now a small minority everywhere, were effectively excluded from decision making.

The establishment of Autonomous Okrugs completed the totalitarian pyramid of power. They were never regarded as a form of national/ethnic self-administration but were simply administrative units at a certain level: higher than Raions but lower than Oblasts. All matters concerning divisions within the Autonomous Okrugs and between Autonomous Okrugs and other units, also questions about the setting up or closing down of villages, towns, Raions and village Soviets, were, according to the law (Article 3), placed under the jurisdiction of the higher administration: the Oblast, Republic and, finally, the Union. Local Soviets now had a purely consultative role, and that was all.

Self-determination was no longer possible since economic and social planning (Article 7) became part of the respective Oblast or Krai responsibilities. The only right the local administration had over industrial enterprises functioning on their land was the right to be informed about their activities and to pass suggestions to higher levels of administration (Article 16).

Article 13 did appear to give the local Soviet some rights: the right to control whether the industrial enterprises kept the law; the right to coordinate and control their land usage and to protect the environment, and so on. In fact, however, the Soviet had no means of implementing control and coordination. Even to establish or to close down an industrial enterprise of their own, the Autonomous Okrug had to ask for permission at a higher level (Article 16).

Given that Autonomous Okrugs replaced National Okrugs, it would be natural to expect special articles securing social, economic and cultural rights and providing for some kind of autonomy for the native peoples to be outlined in the law. However, Article 21, dealing with the agricultural and industrial rights of Autonomous Okrugs, says nothing about the traditional native occupations and system of subsistence. Article 28, regulating the rights of the Autonomous Okrug in education and science, does not mention the teaching of Northern Minority languages, culture and history in schools. The only mention of the indigenous peoples is a vague half-line in Article 29, that local Soviets should 'take measures to develop native culture, art and literature'.

The law was not accompanied by statutes on administrative territorial units which ought to have contained detailed descriptions of their legal basis and the ways they could be established or reorganized. Nor did it discuss border changes and land transfer issues. Thus, the population of the Northern areas could not enjoy effective legal security.[78]

In the same year as the Autonomous Okrug law, a party decree was published: 'On the Measures for Further Economic and Social Development of the Areas Populated by the Peoples of the North'. The document seems to be concerned about the Northern Minorities since new funds were allocated to the North and new educational and social projects were launched. However, the (perhaps deliberate) ambiguity of the wording: 'Development of the Areas Populated by...', not 'Development of the Peoples of the North', made the decree useless in practice for the Northern Minorities. All the funds went directly to the Oblast and Raion authorities and were used to cover the needs of the whole population, of which the Northern Minorities constituted but a very small percentage. Needless to say, they had no influence on the distribution of funds.

Ecological disaster: 1955 onwards

The avalanche of industrial development hit the North in the mid-1950s, although attempts to industrialize it had already been made in the mid-1930s. In the following three decades, the area was not colonized but conquered, for it turned out to be extremely rich in timber, gold, coal, ore, oil, gas and other natural resources. However, there were laws neither for the geologists, nor for the road-or house-builders. A new mine or a new timber-cutting site could be started at any time, in any place, by a decision of the Moscow administration. Any parcel of land could be alienated from the native people by a stroke of the pen. Everything was explained and excused by the extraordinary state importance of the task which the 'pioneers' had to fulfil: gold for the state, oil for the state, and so on. Lyudmila S. Bogoslovskaya, a well-known expert on the Northern ecology and traditional subsistence models, stated that the state ownership of the land declared in the Constitution 'is a myth: what we really have is bureaucratic "departmental property", especially in the North'.[79]

The result was that the fragile ecological systems in the North, and the small ethnic groups of the Northern Minorities, were not able to withstand this industrial pressure, this 'permanent ecological aggression',[80] and it had an enormous effect on both the social and natural environment. The North's extraordinary vulnerability was seen, for example, in 1984 when it was calculated that, if one man in one caterpillar vehicle furrowed the Taymyr tundra eight hours a day for three summer months, he would succeed in turning the entire Taymyr Peninsula into a desert by the end of the century. The native population were unable to oppose these pressures because they had no legal structures they could use on their own behalf.

Timber

The first to attack the North were the timber concerns who were allocated taiga lots by the central government, without consulting or even informing the local administrations. A local Soviet would frequently learn that part of its territory had been given to a timber-cutting enterprise only when the employees arrived to prepare the trees for felling. For example, in December 1987 the hunters and reindeer breeders of an Evenk village called Tyanya (in Okleminsk Raion, Yakutiya) received an order to the effect that 450 sq. km. of taiga, amounting to five million cubic metres of trees, were to be alienated from their traditional hunting grounds. The document allotted to the native population a parcel of land only 20 x 40 km. for their own use. The village assembly sent delegates to the Raion Soviet, then to the administration of Yakutiya Republic, but nobody would listen to them. They were sent back rudely with the verdict: 'This is a decision taken in Moscow, nothing can be done about it.'[81]

From the mid-1950s onwards, first-class forests, the traditional hunting and fishing grounds of the Northern Minorities, were cut down on a massive scale. For example, a one-year plan in Gornaya Shoria in 1990 resulted in the felling of 1.4 million cubic metres of timber using powerful machinery and in such a mechanically and ecologically unsound manner that in many cases almost 40 per cent was wasted, left to rot where it had been cut. The remainder was floated down the rivers, many of which became so choked up that it was possible to cross from one bank to the other without wetting one's feet. The damage done to Siberian forests was enormous: the far east of the country lost 30 per cent of its forests, including 21 per cent in Magadan Oblast, 34 per cent in Primorskiy Krai, 34 per cent in Khabarovskiy Krai, 39 per cent on Sakhalin and 42 per cent in Amur Oblast. At the same time, there was also a sharp decrease in the number of fur animals.[82]

International companies also played a part. According to a 1987 agreement between the USSR and Cuba, the Sukpai Timber Company was established in the far east and given a licence to cut timber in the lands of the Udege, whose livelihood depends entirely on the forests. Similar treaties were signed with North Korea. Today, while cutting the timber, Korean workers poison the rivers, poach and recognize no laws – and the local administration can do nothing to stop them.[83]

Oil and gas

Oil and gas extraction began in the mid-1960s and also had a negative effect on the North. The largest oil deposits (Surgut and Samotlor) lie in the land of the Khants but they received no compensation for the oil pumped out of their land, while the land itself was destroyed.[84]

One of the most graphic examples of the 'oil war' in the North is the story of Yamal Peninsula. After large gas and oil deposits were found there, a decision was taken to start quick exploration and development of the area even though some experts maintain it is not economically profitable. A technical plan was drawn up which included a south–north railway, a gas-main and several oil wells and rigs. As usual, the rights and needs of the native population were not taken into account so that, for example, the railway was planned in such a way that it cut off the summer deer pastures from the winter ones. The machines moving north destroyed the tundra with the result that five state deer farms in Yamalo-Nenets Okrug lost 594,699 hectares of pasture in a few years and more than 24,000 deer. The same happened in other areas, for example, in 1970-87 the deer herd decreased in Magadan Oblast by 15 per cent, in Krasnoyarsk Krai by 30-40 per cent while in Sakhalin it almost ceased to exist.[85]

A. Pika, a Moscow ethno-sociologist who worked in the late 1970s with the Khants near Lake Pyaku-ot, gave the following description of what he saw there ten years later:

> 'It is difficult to recognize the place. Where there was a realm of virgin land, where one would only seldom meet a fisherman's hut or a deer-breeder's or a hunter's tent, a city has been built. One sees settlements, cross-roads of asphalt highways stretching as far as the eye can see. And between them – black patches of burned forests, vast spaces of man-made deserts, the moss uprooted by caterpillars, oil overflows surrounding oil rigs, gas torches burning day and night, the smoke of forest fires. One gets an impression that man declared war on nature here.'[86]

The indigenous people had no legal rights of redress. All they could do was look in despair as their land, their way of life and their future were quickly and ruthlessly being destroyed. The author remembers, for example, horror on the faces of Eskimos from southeastern Chukotka when, in 1980, rumours came that oil had been found nearby. One said, 'This is the end, we'll be finished very soon now.' He looked desperate, helpless and resigned. Luckily, the rumours proved untrue.

Discussion and resistance

After 1985, the situation began to change. In 1987, the Yamal Okrug administration made the first attempt openly to oppose the unchecked industrial development of the area. They openly criticized the Ministries of Oil and Gas, Energy and Transport for their singleminded concern with oil and gas, for ignoring the peoples of the targeted areas and for violating the few laws that were supposed to guard their interests. In actual fact, the Okrug authorities were interested not so much in protection of the natives and their land but in the opportunity to get compensation and additional funding for the Okrug.

In 1988, the Yamal Okrug Soviet banned the building of the railway but the ministries involved simply ignored their decision. In 1989, the Director of the Arctic Department for Oil and Gas Construction (Arktikneftegazstroy), I. Shapovalov, answered a journalist as follows:

'We'll have to come to Yamal anyway. The gas must be supplied by 1991, as planned...No one will change the agreed dates. And we'll not be able to avoid it...we hear so much idle talking, senseless indignation, silly shouts about "saving" a strip of Yamal land. Come to think of it, it isn't land at all...it has 60% of ice in it.'[87]

The opposite position was expressed by an Evenk poet, A. Nemtushkin, who wrote about another large-scale industrial project, the Turukhan hydro-electric plant:

'Many people think that this [the ecological damage resulting from Northern industrial development] is an unpleasant but necessary evil compared to the advantages that billions of new kilowatts will bring...However, in reality it means destruction of the very basis of the native way of life, comparable to the consequences of a nuclear war. The only difference is that the war would instantly destroy all the life on earth, while ecological disaster will have the same effect, but gradually.'[88]

The devastating activity of industrial giants in the North is caused neither by any special intention to harm the native people, nor by their ecological ignorance (though the latter surely is there), but by the way the economic system itself works. The success of a ministry under central control has been evaluated by only one criterion: how much money it spends. Neither the negative ecological consequences nor even the profitability are of any interest. It should be obvious that the losses incurred by building a mine and a concentrating mill in the centre of Kamchatka would be higher than any possible profit this project might give, but the ministry is indifferent: the more the project costs, the better for them. The local administration, on the other hand, is very interested in what is built on its land but has no rights.[89] The result is that the only way to affect the final decision in these cases is through publicity.

In February 1989, the Presidium of the Council of Ministers of the USSR decided that the existing development plan for Yamal should be suspended, basing its decision on the lack of concrete information on how industrial development would affect the local ecology and relations with the native population. However, the ministries at first ignored even the Presidium. Acting through old and well-established ties of personal and party influence, they forced the government to issue 'temporary permissions' – and continued their work. In 1990, the struggle was still going on.

Another example comes from the area where the Khants live near the Sob River. In 1984, large-scale extractions of gravel from the river bed began. As usual, nobody asked for permission either from the local administration or from the Khants. The machinery was shipped in, together with workers from other parts of the country, and the consequences soon became evident: the water balance of the river was destroyed, the river bed and the river bank were altered and, before long, the stocks of sturgeon, formerly plentiful, went down drastically. Also, the incomers robbed the winter huts of the native hunters and the ancient Khant cemetery was vandalized.[90]

The natives tried to protest but without results. Then the people from Katravozh, a village on the bank of the Sob, called a meeting and decided to oppose the intruders by other methods. They blocked the river with buoys and fishing boats and refused to let the dredgers go upstream. The Okrug Executive Committee recognized this act as legal. In 1987, it transpired that the excavations were unprofitable and the gravel company withdrew, leaving behind a crippled river.

The saddest part of the story is that the legality or illegality of what the Khants or the gravel company did was not evaluated by the court but by the Okrug executive administration. The idea that the gravel company could be taken to court never occurred to any group in the conflict – to the Khants, the administration, the company – because of the complete dominance of the courts at all levels by the Communist Party structures. The courts always rubber stamped party decisions.

An illustration of what awaited a native if he or she went to court against an incomer occurred in 1985. An old hunter lived alone on Sakhalin in a small Nivkh village which had been abandoned in the 1960s. He had a licence from the Oblast administration for hunting in the area and also a part-time job as a poaching inspector. Several kilometres away from the village there was a lighthouse where a new keeper, a Russian, came to work. Very soon the Nivkh hunter noticed that the Russian was poaching in his territory, hunting seals and foxes. Finally, he killed a bear.

Bears are sacred animals in Nivkh culture. There is a very elaborate bear cult and a bear may only be killed after a long and complicated ceremony. The old hunter was enraged and, since the law was obviously on his side, took the Russian to court. Yet the court acquitted the Russian and started a case against the Nivkh accusing *him* of poaching. The police searched his house without a warrant, his guns were confiscated even though all were properly licensed, and skins were taken. During the search, a policeman said to the old man, 'You shouldn't have acted against a Russian. See what's going to happen to you now!' The old man was fined by the court, firstly 500 then an extra 200 roubles. The story, one of many, became known for the sole reason that the old man's brother was a well-known Nivkh writer, Vladimir Sangi, who lives in Moscow and is now President of the Association of Northern Minorities and who was influential enough to make the episode public.[91]

The prosecution and punishment of natives who sought justice against the violence of the incomers were common in the 1970s and 1980s. This was the time when the courts, the police, the KGB, the administration and the press were closely bound by mutual guarantee and by membership in the party structures, and were ready to bring the immense power of the state down on any 'troublemaker' who dared to question their right to violate the law.

A standard accusation was that of 'nationalistic activities' and, from the early 1930s until recently, this was used many times against natives who tried to oppose the large-scale industrial offensive or to protect traditional culture. The supposed logic behind the accusation was that when an ethnic group opposed the interests of the state, they were thereby committing a 'crime' against the state. To give an indication of the scale of the problem, in Yakutiya, about 3,000 people were arrested between 1950 and 1985 for nationalistic activities.[92] The same crime was used to arrest and incriminate the majority of the Shor intelligentsia.[93]

Servernye Prostory journal is full of bitter letters by native people who mourn their dying motherland, and protest against their lack of rights and denial of free speech. One states:

'I am an Evenk...In our village we now number only about 409 people. Our traditional reindeer-breeding is gradually being curtailed as unprof-

itable. We have forgotten our language, our traditions, our culture, our arts. There are no natives in the local Executive Committee; outsiders have all the power, but they are not interested in our local problems including ecological ones. A hydro-electric plant is being built on the Adycha river – this means death for nature, as well as for us. Three million cubic metres of timber will go under water, many villages will be pulled down. Where shall we live, what shall we do, where shall we hunt and fish, where shall we get drinking water?... I once had an opportunity to ask A.M. Zoteyev, the Deputy Chairman of the Council of Ministers of the Russian Federation: Why don't you take into consideration the interests of the native people? He answered without hesitation: "The interests of the state go first, the interests of the people are subordinate".[94]

Before 1985, it never occurred to those in power in the North that indigenous people could make a compensation claim for their devastated land. The Norilsk mining enterprise, one of the largest and richest in the country, which is located in the heart of Taymyr Autonomous Okrug, succeeded in providing relatively high wages, decent food supplies (at least before 1988) and tolerable living conditions for its workers. Yet for several decades it refused to notice the impoverished native population that lived on the land from which it extracted its wealth.[95]

Inequalities
The difference in living standards between the Northern Minorities and the incomers is vast. In the Kamchatkan villages of Oklan, Khairyuzovo, Voyampolka and others, average living space per person is 3–7 sq. m. – about the size of a graveyard plot. Most villages lack the basic utilities: no running water, no central heating, sometimes no electricity. The same disparity in wages, which began in the 1930s, between the native population and incomers remains today.[96] The average monthly wage of an Eskimo sea-hunter in 1988 was generally around 80 roubles while the monthly wage of a Chukotkan miner in 1985 was around 900 roubles and those of a Norilsk miner in 1990 around 1,700 roubles. The living conditions of a native in the Northern villages is three to four times worse than in the Russian Federation[97] in general. At Vostok collective farm on Sakhalin in 1981, the distribution of income was similarly unequal: 36.8 per cent of natives and only 8.4 per cent of non-natives had a salary of 2,400 roubles or less, while 56.6 per cent of non-natives and only 18.7 per cent of natives had a salary of over 4,800 roubles.[98]

The native population is able to find only the lowest paid and least qualified jobs. Unemployment amongst the natives is very high, since their traditional activities have been undermined, declared unprofitable and shut down. In the new jobs, the Northern Minorities can seldom compete with the incomers, not only because their training is worse and their education of poorer quality, but also because many of the key positions in the village, Raion and Oblast administration are taken by non-natives who are often prejudiced against hiring natives. For example, only one director of the 18 Taymyr state farms was a native resident.[99]

Until recently, the law of 'Northern increments' offered an increase of up to 200 per cent for long-term contracts in the North but was given only to the incomers. Around 1985, the law was changed but in practice the wages still differ. For example, in Yamal, the incomer still receives 170 per cent more than is paid for the same job done in the European part of Russia, while a native is only offered 150 per cent more. This contradicts Convention 169 of the International Labour Organization (especially Article 20 that demands equal payment for equal labour irrespective of the worker's ethnic affiliation). On the whole, it is difficult to find a single line in this Convention that has not been violated in the North.

Glasnost and beyond: 1985 onwards

As already shown, there was no possibility before 1985 of successfully protesting against policies of the state since the latter had a whole variety of instruments to silence opposition, which it did not hesitate to use. However, by the mid-1980s, even elements within the Communist Party began to realize that the entire Soviet system was moribund, especially in its economic inefficiencies. Cautious changes came initially from the top and, after Mikhail Gorbachev succeeded as General Secretary of the Communist Party in March 1985, these accelerated. Countless popular movements developed throughout the USSR – democratic, nationalist, environmental – and the situation rapidly took on its own momentum.

Grassroots protest
Change came later and more slowly for the Northern Minorities than for the rest of the country, perhaps because of the vastness of their territory. The following stories of two villages, Sikachi-Alyan in Khabarovskiy Krai and Paren in Kamchatkan Oblast, are helpful in illustrating the effects of this change on the indigenous peoples in general.

In 1970, a Nanai fishing cooperative was closed by the local administration in Sikachi-Alyan. As a result, unemployment soared, alco-holism and crime increased and the younger people moved to neigh-bouring towns. Next, the village Soviet was disbanded and the admin-istration moved to a larger Russian settlement. The inhabitants were forced to hand over to the state taiga land which had belonged to the village, as well as to give up their fishing sites to a state-owned fishing company. Without the permission of the Nanais, health centres for workers from neighbouring towns were established in and around the village, along with private *dachas*.

In the summer of 1989, however, the picture suddenly changed. People began to protest against the building of these *dachas* and health centres and the village council was re-established. Also, a 25-strong fishing team was organized to supply the village with fish while a con-struction team of 15 people was created to build new houses. Unem-ployment disappeared.

Currently, the Nanais' main demand is that land which belonged to their community before 1960 should be restored to them. At the same time, the village administration is studying the legal problems posed by the health centres and *dachas*. They would like to set a rent for the land and use the money for the needs of the village but, if this is refused, they are ready to take the matter to court with the help of the Association of Northern Minorities.

In Kamchatka, as late as 1986, the Raion Council launched a cam-paign to shut down the village of Paren because of its alleged unprof-itability. At first, they tried to talk the people into moving voluntarily and to switch to the work of reindeer breeders. Then, when they failed, they threatened to dismantle the electric power plant and to shut down the shop.

However, the times had changed. When the Raion Council's delega-tion came to the village to 'persuade' and threaten, it was met by a well-organized rally and posters saying, 'The Poytylo tribe will never leave the land of their ancestors!' The local and central press heard of the protests and published scores of articles and letters from the vil-lagers. One letter read: 'The relocation of Paren population will mean one thing: we, the Paren Koryaks, will lose our language, our customs, traditions and skills. What could be worse than that?' Currently, the joint efforts of the Poytylos, the press and some politicians, have suc-ceeded in at least suspending the elimination of the village.[100]

Independent political and social structures began to appear through-out the North and 1989 was an especially fruitful year in this respect. For example, an association called 'Yamal for Our Descendants' was established which opposed the ecological destruction of the Yamal

Peninsula. In Leningrad, the Siberian Cultural Centre was founded with the aim of uniting all Northern Minority people who live in the city and of supporting their political and cultural actions against the local Russian administration in the North.

In 1989 in Kolpashevo, a village of the Tomsk Oblast, a constituent assembly of 87 delegates established the Society of Tomsk Sel'kups. One of its major demands was the restoration of ethnic Sel'kup village Soviets in areas of high-density Sel'kup population.[101] In the same year, the Association of Kola Saami was set up by Saami people. 'The Association is an independent non-governmental organization which is called upon to promote the social and economic development of this ethnic minority, to preserve its traditions based on the harmony of man and nature, and to study and develop its cultural and spiritual heritage.'[102]

Another constituent assembly took place in the summer of 1990 in Provideniya (Chukotka). This was the Regional Society of the Eskimos and its 52 delegates came from six important villages in the area. The main goals of the society are to fight for the right of native priority to land usage, for the right to pursue traditional industries, for the introduction of taxation of all organizations using the land and for cultural revival.

First Congress of Northern Minorities

A very important event in the history of Northern Minority political struggle occurred in March 1990 when the First Congress of Northern Minorities took place in Moscow. Despite an element of government manipulation, especially at the beginning, the Congress overcame this and adopted several important resolutions as well as establishing the Association of Northern Minorities with Vladimir Sangi as chairman. Its goal was bluntly formulated: 'To unite all our strengths in order to survive'.

The main resolutions were as follows: the delegates stressed that only seven out of the 26 Northern Minorities have formal ethnic autonomous structures. Therefore, alongside the necessity to re-establish National Raions and indigenous village Soviets, the Congress recommended a return to tribal Soviets and Councils of Elders as forms of self-administration. They also demanded legal confirmation of traditional land usage in areas populated by the Northern Minorities and that industrial projects in the North should be evaluated by a local indigenous organization. Thus, indigenous village Soviets should be given exclusive rights to control both land and water usage and reserved territories might be established to protect traditional life. The Congress also noted a very low level of education and medical service amongst the Northern Minorities and called for special measures concerning their languages and cultures.

The Congress addressed the Soviet government and demanded immediate ratification of the 'Convention Concerning Indigenous and Tribal Peoples in Independent Countries'. This had been adopted by the International Labour Organization (ILO) in June 1989 but its principles needed to be observed throughout the USSR.[103]

However small in numberss the Northern Minorities may be, they do have an intelligentsia of their own, including well-known writers, social workers, scholars and politicians who live in the larger cities and have access to the information and to decision-makers on Northern Minority policy, both on a national and international level. This group, together with the educational, cultural and social workers in the villages, plays an important part in formulating and promoting ideas that can help all the Northern Minorities. Undoubtedly, their membership and participation in the movement are sure to grow.

Government actions

A widespread discussion of the catastrophic situation facing the Northern Minorities started after 1985 and has already begun to cause changes in government policy.[104] For example, in the cultural sphere, the Council of Ministers issued an edict in 1989 that school classes in the Ul'chi, Yukagir, Itel'men, Dolgan and Nivkh languages should be resumed. New programmes for instruction in reindeer breeding, hunting and fur farming have been introduced. Northern Minority newspapers which were closed in the early 1930s (the only exceptions were the Khants, Nenets and Chukchee papers) are now slowly reappearing.

In August 1989, the Even-Bytantai National Raion was established. It was the first in several decades and serves a compact group of about 1,000 Evens who live in a territory of 55,600 sq. km. The National Raion is a reserved area and the Raion Soviet has a deciding vote on all questions of industrial and other development in the region. The right of the Evens to their traditional way of life is secured by local law.[105]

In 1990, the Soviet Parliament passed two laws which have a direct bearing on the Northern Minority situation. One of these, 'On General Principles of Local Self-Administration' (9 April),[106] contains several sections which can be used by the Northern Minorities to improve their situation.

Section 2, paragraph 3, states: 'Village Soviet, settlement, Raion, town and part of town can be considered as primary territorial units of self-administration.' This allows an ethnic group to establish its own administrative body which would include local people.

Section 8 sets an economic basis for self-administration: natural resources (land, minerals, water, forests, vegetable and animal life), communal and other property are to serve as a source of local income and to satisfy the social and economic needs of the population of a given territory.

Section 11 states: 'Economic relations between local administrations and industrial enterprises, and organizations that are not communal property, should be based on taxation and agreements.'

Section 23 is also very important: 'The establishment and reorganization of industrial and social enterprises that are using natural resources of a given territory should be carried out only in accordance with the consent of local Soviet...Enterprises...irrespective of their affiliation...should get permission from the local Soviet for any kind of activity affecting the ecology, demography etc. of a given territory.'

The other law passed in 1990, 'On Free Ethnic Development of the Citizens of the USSR who Live outside their Ethnic Territories or have no such Territories within the USSR' (26 April),[107] is even more important. This allows for the establishment, in areas which are heavily populated by an ethnic group, of indigenous territorial units like National Raions and indigenous village Soviets. These can be created if, through an expression of free will, the majority of the population demands them (Section 7). At the same time, an ethnic territorial unit may be established if an ethnic group does not constitute a majority of the population: an extremely important provision for the majority of the Northern Minority population at the end of the 20th Century.

The political situation in the Russian Federation is now changing rapidly since normal political life has emerged from fear and muteness. After the 1989 elections to the Supreme Soviet (the Union Parliament), many deputies began to make public the violations of human and indigenous rights that had been occurring in the North for decades. Papers and journals were filled with inquiries from deputies and perplexed and helpless replies from ministers, who had previously been accustomed to accounting only to the Communist Party. As a result, many industrial projects in the North were cancelled or suspended.

The establishment of the Association of Northern Minorities became a powerful stimulus for political movements of Northern Minorities all over the country. Groups of qualified experts worked on the legal, economic, ecological and social aspects of the Northern Minorities' situation. New laws provided the indigenous peoples, at least theoretically, with a vastly improved legal standing.

In December 1991, the USSR finally broke apart. The new Russian state, formerly the Russian Federation, took over all the international and internal obligations and problems of the former USSR, including those of the Northern Minorities. However, much of the former opposition is still in existence in the form of the Oblast, Okrug and Raion administrations and the industrial lobby. The major economic switch from a centralized economy to a free market one is bound to affect the Northern Minorities, as it will all the population, although the long-term effects will take some time to emerge.

The actual situation of the indigenous peoples has yet to change dramatically but today there is hope that, protected by consistent laws and assisted by a free press that gives their voices a chance to be heard, Russia's native peoples will find the moral strength to rise from the catastrophic situation in which they have found themselves after 70 years of totalitarian rule.

The way ahead

Much of what has happened in the North probably could not have been avoided. The incomers would have arrived in any case; the industrial development, timber cutting, oil and gas extraction would have started under any conditions; the influence of the Russian language and the process of cultural divergence were inevitable. Developments like these take place all over the world, and it would be naive to pretend that they can be reversed or ignored. One estimate is that up to 50 per cent of the world's languages will become extinct during the coming century.[108]

Is there hope for Northern Minorities?
Governmental wisdom is needed, together with knowledge and patience, to make the process of development as painless and uncomplicated as possible for indigenous peoples. The world presents many different models and patterns of transition. For example, in Greenland, Denmark conducted for centuries a policy of total governmental control over all the native populations' contacts with the outside world. The United States and Australia chose to set up reserves for their remaining indigenous peoples. Today, these three countries are attempting to rectify the mistakes of the past.

Unfortunately, the Soviet experience seems to be the least successful. Instead of trying to mitigate the negative consequences of its policies, government actions have reinforced and intensified them by speeding up assimilation and by aiding the disintegration of traditional social organizations, cultures and indigenous languages. Its obvious ultimate goal was the 'melting down' of various ethnic groups into one single unit, 'the Soviet people'.

It is possible that the original intentions were good. Those who determined the policies in the North may have believed quite sincerely that they were beneficial: that the Nivkhs of Sakhalin would be more comfortable in larger modern settlements; that the Eskimos, born sea-hunters, needed protection and should not be allowed to hunt in their skin-boats for their own security; that the Naukan Eskimos would be happy to leave their cliffs and settle down in a Chukchee village. However, even good intentions, implemented by force, unsupported by knowledge and without an effective mechanism of two-way communication between the central power and the people, inevitably fail.

This failure was marked by the fact that the Northern Minorities had no administrative territorial units and local organs of power that could secure their rights and protect traditional forms of economic, social and cultural life in accordance with an effective legal code. From the late 1920s, all the essential decisions in the North were made at higher administrative levels: in Oblast, Republic, Central Parliament, ministries, or, more often, Communist Party structures.

The Northern Minorities suffered the same tragic consequences of the totalitarian Communism that embraced the whole country. However, since they were small in number and much more vulnerable, the pressure on them was much stronger. 'The people of the North live a completely different life compared to other peoples of the USSR, to the extent that the constitutional equal rights they have do not mean real equality. Special protection is needed of their environment, their way of life, their right to control their economic development.'[109]

To find a way forward, great efforts are needed. Much work will be required from the Northern Minorities themselves, as well as the special attention and professional work of experts and politicians over the coming years.

Possible solutions
One possible solution may be in reserved territories of a specific type. This is partly a revival of Vladimir Bogoraz's approach which he formulated in the early 1920s, that the only way to protect and save the native peoples was to establish and secure by law special areas of taiga and tundra, rivers and seas, for their exclusive use. These ideas, that would have been considered 'seditious' and 'anti-Soviet' before 1985, are today rapidly gaining support.

Yet, in fact, over a decade before glasnost, the creation of reserves had been tentatively suggested. For example, in 1970, a Leningrad biologist, B.A. Tikhomirov, recommended the establishment of a chain of national parks on the Taymyr Peninsula where only the Northern Minorities would be allowed to hunt. This suggestion, presented to an academic symposium on wild reindeer, was heavily criticized as 'propaganda of reserves', and was never published. Similar ideas applying to other areas came from a Leningrad linguist and anthropologist, E.A. Kreinovich, but were not published either.

The concept of 'biosphere' national parks was also put forward. In the early 1980s, Soviet economist N.I. Chesnokov proposed the establishment in western Siberia of a network of a new type of national parks, which were to include both territories reserved for the traditional economic and cultural activities of Northern Minorities, including hunting, and also areas where hunting, fishing and even entry would be forbidden to anyone.

When, in 1982–5, such a national park was established close to the border of Evenk Autonomous Okrug and Turukhan Krai, it included a 'core' where no hunting was allowed and also large parcels of land for Kets, Evenki and Sel'kups.[111] Professor L.S. Bogoslovskaya, a Moscow ecologist, and her colleagues are working on plans for a similar national park ('Beringia') to cover the ethnic territory of the Eskimos and the Maritime Chukchees in southeastern Chukotka and southwestern Alaska.

The Samotlor Practicum
In 1989, a representative meeting of 35 scholars expert on the Northern Minorities took place in Tyumen.[112] The 'Samotlor Practicum' suggested three possible paths for the future evolution of the North. The first was 'non-interference', the second was 'reserved territories' and the third was 'cultural assimilation'. The majority of the experts voted, with certain additions and changes, for the second path.

They stressed that the previous paternalistic approach of 'Big Brother' was both immoral and non-productive and that every ethnic group, like every individual, should have a right to choose between a traditional and a modern way of life (or a combination of the two). This choice should not be offered only once in a lifetime but opportunities for choosing either way should be permanently available.

One group of experts (L. Bogoslovskaya, V. Kalyakin, I. Krupnik, V. Lebedev, A. Pika) insisted that the concept of 'ethnic territories' and the basic idea of the priority of indigenous subsistence and economic activities should be legally recognized and secured by law. They suggested any future law should contain the following principles in order to regulate relations between indigenous peoples and the state:

1 A Northern Minority village that traditionally uses certain land, forest, tundra, river, etc. should have the deciding vote in all questions of allocations of these territories to any industrial enterprise or ministry.
2 Any 'amalgamation', relocation or liquidation of villages by an outside decision should be legally forbidden.
3 The environmental protection law should be extended to cover preservation of traditional industries and subsistence systems.
4 General, large-scale programmes for the economic and social development of the North should be replaced by specific small-scale projects for smaller areas, with careful regard to specific ecological systems and traditions.
5 Large-scale industrial projects in the North should be submitted not only to independent ecologists but also to independent ethnologists.[113]

Many experts from the Samotlor Practicum agreed that Northern Minorities should be given effective instruments with which to choose their future themselves, such as referenda. Theoretically, the idea of self-determination is an excellent one, but considering the immense social, cultural and psychological effects of totalitarianism, are the Northern Minorities still capable of finding enough energy and knowledge to take their destiny completely into their own hands?

In all probability, some outside help will be needed, including economic assistance as well as social and psychological support, in order to restore the initiative and to return the native people socially and psychologically to the integrity of the early 1920s.

All the experts came to the conclusion that every attempt to improve the situation of the Northern Minorities would be ineffective without profound legislative change. First, the areas populated by the indigenous peoples must be given effective autonomy. They must also be as decentralized as possible, in the form of indigenous Raions or, preferably, indigenous villages. These should be underpinned by two principles: legal guarantees to land and budgetary allocations made directly to the minorities.

The first principle would include a government programme to support the traditional use of land and resources. It would contain legal guarantees of rights to an indigenous area, Raion, village etc. as well as a final veto on forced alienation or rental of land in any form and for any purposes. The establishment of the Even-Bytantai National Raion in 1989 was a step towards this goal.

The second principle of budgetary allocations creates complications.

At present, when the central government (be it Soviet or Russian) allots certain funding with the aim to 'secure development of the areas populated by Northern Minorities', the money almost invariably goes to the existing industrial and agricultural structures of the Raion, Okrug or Oblast: factories, collective and state farms, where the Northern Minorities are often a minority.

To reverse this, compensations and royalties should be paid directly to Northern Minorities, both to recompense the people for past exploitation and damage and to pay for future use of their natural resources. In addition, they should be allotted not a proportional part of the national budget but, in accordance with European experience of regional support, a larger share: after all, they are much more vulnerable and comparatively poorer than the rest of the population.

However, the main problem is not the amount of money but its distribution for, at present, the latter remains under the full control of Oblast, Okrug and Raion administrations and these include very few indigenous representatives. Even if the compensations are paid, they will be channelled to build housing and new public buildings in larger settlements and towns, to improve the road system in and around the towns, to import furniture, food, clothes, cars and so on. They will never be used to support the development of traditional indigenous villages, life or cultures.

It is understandable perhaps that the democratically elected Oblast government should try to satisfy the needs of the majority but the rights of the Northern Minorities can never be secured if they are not protected by special laws aimed at putting them in a privileged position. This is the only effective instrument to secure equality. The importance and indispensability of special legislation for the Northern Minorities have become self-evident.

Language and culture

Although the languages of the Northern Minorities are taught in schools in the North, education in its present form can provide little or no support for their preservation. There is a shortages of teachers, schools and books. The teachers are often young people who are themselves not proficient in the Northern Minority languages while the technique of teaching them as 'mother-tongues' through primers, reading and writing, a technique which was developed in the 1930s, is now hopelessly outdated.

In Surgut and Nizhnevartovsk (inhabited by the Khants), there was not one qualified Khant-speaking educationalist in 1988. No Yukagir language teacher could be found for the primary school in Nelemnoye in 1987 and no Aleut language teacher could be found for Nikolskoye school in 1984. In 1991, when an announcer for the Anadyr-based Eskimo-language radio programme retired, no substitute could be found.

The terrible blows suffered by the Northern Minorities may prove to be fatal for many of their languages. Yet it may not be too late for some of these to be revitalized, as has happened elsewhere in the world. Referring to the Canadian Inuits, Louis-Jacques Dorais states: 'The future of Inuit language and culture is linked to the preservation of a strong local identity, which, in turn, stems from a world-view where native and non-native knowledge are harmoniously integrated.'[114]

Even so, the complete loss of their native language by the younger generation does not necessarily signify total assimilation and loss of ethnic identity. Evenk in Buryatiya, for whom either Russian or Buryat is now their native tongue, still consider themselves Evenk. The Nenets, assimilated linguistically to the Komi, call themselves Nenets. The Eskimos who now speak only Russian identify themselves as Eskimos.[115] To build on the remaining languages, whatever they may be, provides hope for the cultural survival of the Northern Minorities.

3

THE ALASKA NATIVES

by Fae L. Korsmo

Introduction

From the moist coastal climate of the southeast panhandle, with its towering cedar trees, to the bare, windswept tundra, Alaska hosts a diversity of cultures. Long before Russian explorers plied the coasts in the 1700s, the forebears of the Alaska Natives had established themselves as distinct societies. The term 'Alaska Natives' encompasses the Yupik, Inupiat, Aleut, Athabaskan, Tlingit, Haida and Tsimshian peoples. Together, they constitute just over 15 per cent of the state's population, or more than 85,000 people out of approximately 550,000 statewide.[1] They speak twenty different languages.[2] Fifty-six per cent of the Alaska Natives are concentrated in non-urban areas, including more than 200 small villages with populations smaller than 2,500.[3] However, the state's most populous city, Anchorage, is home to more than 14,000 Native people.[4] Alaska Natives can be found in a variety of occupations and ways of life, from subsistence hunting and fishing to state and corporate office. Despite the cultural, linguistic, occupational and geographical differences, the Alaska Natives have shared similar challenges as a result of colonization and pressures to assimilate to the dominant culture. Perhaps the most pressing concerns of the Alaska Natives today involve self-government and tribal jurisdiction over land and water, in addition to health and social problems such as alcohol abuse, suicide, unemployment, housing and sanitation.[5]

This chapter will give a brief overview of the controversies and recent developments surrounding Alaska Native rights, beginning with the history of contact between Alaska Natives and first the Russians and then, after 1867, the United States. After the historical treatment, we

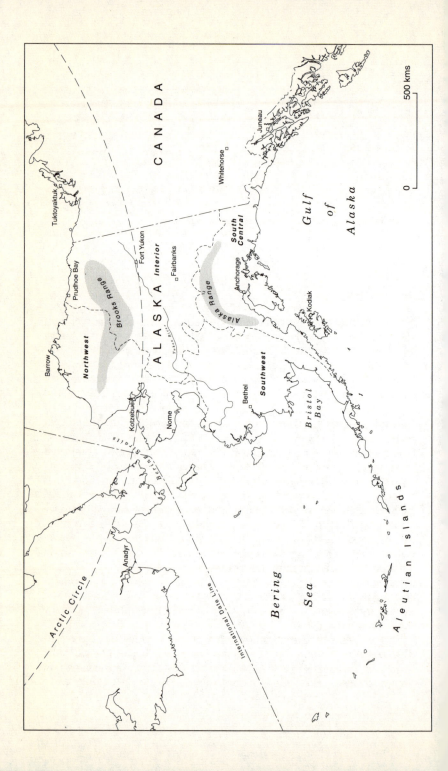

shall turn to the issues of subsistence, tribal sovereignty and future prospects. Space does not permit more than a few details about the separate and distinct Native cultures in Alaska, or more than a cursory glance at the complex evolution of US policies. Throughout the chapter, however, a single theme emerges: Alaska Natives are neither the passive victims of aggressive colonization nor the single most important arbiters of their own lives, but independent actors who are nevertheless subject to powerful economic and political forces beyond their control. The recognition of Alaska Native rights evolves and shifts accordingly in the ever-changing context of minority–majority relations.

Russian America, 1741–1867

When Vitus Bering and Alexii Chirikov and their crews landed on the Alaskan coast in 1741, they opened the way for more than a century of Russian fur trade. Russia extended its empire to Alaska as part of the sweep across Siberia. Whereas peasants were brought to till the soil and colonize Siberia, in addition to hunters and trappers of fur-bearing mammals such as sable, farming made little headway in Alaska. Few Russians actually settled in Alaska. Instead, the sea otter became the main object of the Russian hunter-traders (*promyshlenniki*) who stayed long enough to accumulate their bounty. The Russians forced the Aleuts to hunt sea otters and fur seals for them, taking advantage of the expertise and equipment the Aleuts had developed over thousands of years of living in their marine environment. As a result of the harsh treatment as well as new diseases brought from the European continent, the Aleut population declined by at least 80 per cent during the first and second generations of Russian contact.[6]

Along with population loss came culture change. Because Russian settlement was largely confined to the coasts and the mouths of major rivers, not all Alaska Native groups experienced daily contact with the newcomers. Who were these different peoples the Russians encountered? How were they treated?

The Aleuts experienced the longest and most intensive history of non-Native contact.[7] Prior to contact, the Aleuts lived in villages and seasonal subsistence camps along the coasts of the Aleutian Islands. Food sources included marine mammals, marine invertebrates, eggs, birds, fish and plants. Villages consisted of multi-family semi-subterranean dwellings, or *barabaras*, made of stones, driftwood and whalebone. With their water-repellent clothing made of gut and their sturdy canoes or *bidarkas*, the Aleuts were well adapted to the marine climate. When forced into Russian service, the male Aleut hunters

Alaska Native Languages

Language family	Language
Eskimo-Aleut	Aleut
	Alutiiq
	Central Yupik
	Siberian Yupik
	Inupiaq
Tsimshian	Tsimshian
Haida	Haida
Athabaskan-Eyak-Tlingit	Tlingit
	Eyak
	Ahtna
	Tanaina
	Ingalik
	Holikachuk
	Koyukon
	Upper Kuskokwim
	Tanana
	Tanacross
	Upper Tanana
	Han
	Kutchin

were often taken from their homes and families, leaving the women and children to fish and gather. Settlement patterns were broken, and some Aleuts were relocated to other islands such as the Pribilofs. In addition, Russian Orthodoxy replaced traditional spiritual beliefs and rituals associated with the hunting and gathering life.

Other coastal peoples affected by Russian contact included the Koniag of Kodiak Island, the Yupik of southwest Alaska, the Kenaitze of the Kenai Peninsula, the Chugach, and the Tlingit in southeast Alaska. The Koniag numbered 10,000 or more at the time of Russian contact. Archaeological evidence reveals a complex society based on extended families (again we see the multi-family dwellings, housing perhaps 18 to 20 people), ritual observances centred around spiritual transformations and a fisher-hunter-gatherer economy where the salmon played an important part.[8] Linguistically related to the Koniag, the Yupik of the Yukon–Kuskokwim delta first encountered Russian explorers and missionaries in the early 1800s.[9] The Yupik may have numbered as many as 15,000 at the time of Russian contact, spread out in villages along the delta. Rich in fish, including salmon, whitefish and trout, the rivers and streams braided through territory that supported abundant game – moose and caribou as well as smaller mammals like otter, muskrat, fox and mink. People followed the movements of fish and game, with extended families occupying fishing camps along the rivers during the summer and larger, more permanent villages during the winter.[10]

To the south and east, the Russians attempted to gain a foothold in Tlingit territory, using Koniag and Chugach men as hunters and warriors to raid the Tlingit villages in the late 1700s. The Tlingit were trading with the British and initially fought the Russians.[11] The northernmost of the northwest coast peoples who built large wooden houses, totem poles and dugout canoes, the Tlingit were known as skilful warriors and traders who gave away their many luxuries at elaborate ceremonials called potlatches.[12] They temporarily succeeded in expelling the Russians, but after 1804 it appeared the Russians were determined to maintain a settlement at Sitka. The Tlingit simply went on with their lives and tolerated the Russian presence.

People living in the far north and interior regions of Alaska saw far less of the Russians than the coastal and riverine groups, simply because these areas were inaccessible or undesirable from the Russian perspective.[13] For the Inupiat and Athabaskan peoples living in north and interior Alaska, contact with the Russians was predominantly indirect; trade with other Native groups further south brought Russian goods into their hands, but Russia established no settlements.[14]

According to Kostlivtsev, commissioned by the Russian government to investigate property rights in Russian America in 1860:

> *'the further from the coast, the more rough and independent the charac-*
> *ter of the savages; every symptom not only of social, but even of settled*
> *life, disappears, because these natives, having no other occupation but*
> *hunting, migrate in the track of game from one part to another, estab-*
> *lishing but provisional settlements for the winter season.'*[15]

Kostlivtsev may have been describing the Athabaskans, hunter-fisher-gatherers of the northern forest. Northern Athabaskan groups can be found across both Alaska and Canada. They were extremely mobile, and their temporary and semi-permanent dwellings reflected their seasonal movements according to wildlife migrations and weather patterns.[16] While the Russians dismissed them as savages, the Athabaskans had elaborate kinship networks and powerful tribal chiefs or councils comprising a rather complex political system. The same could be said of the Inupiat, who in general were more oriented towards the north coast and depended on the sea-mammal harvest. The most important early contact with the Inupiat, in fact, was made not by the Russians but by whaling ships from New England and California which followed the bowhead whale along the north Alaskan coast and across the ocean to the western Chukchi Sea during the middle 1800s.[17]

Russian presence, then, had varying impacts on Alaska Natives, ranging from the virtual enslavement of the Aleuts to little or no interest in the more remote groups of Athabaskans and Inupiat. Given the mistreatment of Aleuts and other coastal societies, it seems incongruous that Russians accepted Creoles, or people of combined Native and Russian heritage, as Russian subjects and devoted considerable energy to teaching and preserving the Aleut language.[18] Perhaps an explanation lies in the inclusive form of colonialism the Russians practised, whereby local leaders willing to cooperate were co-opted and their followers integrated into Russian society.[19]

The 1844 Charter of the Russian-American Company, the fur-trading monopoly established as a hybrid governmental and economic concern in Alaska, recognized three categories of Natives. First, the dependent or settled tribes were considered Russian subjects, and these probably included the Aleuts, Koniag, Kenaitze and Chugach. Second, the not wholly dependent tribes lived within the reach of Russian settlement, but did not enjoy the duties or privileges of Russian settlement. The second category most likely referred to the Tlingit, who resisted the Russians. Third, the independent tribes (further north and inland, such as the Athabaskans and Inupiat) had little interaction with the Russians.[20]

The Russian classification system became an important source of knowledge for the United States when the latter purchased Alaska from Russia in 1867. It is hardly surprising that neither Russia nor the United States consulted the societies living in Alaska before making this transaction. To this day, some Alaska Natives refer to 1867 as the year that 'the occupation rights' to Alaska were transferred; Russia never had legitimate possession of Alaska, so how could Russia sell something it did not own?[21] In any case, the Treaty of Cession between Russia and the United States recognized three groups of Alaskan people: (1) Russian subjects who preferred to retain their allegiance and were permitted to return to Russia within three years; (2) Russian subjects who preferred to remain in Alaska and enjoy the rights and immunities of US citizens; and (3) the uncivilized tribes who would be 'subject to such laws and regulations as the United States may, from time to time, adopt in regard to aboriginal tribes of that country'.[22]

But these categories did not translate directly into US law. Who were US citizens? Prior to 1924, Native Americans could become citizens of the United States only on the condition that they applied for an allotment of land and gave up their tribal ways. Were the children of Russian fathers and Alaska Native mothers US citizens or members of 'uncivilized' tribes? Were Alaska Native societies 'tribes' under federal Indian law?

Early US administration and aboriginal rights

Immediately after the 1867 Treaty of Cession, the United States occupied Alaska militarily, using both the army and the navy. The 1884 Organic Act ended military rule in Alaska and made Alaska a customs district governed by several federal officials. The Second Organic Act of 1912 made Alaska into a territory of the United States and provided for a legislature.[23]

With regard to Native rights, US rule consisted of a mixture of neglect, assimilation and segregation. Schools were segregated. During the first twenty years following the Treaty of Cession, the United States made no provision for education; instead mission societies provided education. From 1885, the US government began to establish state schools and contracted with the missionaries to continue to provide education. Around the turn of the century, however, a dual system of education was inaugurated. Under the governor of the District (and subsequently Territory) of Alaska, schools were established for 'White children and children of mixed blood leading a civilized life'. Native schools, however, were under the jurisdiction of the federal government.

Segregation also existed in the realm of political participation. In 1925, the Alaska territorial legislature enacted a literacy law, requiring that voters be able to read and write the English language. Similar laws in other parts of the United States were designed to keep minorities from voting, and the same motivations were present in Alaska.[24]

Policy concerning Alaska Natives' rights to land and water was marked by neglect and, whenever a conflict arose between Native and non-Native, a confusion of two approaches: assimilation and aboriginal rights of possession. The 1884 Organic Act had provided that 'Indians or other persons in said district [Alaska] shall not be disturbed in the possession of any lands actually in their use or occupation or now claimed by them, but the terms under which such persons may acquire title to such lands are reserved for future legislation by Congress.'[25] However, on what basis did the Alaska Natives possess title to their lands? Was it aboriginal title or did the Natives and non-Native settlers possess equal rights to landownership? The courts said yes to both. In the first instance, Alaska Natives were legally equivalent to Native American tribes and held land in common based on aboriginal occupancy.[26] In other words, Alaska Natives held separate but not inferior systems of land tenure, and these systems had their own internal validity independent of recognition by a European power. Once the discovering nation established a foothold, though, the power of the Natives to sell their lands to anyone else but the discovering nation was curtailed. Thus, when the United States signed the Treaty of Cession, Congress assumed the ultimate power to extinguish aboriginal title and dispose of Native lands. The Alaska Natives still had the right to possess those lands, however.[27]

In the second instance, the courts determined that Alaska Natives held individual rights equivalent to those of white, non-Native settlers who came to homestead.[28] This approach was in tune with the assimilationist policy favoured by the United States during the late 1800s and early 1900s. The purchase of Alaska from Russia and its territorial incorporation occurred concomitantly with the selling of Indian reservation lands in the rest of the United States and the accompanying efforts to make Indians into farmers. The General Allotment Act (also known as the Dawes Act) of 1887 divided tribal property into individual allotments, sold the 'surplus' Indian lands and provided for citizenship to be conferred on Indians who abandoned their tribes, took up the plough and adopted the habits of civilized life.[29] Congress passed a separate allotment act for Alaska in 1906, even though there was very little reservation land to break up. In fact, the small reservations that the US government did establish in Alaska during the early years were primarily for schools, hospitals and reindeer herding. They represented the efforts of the US Commissioner of Education and his agent, Sheldon Jackson, to provide tools for self-sufficiency and a settled, civilized life, not a means to reaffirm and strengthen Alaska Native cultures.[30]

These reservations were designed to aid the transition from a hunter-gatherer existence to a cash economy through vocational training, the establishment of reindeer herding and the protection of fisheries.[31]

The question, then, of whether the Alaska Natives possessed collective aboriginal title (as had the Native American tribes of more southerly regions before they signed treaties with the United States), or whether they held individual rights equivalent to non-Native homesteaders, remained unresolved and confused, often decided in favour of more powerful interests, such as the fisheries and mining industries.

Retribalization, reservations and statehood

During the 1930s, the United States turned away from the allotment policy. The Dawes Act had failed to assimilate Native Americans or to eliminate the tribe as a fundamental unit. Instead, the land losses and dislocations resulting from the policy seemed to exacerbate problems of poverty. The new policy under the Roosevelt administration, then, recommitted the United States to maintaining tribal identity. The Indian Reorganization Act (IRA) of 1934 repealed allotment, appropriated funds for the purchase of lands for landless Native Americans, set up a credit fund for loans and authorized tribal organization and incorporation. Tribes had the right to adopt constitutions, employ legal counsel, protect tribal lands and negotiate with federal and state governments. They also acquired the right to own, manage and dispose of property. Two years later, the policy was extended to Alaska in the Alaska Reorganization Act of 1936.[32]

US Interior Secretary Harold Ickes gave three reasons for establishing Alaska Native reservations. First, they would define Native groups as tribes. Second, they would stipulate the geographic limits of tribal jurisdictions. Third, they would allow the United States to protect the economic rights of the Natives against outside commercial interests.[148] As a result of the Alaska Reorganization Act, 69 villages chose to reorganize their form of government and adopt the constitutions recommended by the provisions of the Indian Reorganization Act. In addition, six villages established 'IRA' reservations.[34]

Why so few reservations in Alaska? Opposition to reservations came from several sources. First, commercial fishing and cannery companies opposed any reservations that would limit their access to rivers and coastlines. Second, politicians, including the territorial governor of Alaska Ernest Gruening, opposed segregating Alaska Natives and equated reservations with powerlessness, poverty and subsistence. Third, in some cases the Natives themselves voted down proposed reservations. For example, the Inupiat of Barrow and Shungnak voted against establishing reservations, reportedly because they thought a reservation would not encompass a large enough area for hunting and fishing.[35]

In the United States as a whole, the policy to encourage the maintenance of tribal identity was short-lived. It was replaced by 'termination', or several legislative acts authorizing the cessation of a special federal–tribal relationship for specific tribes and the removal of responsibility in Native American affairs from the federal to the state level. For example, Public Law 280 transferred civil and criminal jurisdiction over Native Americans from the tribes to the states; the states also assumed many educational responsibilities formerly carried out by the tribes and the federal government.[36] In Alaska, the campaign for statehood after the Second World War coincided with the termination era in federal Indian policy. For those interested in the economic and political success of the new State of Alaska, reservations and the federal–Indian trust relationship seemed like obstacles to the development of resources and the collection of tax revenues.[37] After considering various options for statehood, including the revocation of Native reservations in Alaska and the transfer of practically all lands to the new state, Congress passed a bill that would grant 103.5 million acres, or nearly one-third of Alaska's territory, to the new state. Thus, when Alaska became a state in January 1959, it had the power to acquire a great deal of land, including land still claimed by Alaska Natives.

The Alaska Native Claims Settlement Act

During and after the Second World War, Alaska experienced a construction boom, and the territory's population nearly doubled, mostly as the result of in-migration. Alaska Natives constituted 45 per cent of the territory's population in 1940; by 1950 they were only 26 per cent.[38] Increased population meant higher demands on resources. More importantly, however, the strategic importance of Alaska in the Cold War and the newly achieved statehood made both the state and federal governments powerful contenders for Alaska's land and water. The federal Atomic Energy Commission (AEC), for example, proposed to use a nuclear explosive to blast an artificial harbour at Cape Thompson on Alaska's northwest coast. In 1958, the AEC requested 1,600 square miles of land and water for the proposed explosion. The village of Point Hope voted against the project and wrote a letter of protest to President John F. Kennedy. Eventually the plans were abandoned. Similarly, the state proposed to acquire as part of its 103.5 million acres of land an area near the Athabaskan village of Minto, not only for a recreation site but also with future oil development in mind. Minto and other nearby villages protested the state's plan.[39] The village of Minto filed a counter-claim to the land and water they had occupied for many generations. In fact, villages all over Alaska began filing claims with the US Department of the Interior.

Increased competition for Native land and water not only sparked local resistance but helped to mobilize the Alaska Natives on a regional basis. In 1966, these regional Native associations met and formed a statewide organization which would become known as the Alaska Federation of Natives. In addition, the Native villages and associations across Alaska filed claims covering the entire state in an effort to block the State of Alaska from acquiring land and water the Alaska Natives had never ceded.[40] The US Secretary of the Interior, Stewart Udall, responded by stopping the transfer of public lands to the state until Congress could settle the Alaska Native claims. Congress was just starting to look at the issues when significant oil reserves were discovered on the North Slope of the Brooks Range. The oil companies wanted to build a pipeline to the port of Valdez to transport the oil out of Alaska, but Native claims held up their plans. Because the economic stakes were so high, Congress acted rather quickly to open up negotiations with the oil companies, Alaska Natives, environmental groups and the State of Alaska.

The result, the Alaska Native Claims Settlement Act (ANCSA) of 1971, created twelve regional for-profit corporations that would have title to the surface area and subsurface minerals of land selected for development across the state up to a total of 18 million hectares (44 million acres) statewide. Villages in each region could also create their own corporations, and the village corporations would retain surface title to local lands as part of the settlement. Monetary compensation for lands given up by the Natives would total $962.5 million, about half from funds supplied by Congress and half from mineral revenues collected on state and federal lands. On the surface, the ANCSA seemed like a generous settlement, one that embraced the need to modernize economically yet empowered the Natives to do so themselves and on their own terms. As time went on, however, it became clear that the settlement was not at all 'a settlement' but rather left several questions unresolved.

First, the settlement was a transitional mechanism that provided a 20-year period during which stock in the Native corporations, both regional and village, could be held only by the Alaska Natives. After that 20-year period, however, the restricted stock would be replaced by at-large shares on the open market. If non-Natives bought up the corporate stock in 1991, they would then acquire title to Native lands, for the corporations were the entities that held the title. The Alaska Natives would not only lose control over the corporations, but they would also lose their land. The year 1991, then, loomed large.

Second, Congress postponed the issue of subsistence. The settlement act extinguished aboriginal rights to hunt and fish, with the implicit assumption that subsistence practices would decline as Natives moved into the modern cash economy. At the time of the settlement, the State of Alaska promised to provide for Native subsistence needs in state fish and wildlife regulation. The State of Alaska has not recognized any Native right to hunt, fish and gather, however, and the regulation of fish and game has been riddled with controversy. Additionally, contrary to the assumption that they would move away from subsistence, Alaska Natives continue to practise a mixed economy, where wage earning provides cash for subsistence hunting and fishing technology: boats, rifles and snow machines. Subsistence is not merely a means to survive in the Arctic and sub-Arctic, but also a way of life. Identity, self-worth and life itself for the Alaska Natives are inextricably linked with subsistence activities.[42]

Third, the status of Alaska Native villages as legal and political entities and the existence of Indian Country in Alaska remain subject to dispute. 'Indian Country', or the territory over which tribes exercise jurisdiction, and tribal sovereignty, or the domestic dependent sovereignty described by Chief Justice Marshall, are issues that continue to surface in the courts. Before we consider subsistence, the ANCSA corporations, Indian Country or village status, however, we must turn to those very doctrines of federal Indian law which have engendered such controversy: aboriginal title and tribal sovereignty.

Powers of tribes: Indian Country, sovereignty and Alaska Natives

As the legal basis for Alaska Native claims prior to the ANCSA, aboriginal title is one of the ways Indian tribes have acquired property held in common. Enshrined in early US Supreme Court decisions from the early 1800s written by Chief Justice John Marshall, one of the most famous Supreme Court Justices to articulate the principles of federal Indian law, the doctrine holds that American Indian tribes have separate but not inferior systems of land tenure. Certain limitations were imposed on the powers of the tribes to cede lands to others, however, when the European powers began treating with the tribes. Through the principle of 'discovery' the Europeans divided up the right to enter into relations with the native inhabitants of the country discovered. Each European power gained the exclusive right to acquire land from the Indian tribes within their respective spheres of influence. Until the European power actually purchased Indian lands, the tribe still possessed those lands as the rightful occupants.[43]

In addition to land title, Chief Justice Marshall ruled on the legal and political status of tribes in relation to the state and federal governments. The doctrine of tribal sovereignty arises out of the treaty relationships between the Indian tribes of North America and Great Britain (later the United States). For example, the Cherokee signed a treaty in 1791 ceding certain lands to the United States, and the United States in turn guaranteed other lands to the Cherokee, lands that happened to be within the boundaries of the State of Georgia. But the State of Georgia demanded that the United States extinguish Indian title and remove the Indians from the state. When the federal government did not respond, Georgia extended its laws to Cherokee territory, despite the fact that the Cherokee Nation had its own constitution and legal system. The Cherokee took the case to court, and in this as well as related cases involving the Cherokee, Chief Justice Marshall ruled that the Cherokee Nation had the status of domestic dependent nations; within the lands they possessed, they retained sovereign powers of self-government. With respect to external diplomacy, however, the Cherokee had by treaty given up their powers to establish relations with other nations to the federal government of the United States. State governments could not assume jurisdiction within Indian reservations, then, but the federal government could limit the activities of Indian Nations beyond the boundaries of Indian Country.[44]

Powers of Indian tribes include the ability to determine the form of tribal government and tribal membership; the power to legislate, including the power to levy taxes, establish schools and control economic activity; the power to administer justice and exclude persons from tribal territory; and certain powers over non-Indians, except in criminal matters.[45] This 'domestic dependent sovereignty' assumes that a distinct territory exists, such as a reservation, over which the tribal government can exercise its power. Furthermore, jurisdiction is related to possession, a trait of Anglo-American law; the sovereign holds title to the land under its administration.

Chief Justice Marshall, in his Supreme Court decisions, characterized the relationship between the federal government of the United States and the Indian tribes as that of a guardian and ward. The stronger nation, the United States, protected the weaker nation, and in return, the tribe necessarily gave up some of its sovereignty. This 'trust' relationship between two governments implies that the United States has a continuing duty to protect tribal resources and act in the tribes' best interest. Here enters a paradox: tribes have the power to govern themselves, yet the federal government has established itself as a paternalistic protector.

What are the implications of this paradox for the Alaska Natives? Do Alaska Native villages constitute federally recognized 'tribes' or do the unique circumstances of Alaska make the Natives an exception to federal Indian law?

The State of Alaska has argued that the Alaskan situation is indeed unique compared to the history of the Indian tribes in the contiguous states.[46] According to the state's argument, Congress generally intended Alaska Natives to be governed by the same federal laws applicable to all other residents of Alaska, at least until 1936. Furthermore, the state points out that Congress never signed treaties with Alaska Natives, never regarded them as anything more than dependent subjects. The brief interlude of creating reservations according to the Alaska Reorganization Act of 1936 was merely an administrative attempt to settle Alaska Native claims and, because of the opposition it engendered, was not fully applied to all Alaska Natives. Within this argument put forth by the State of Alaska, the Alaska Native Claims Settlement Act merely continued the federal policy of treating Alaska Natives as individuals rather than tribes. The state relies on three features of the ANCSA to support this claim. First, the Native corporations would hold land in fee simple title rather than tribal reservations. ('Fee simple title' means that the owner can sell or otherwise alienate the land, while reservation land has been set aside by the federal government for tribes and cannot be sold to or settled by outsiders. The United States holds reservation lands in trust for the tribes, while the tribes exercise their rights of self-government on the lands.)

Second, as part of the settlement act, Congress encouraged Alaska Native villages to form municipal, or city, governments. These municipalities would be instruments of the State of Alaska and would therefore lack the capacity to form a government-to-government relationship to the United States. Third, the ANCSA shielded undeveloped Native lands from taxation for twenty years. According to federal Indian law, Indian Country is not subject to taxation. Therefore, Congress could not have considered Native corporation lands to be Indian Country.

The State of Alaska, then, has argued against special Native rights based on the tribal model of Indian Country and domestic dependent sovereignty. Because of the shifts in federal Indian policy, and the ambiguity of US policies concerning Alaska Natives, the state's position is not entirely unfounded. However, as the following three sections on ANCSA amendments, subsistence and tribal status show, the state's argument has not always prevailed.

The '1991' amendments

During the 1980s, a highly charged debate took place about the viability of the regional and village corporations created under the ANCSA. By 1981, ten years after the settlement, the Native corporations had received less than half of the land allocated to them. The regional corporations had only marginal profits, with at least one in danger of failing.[47] Furthermore, the ANCSA required the automatic cancellation of restricted stock in December 1991 and its replacement with ordinary stock. This would give the Native shareholders the option to sell their shares. If enough Natives sold their shares to non-Natives, they would lose control over the corporations. In turn, the loss of corporate control meant loss of the land. Because few of the corporations were successful, the danger loomed that non-Native interests would be in a position to take control of the corporations and the land.

Efforts to amend the ANCSA to eliminate this danger took place on two levels. First, the Alaska Federation of Natives and Native corporate leaders sponsored conferences and workshops to gather ideas on how to amend the ANCSA to protect Native ownership and control. Second, village leaders and the Inuit Circumpolar Conference investigated alternative forms of land tenure that would guarantee Native rights to land and water for generations to come. Specifically, the Inuit Circumpolar Conference commissioned Thomas Berger, a respected advocate of Native rights and a former judge on the British Columbia Supreme Court, to visit Alaska Native villages and gather the views of rural

Alaska Natives. After gathering volumes of testimony, Berger observed:

> *'Alaska Natives wish to choose a form of landholding that reflects their own cultural imperatives and ensures that their ancestral lands will remain in their possession and under governance...At every hearing, witnesses talk of the corporations, shares, profits, sometimes even of proxies, but then, emerging from this thicket of corporate vocabulary, they will talk of what they consider of most importance to them – land, subsistence, and the future of the villages.'[48]*

Berger concluded that the corporate form of land tenure, with its risk-filled profit-making imperative, did not accommodate the aspirations of the village people to hold on to tribal lands. Instead, he recommended that Native shareholders concerned about land loss vote to transfer land from the village corporations to the tribal governments. If a minority of shareholders voted against the transfer, however, they could exercise their dissenters' rights and exact compensation. Berger suggested Congress enact legislation to facilitate the transfer of land by the village corporations to tribal governments without regard for dissenters' rights.[49] Alaska Native associations concerned with village government, such as the United Tribes of Alaska and the Alaska Native Coalition, lobbied for such legislation.

The Alaska Federation of Natives (AFN), its leadership dominated by the regional corporations, did not support the transfer of lands to tribal governments. Rather, it proposed extending the stock restrictions indefinitely, reserving the option for each corporation to permit stock alienation, subject to shareholder vote. In an effort to create a united front, AFN leaders and tribal advocates forged a compromise with tribal government leaders and included in their proposal an option to transfer land and assets to other Native entities (such as trusts or non-profit corporations) without the burden of dissenters' rights.[50]

Congress did not approve the land transfer provision, but did agree to extend the stock restrictions and keep the corporations in Native hands, unless the corporations themselves opted to sell shares.[51] Thus, with the so-called '1991' amendments (passed in 1988), the Alaska Natives could at least be assured of continued control over the corporations. Other amendments to the corporate provisions of the ANCSA were less satisfactory. For example, the original legislation failed to provide for Alaska Natives born after December 1971. These 'new Natives' or so-called after-borns were not assigned shares of stock in the village or regional corporations and therefore had no legal ties to the land unless they interited stock. Over the generations, the interited stock would be divided and redivided, eventually worth very little. The amendments to the ANCSA passed in 1988 allowed each corporation to issue stock to the new Natives if that corporation so desired. Of course, if the corporation decided to issue new shares, this would dilute the value of existing shares. It is not surprising that the few regional corporations that voted to issue new shares were among the most financially sound and thus able to extend the sphere of share-holders.[52] While it may seem a minor problem, the option to distribute shares to Natives born after December 1971 demonstrates the inadequacy of the ANCSA as legislation defining Alaska Native rights. Differences between corporations can result in disparate treatment of Native people.[53] For all its complexity, the ANCSA remains a land settlement rather than the last word on the status of Alaska Natives.

Subsistence

Although the ANCSA extinguished aboriginal hunting and fishing rights, Congress urged the State of Alaska and the US Secretary of the Interior to protect the subsistence needs of Alaska's indigenous peoples.[54] The Alaska Natives became increasingly alarmed at the prospect of losing subsistence rights, especially since more and more people were moving to Alaska during and after construction of the oil pipeline, and the State of Alaska was doing little to adjust for the increased pressure on natural resources. In the late 1970s they lobbied both the state and federal governments for subsistence protection. Anticipating congressional action on the matter, Alaska adopted a subsistence law in 1978, providing a preference for customary and traditional use of fish and game. 'Customary and traditional' referred to historical uses of fish and animals for food, shelter, fuel, clothing, tools and transportation, implying a continuous dependence on the resources over time.

The federal government's subsistence law came in the form of Title VIII of the Alaska National Interest Lands Conservation Act (ANILCA) of 1980. The ANILCA set aside public lands in Alaska for national parks, forests, refuges and wilderness preservation. The subsistence provisions of Title VIII recognized the priority of rural residents, both Native and non-Native, who depended on local resources. When the populations of fish and wildlife species reached levels that could not be sustained, sport and commercial harvests would be curtailed, while the subsistence users would be able to meet their needs. If the suspension of sport and/or commercial uses were not sufficient to sustain the species, then reduced subsistence harvests could be allocated among subsistence users, subject to three criteria: (1) customary and direct dependence on the species as the mainstay of livelihood, (2) local residency and (3) availability of alternative resources. Subsistence uses are defined in the ANILCA as 'customary and traditional uses by rural Alaskans of wild fish and game for personal or family consumption, barter, or customary trade'.[55]

The state had one year after the passage of the ANILCA to enact and implement laws and regulations on subsistence; if the state did not act, then the federal government would assume management. The state did adopt the rural subsistence priority, but not without a great deal of controversy. For example, the state's definition of a rural area as 'a community or area of the state in which the noncommercial, customary, and traditional use of fish or game for personal or family consumption is a principal characteristic of the economy of the community or area' came under fire from the Kenaitze Indians of the Kenai Peninsula. According to the state's definition of rural, the Kenai communities did not qualify for subsistence priority. The Kenaitze filed suit, challenging the state's definition, and a federal court ruled that population size, rather than the economic characteristics of a community, was a more appropriate definition of 'rural'. The court concluded that the State of Alaska was attempting 'to take away what Congress has given, adopting a creative redefinition of the word rural, a redefinition whose transparent purpose is to protect commercial and sport fishing interests'.[56]

The Kenaitze case was only one sign of disagreement over subsistence. The next major challenge came from urban dwellers, including two Alaska Natives who lived in Anchorage. They objected to the geographical requirement, claiming that individual need rather than place of residence should determine subsistence preference. Since a large portion of the Alaska Native population live in non-urban areas, the rural subsistence priority benefited them. But what about urban Natives? The McDowell lawsuit pointed up the imperfect fit between a rural preference and a Native preference; neither Congress nor the State of Alaska was willing to adopt the latter option. In its decision, the Alaska Supreme Court ruled that the state subsistence statute unfairly discriminated against the urban population and violated Article VIII of the Alaska Constitution, which states that the fish and wildlife resources must be reserved for the common use of all Alaskans, that subsistence laws could not create an exclusive right or special privilege of fishery, and that state laws must apply to all persons similarly situated. The court decision against a rural subsistence priority threw the state out of compliance with the ANILCA.[57] While the federal government still uses the rural criterion for subsistence hunting and fishing on federal lands, the state recognizes all Alaska residents as potential subsistence users.

The implications for Alaska Native rights are troubling. To assert their resource rights, Alaska Natives are pursuing a variety of strategies. These include (1) efforts to amend the state's Constitution to provide for a rural subsistence priority; (2) closing Native corporation lands to prohibit trespass by non-shareholders; (3) contracting as tribal entities with federal subsistence managers; (4) expanding the tribal government's role in regulating hunting and fishing; and (5) arguing for the inclusion of indigenous customs and traditions in both state and federal regulation.[58] Currently several Native organizations, including the Alaska Federation of Natives and the Alaska Inter-Tribal Council, are asking the federal government to assume control of fishing regulation on major rivers in Alaska.[59] At the time of this writing, navigable waters are subject to state control. In the autumn of 1993, the state closed subsistence fishing on the Yukon River and its tributaries because of a low run of chum salmon. Natives protested vigorously, fished for chum illegally and argued that the low numbers of salmon were caused by heavy commercial fishing off the coast of the Alaska Peninsula. The Alaska Natives argue that the federal take-over of fishing regulation is necessary to ensure subsistence rights promised in Title VIII of the ANILCA.[60] In addition, the Alaska Natives will continue to press for an amendment to the state's Constitution to allow a subsistence preference.

At stake in the subsistence battle are not only competing interests (commercial, recreational and subsistence users), but competing ideologies. Natives who define subsistence as essential to cultural survival invite the scorn of a non-Native who supplements the family diet with salmon and caribou. The urban dweller who charters a plane out to western Alaska and leaves fish parts lying around the river banks is seen as a disrespectful and dangerous invader by a Native villager. There is more to the controversy than who gets what. Western biologists seek to limit the harvest to ensure sustainable yield, while Native villagers may be more focused on preventing waste.[176]

Some advocates of Native rights maintain that the best solution is ultimately local control over resources. Indian tribes enjoy the exclusive right to hunt and fish on land and water reserved to them, while off-reservation rights are usually negotiated through treaties or congressional legislation. In Alaska, however, the status of Indian Country remains subject to dispute.

Self-determination, tribes and Indian Country

The debate over tribal status for Alaska Native villages involves more than legal niceties. Whether the villages have the right to determine their own membership, levy taxes, operate their own schools, regulate hunting and fishing, administer their own separate justice systems or adopt and enforce their own legal codes depends on the extent to which they are recognized as tribes. Of course, there are other options; one of the strongest local governments in Alaska is the North Slope Borough, effectively a Native government. This entity, a regional government formed in 1972, has the power to tax, to regulate energy exploration and development, to govern the school system and to have decision-making powers in fish and wildlife management.[62] Another Native-controlled borough, the Northwest Arctic Borough, has exercised important powers of taxation and economic regulation. But Native dominance of these regional governments depends entirely on maintaining a majority population in the region. A tribal government, on the other hand, can limit membership and participation to Native people, even if they have left the village for employment in a larger city. In 1990, 41,380 or 48.3 per cent of all Alaska Natives lived in areas where Natives made up more than half the population, a decline from 54.5 per cent in 1980.[63] Congress encouraged Alaska Native villages to establish municipalities through the ANCSA. Many villages have done so, but other Native communities oppose municipal status; municipalities are instruments of the State of Alaska and have no special government-to-government relationship with the United States.[64] The State of Alaska, on the other hand, prefers to deal with municipalities rather than traditional tribal governments.[65]

The status of Alaska Natives is more a political than a legal question, but that is the nature of federal Indian law. Throughout history, the US policy shifts from assimilation to retribalization to termination have made themselves felt in Alaska, as outlined above. The most recent trend in federal Indian law is self-determination. During the 1960s and 1970s, Congress enacted laws that guaranteed civil rights to Native Americans both on and off reservations (the 1968 Indian Civil Rights Act) and demonstrated acceptance of tribal autonomy (the 1975 Indian Self-Determination and Educational Assistance Act). The Indian Child Welfare Act of 1978 gave tribes the authority over decisions about child custody, or when to remove children from their families, decisions that had previously been made by state governments. Similarly, the American Indian Religious Freedom Act of 1978 promised to protect traditional religious practices.[66] Increasingly Congress has recognized the right of tribes to self-govern. Despite the ambiguities created by the ANCSA, it is clear that Alaska Natives are included as beneficiaries of the self-determination era. In October 1993, the federal government confirmed tribal status for Alaska Native villages through the publication of a list of federal recognized tribes. Approximately 250 Alaska Native villages were listed as 'recognized and eligible for funding and services from the Bureau of Indian Affairs'.[67]

While the federal recognition of tribes in Alaska is an historic event, the existence of Indian Country has yet to be resolved. Several villages have transferred ownership of their lands from the village corporation created under the ANCSA to the tribal governments, hoping to establish it as Indian Country to be held in perpetuity by the tribe. Tribes have the power to prevent the taking of tribal lands without the tribe's consent. Lands held by the ANCSA corporations are currently thought to be vulnerable to loss through procedures such as condemnation (the process of taking land for public use against the will of the owner) or seizure by creditors (in cases of non-payment of debts where land is used as collateral for loans). Establishment of tribal property could help to establish Indian Country, or the territory over which tribal governments have jurisdiction.[68] Of course, it is not out of the question that the courts may some day rule that ANCSA corporate lands constitute Indian Country.[69] As yet, the status of Indian Country in Alaska remains to be decided.

An important but largely unexplored area of tribal jurisdiction in Alaska is education. Until Alaska became a state in 1959, there was a dual system of education, with the federal government (Bureau of Indian Affairs) responsible for Alaska Native schools and the territorial legislature responsible for educating white children. After statehood, the federal government agreed to gradually merge state and Bureau of Indian Affairs schools into one system. In 1974, a lawsuit filed against the state on behalf of a 14-year-old Yupik student, Molly Hootch, for not providing local secondary schools in villages, led to dramatic changes. Due to the lack of secondary schools in rural Alaska, village students had to be sent to Bureau of Indian Affairs boarding schools in southeast Alaska or other western states. In the mid-1970s, as a result of the challenge brought on behalf of Molly Hootch, the state agreed to build secondary schools in the villages. Today there are approximately 120 small high schools in Alaska villages operated by regional and local boards. The state invested millions of dollars in these schools, and yet academic achievement among village students remains relatively low. This may be partly a consequence of the tension between the objectives of education for community use and education for success in Western culture. Some school districts have made an effort to introduce the study of Native languages and cultures into the classroom. In 1987–8, for example, a total of 7,781 Alaska Native students were enrolled in bilingual education programmes, the majority located in the Yupik and Inupiaq regions.[70] A major obstacle to providing bilingual education is the shortage of Native speakers. According to one linguist, most Alaska Native languages (with perhaps the exception of Yupik) are spoken by few or none under the age of 40.[71] It must also be mentioned that rural education remains dominated by non-Natives.[72] Only 2.8 per cent of all teachers in the state are Alaska Native, and the percentage of Alaska Native school administrators is even lower.[73]

Currently six Alaska Native communities are applying for federal funds to operate their own schools. These would be tribal schools, separate from the state education system, governed and operated by the tribes themselves.[74] Under current federal law, tribes can control their own schools.[75] The major obstacle is the reluctance of the State of Alaska to transfer existing school facilities, since the state opposes tribal sovereignty in Alaska. Federal recognition of tribes in Alaska may force the state to abandon its opposition, however; in that case, tribally operated schools may become more common throughout the state.

Problems of alcohol abuse, suicide, unemployment and poverty among Alaska Natives are often traced to two sources: first, the severe social and psychological dislocation caused by rapid change in terms of population growth and billions of dollars in oil revenues and, second, the increased dependence of Native communities on outside factors (such as markets and governments) over which they have little control. Enhancing the capacity of local institutions to incorporate Native traditions and beliefs, it is argued, would mitigate the effects of rapid change and dependence. Yet the fact remains that Alaska Natives in the remote villages rely on the financial support of the state and federal governments. In western Alaska, for example, transfer income, or money and services provided by the state and federal governments, constituted 60 per cent of per capita personal income in 1989.[76] Despite the fact that most Alaska Native villages lack running water systems or adequate waste disposal systems and have a high rate of hepatitis-A and other diseases, it was only in 1993 that substantial federal funding became available to improve wastewater treatment in rural Alaska.[77] Finally, Congress has recently decided to fund research, prevention and diagnosis of foetal alcohol syndrome. Alaska has the highest rate of foetal alcohol syndrome in the country.[78] Alcohol abuse, according to the Alaska Federation of Natives, 'is undermining

102

the ability of Alaska Natives to control their lives. It is the fuel that fires the cycle of violence and self-destruction'.[79] The causes of, and solutions to, such pervasive and complex problems reach beyond the capability of federal dollars and politicians' promises.

Conclusion

From the beginnings of Russian America to the present, Alaska Natives have experienced periods of rapid change, often with tragic results such as epidemics and culture loss. But there has also been a revitalization of Native traditions and a growing grass-roots movement to consolidate self-governance at the village level. Contemporary Alaska consists of contrasts between wealth and poverty, rural subsistence and urban professionalism, wilderness and resource development. These contrasts are also part of Alaska Native society. Alaska Natives own and operate some of the strongest corporations in the state. Cook Inlet Region Inc., Sealaska and Arctic Slope Regional Corporation generated 95 per cent of the total net resource revenues of $398 million for all the Alaska Native regional corporations from 1976 through 1991. Oil and gas leases as well as timber sales accounted for the three corporations' revenues.[80] Yet per capita income for Alaska Natives is less than half of the per capita income for whites in the state.[81]

Contrasts between Alaska Native cultures, state and federal policies, and regional economies is only part of the story. There are also deep ideological divisions between Alaskans, particularly among non-Natives, regarding the future prospects for Native societies. People who look at the material welfare of the Natives often point to the benefits of assimilation into the dominant culture: education, employment and a higher standard of living, as opposed to the subsistence lifestyle of a rural village. People who are concerned about the maintenance of a separate cultural identity in an age of television and electronic communication look to village self-government and local control. With regard to minority rights, those who emphasize the rights and responsibilities of the individual and healthy competition between different interests are less likely to support what they perceive as privileges belonging to Alaska Natives. Those who accept the premises of the federal-tribal relationship are more willing to consider the collective rights of tribes. Shifting policy on the part of the federal government and the absence of treaties with Alaska Natives certainly add to the ambiguity inherent in the current debate on Native rights.

Nevertheless, many Alaska Native villages are sweeping aside the ambiguity and establishing or strengthening their own institutions: tribal courts, tribal councils and schools. Through their own actions, they are contributing to the complex evolution of minority rights in Alaska. No doubt the state government will continue to oppose tribal sovereignty and Indian Country, but the federal government can exert substantial pressure on the state if it wishes. Here is the paradox of self-determination: dependence upon recognition.

4

THE INUIT (ESKIMO) OF CANADA

by Ian Creery

Introduction

The rest of the world has always called them Eskimo. (The word 'Eskimo' actually comes from an Algonkian Indian word meaning 'he eats it raw'.) They have always known themselves as Yupit and Inupiat in Alaska, Inuvialuit in Canada's western Arctic, Inuit on Baffin Island and in the central Arctic, and Kalaalliit in Greenland. In recent years, they have chosen to be known by the term 'Inuit', meaning simply 'the people' in their language, and in Canada at least this has been generally accepted.

There are perhaps 125,000 Inuit in the circumpolar world, with the largest populations in Greenland and Alaska. The 1991 census of Canada counted approximately 32,000 people who self-identify as Inuit. In addition, there is a population of less than 2,000 Inuit in the Autonomous Republic of Chukotka, in the Russian Federation. They speak three main languages of the Eskaleut language family – Yupik in Siberia and southwest Alaska, Aleut in southwest Alaska and Inupiaq (called Inuktitut in Canada and Kalaallitut in Greenland) from north Alaska right across to Greenland.

This chapter focuses on the Inuit of Canada. It outlines the colonization of the Canadian Arctic, and looks at the efforts the Inuit are making to save their way of life. It will also touch on the development of the Inuit circumpolar movement.

Origins
The first humans are thought to have arrived in North America about 30,000 BC. The last Ice Age stretched from 30,000–15,000 BC, covering most of Arctic Canada with glaciers. The huge mass of water frozen

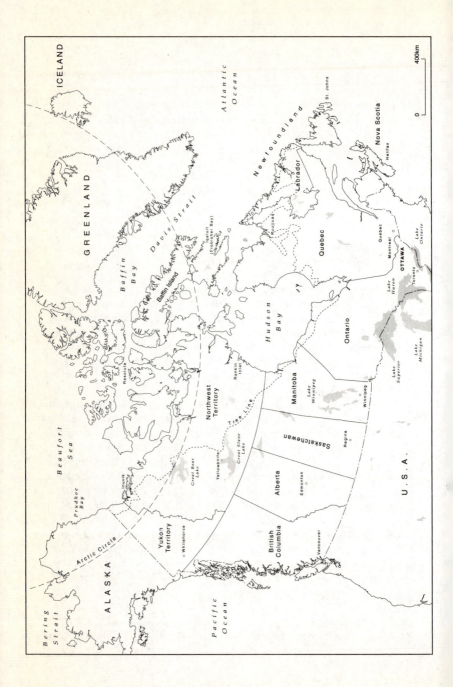

into this glaciation had led to a dropping of the sea level, draining the Bering Sea and exposing a land bridge between Siberia and Alaska. The hunters that followed the herds of game across this bridge were the ancestors of the present-day Indian populations of North and South America. About 15,000 BC the glaciers began to melt, and the Bering Sea encroached on the land bridge. Shortly before it disappeared in about 10,000 BC, a last wave of migration occurred, and these people may have been the ancestors of the Inuit.

The first migration north of the treeline from northern Alaska through Canada to Greenland started about 2,000 BC and lasted until 800 BC. These migrants were the first to adapt to the difficult Arctic environment, but they appear to have died out around AD 1000 for reasons that remain unknown. They were replaced by the direct ancestors of the modern Inuit, who arrived in a second wave of migration from Alaska. They possessed a much more sophisticated technology, and one more adapted to hunting large marine mammals such as whales, than the previous occupants. They spread rapidly across the north, profiting from a warming period in the Arctic climate and from the abundance of whales.

They had reached a high level of adaptation to their environment and lived in security, exhibiting a rich material and spiritual culture, when a cooling trend set in about AD 1200, culminating in the Little Ice Age from 1600–1850. During this period, some parts of the Arctic could no longer supply the Inuit with the game they needed for survival. They drew back into the areas they occupied at the time the Canadian government took an interest in them.

Primitives?

At the time of the first recorded contact in the 19th Century, European explorers brought back tales of primitive savages clad in furs, paddling skin boats and possessing none of the advantages of civilization. Most made no attempt to understand Inuit culture, preferring to see it as inferior. This blinkered view had drastic consequences for some early explorers who were shipwrecked in the Arctic. Rather than accept that Inuit could help them (as other, wiser explorers admitted), they attempted to save themselves and perished.

The Europeans could not understand the sophistication evident in Inuit adaptation to life in a harsh environment. It is evident from archaeological finds that, long before any contact with Europeans, Inuit had attained a high level of development relative to their world. Robert McGhee, a Canadian archaeologist, said of the Old Bering Sea culture of about 2,000 years ago: 'Living between two worlds (Alaska and Siberia), with a technology that gave them an abundant and secure economy, they developed a way of life that was probably as rich as any other in the non-agricultural and non-industrial world.'[1]

He also states that contemporary Inuit culture is far from the sad remains of a glorious past: 'Rather, it should be seen as the result of a recent attempt to maintain the basic elements of a rich and sophisticated culture that could no longer be supported in the deteriorating Arctic environment of the past three hundred years.'[2]

At the time of first contact with Europeans, the Inuit lived as semi-nomadic hunters. They moved from camp to camp according to the seasons and the availability of game (almost their only food source). Travel was by skin boat or by dog team, and on foot in the brief summer. Within their hunting territories, hunters travelled constantly during all seasons, and sometimes were forced to move on long journeys with their families as animals became scarce in one area.

With few exceptions, they were a truly maritime people. Nearly all the Inuit depended for food and clothing on marine mammals – bowhead whale, beluga or white whale, narwhal, walrus and seal – although caribou and fish were also important at certain times of the year. They harvested their food from the sea, and travelled over it in winter and summer. Their spiritual culture also took inspiration from the sea: the most important being in their cosmology was a goddess, variously named Sedna, Taleelayo or Nuliajuk in different regions, who lived at the bottom of the sea.

The basic social unit was the family, and camps usually consisted of several related families in informal association. In spring and summer the camps would split up as each family pursued game in its own area. The families would come together again in winter to hunt cooperatively. It was common to marry outside the loose camp grouping to create links which would minimize feuding between groups. The adoption of children between families was common, and also contributed to social cohesion.

The Inuit governed themselves by a flexible system based on consensus. They took decisions affecting camp life by proposing a point of view and then modifying it through discussion until general agreement was achieved. Each camp had a leader, usually a man, who had superior abilities as a hunter and who greatly influenced the decision-making process.

The camp leaders were strong-willed, sometimes visionary: a good example is Qillaq who, in the 1850s, led the last historical Inuit migration. Through sheer force of personality, he persuaded 38 Inuit to follow him from the Pond Inlet area on a hazardous journey by dog team to north Greenland. Some of his followers died on the way, and others subsequently rebelled against his authority and came back to Canada. The rest remained in Greenland, and their descendants still live there today.

Before sustained contact with Europeans, the Inuit lived in a delicate balance with the natural world. Their existence depended on their ability to interpret that world. They sensed themselves beset by natural and supernatural forces they could not control. Their religion was shamanism. The Igloolik shaman Aua said: 'We do not believe, we fear...'[3] They believed that their world was populated by spirits, both good and evil, which could only be influenced through the mediation of the shamans. The shamans' training was usually long and rigorous, involving a period of exposure to cold, fasting and privation in order to develop mystical powers. They interpreted the natural world, cured sickness and advised on hunting problems, aided by a variety of mystical activity and by a system of taboos.

The Inuit had no writing system, but a rich and resonant oral tradition of passing on legends, songs, parables and hunting narratives. Many of these had shamanistic overtones, but some of the songs have almost Zen-like quality:

'I arise from rest
With the beat of a raven's wings.
I arise
To meet the day.
My eyes turn from the night
To gaze at the dawn
Now whitening.'

Colonization

The first Europeans to set foot in North America were most likely Vikings, who arrived about 1,000 years ago, although there is an unsubstantiated theory that Irish monks made the trip several centuries earlier. Archaeological evidence unearthed in Newfoundland points to the Vikings. Erik the Red had successfully colonized Greenland, and further explorations took him across Davis Strait to Baffin Island. Viking interest was short-lived, however.

Starting about AD 1200 various other Europeans, notably the Basques and Portuguese, made the long voyage across the Atlantic via Iceland to fish for cod in the waters off Newfoundland. Some of them may have briefly turned north. The next visitors to the Arctic were explorers. Between 1818 and 1859 the British Admiralty sent several expeditions to map the Arctic and to look for the northern route to the Indies – the Northwest Passage. The most famous of them was the Sir John Franklin expedition, which vanished in the Arctic in 1845. Subsequent searches for his party captured the European imagination, and led to increased knowledge of the north.

At this time, Europeans began to realize the commercial potential of northern resources. The fur traders of the Hudson's Bay Company gradually extended their activities into the western part of the north to develop its fur harvest. However, the first to colonize and exploit the Arctic in a systematic fashion were the 19th Century American and Scottish whalers.

The whalers ranged the east coast of Baffin Island, and by the 1850s started spending the winters there as well as the summers. They were relentless in their exploitation of the bowhead whale, and by the middle of the century had decimated its population. They then turned to the white whale (beluga), with the same results. It is estimated that between 1868 and 1911, Scottish whalers alone took more than 20,000 belugas from Davis Strait, a figure which does not include the catch of American commercial whalers or Inuit hunters.

On the other side of the continent, American whalers hunted the bowhead all along the north coast of Alaska. By 1890 they had reached the Beaufort Sea in the western Arctic. In little more than a decade they took over $30 million worth of whale products and succeeded in almost wiping out the entire whale population.

The whalers were the first to have a substantial economic interest in the north, and so began to directly affect the lives of nearby Inuit. They needed specialized Inuit knowledge of the water and of the whales that inhabited it. They therefore pressed Inuit into service on their ships in search of the whale and paid them in wages for this work. They also traded for other local goods, and some took Inuit wives during their stay.

The decline in the economic value of the whale hunt drove some of the whalers back to their homelands. The ones who stayed took up the fur trade instead. The fur trade had been the economic foundation of Canada, and by the turn of the 19th Century the traders were increasingly searching for fresh sources of fur. The Hudson's Bay Company was the most important commercial interest, and set up its first Arctic post in northern Quebec in 1909. According to geographer Peter Usher: '...within 15 years the distribution of trading posts and indeed the course of future settlement was virtually set for the entire Eastern Arctic'.[4] The fur trade induced the Inuit into a symbiotic relationship with the traders; they forsook their traditional hunting ways (in which trapping was relatively unimportant) in order to trap the furs which they could trade for goods – guns, bullets, knives, flour, tea and tobacco.

The advent of southern technology brought other changes. Guns made it much easier to kill game so hunters no longer had to rely on the traditional skills of stalking animals and killing them at close range with bows and spears. As Inuit adopted modern technology, so they became vulnerable to shifting economic patterns in the larger world. Fur prices rose and fell, and during lean years many Inuit became totally dependent on the traders for their own survival. In the late 1940s fur prices collapsed, bringing the trade to a halt in most of the Arctic. Many posts closed, leaving the Inuit unable to return completely to their old hunting way of life, merely subsisting precariously in a mixed economy. It was at this point that the Canadian government belatedly took up its responsibilities to the Inuit.

Governmental interest and involvement

In 1670 Britain granted the Canadian Arctic to the Hudson's Bay Company as part of Rupert's Land. The Company owned the land until it sold it in 1870 to the new Canadian government, which renamed it the Northwest Territories (NWT). Canada had adopted the federal system of government, with power divided between the federal government and the provinces of Nova Scotia, Prince Edward Island, New Brunswick, Quebec, Ontario and British Columbia. The Northwest Territories included all the rest of Canada as far north as the Arctic coast.

The Canadian government saw the NWT as a hinterland reserve, awaiting settlement by the immigrants pushing their way west from eastern Canada, but having no intrinsic value. As settlers pushed westward, first Manitoba, then Saskatchewan and Alberta were carved out of the Northwest Territories as new provinces. In 1912 Parliament extended Quebec's boundary northward to include the Ungava district and the Inuit who lived there.

The NWT that remained still held no attraction for the Canadian government. In the late 1800s other countries, particularly the United States, became interested in the high Arctic and their conflicting claims forced Canada to establish and then defend its sovereignty. For this reason more than any other, the federal government established Royal Canadian Mounted Police (RCMP) posts on remote Arctic islands. It also extended the rule of Canadian law to the Inuit and to the Euro-Canadian traders, whalers and missionaries who had settled there.

In part, Canada had seen no need to establish sovereignty in the

Arctic because it had not considered the land to have belonged to any-one else, Inuit included. Canada's view of native people was that they did not have sovereignty over traditional lands, but merely exercised aboriginal rights to use of the land.

Ironically, the Inuit may have helped to perpetuate this idea by their own actions. Generally, they welcomed the Europeans who arrived on their shores. They extended help to early explorers, indeed went out of their way to save them from starvation after shipwrecks. They guided them where they wanted to go, and cooperated uncomplainingly in commercial exploitation of the whales. They never attempted to defend the sovereignty of their land by force. This led the Canadian government to assume that they had no strong feelings of nationhood or of attachment to their country, so there was no need to obtain their approval before taking their land for Canada.

In southern Canada, the federal government had been signing treaties with Indian bands across the country, partly to save them from exploitation by traders and partly to open their lands up for immi-grant settlement. The treaties were based on the agreement that native people had certain aboriginal rights to the land, although this was never recognized as native sovereignty. This agreement has been the foundation of modern efforts to achieve self-government for native people within Canada's new Constitution.

In the north, the government signed treaties with the Indians of the Northwest Territories for economic reasons: Treaty 8 in 1899 paved the way for the Klondike Gold Rush in the Yukon, and Treaty 11 in 1921 came about because of the discovery of oil and gas in the Mackenzie Valley. There was a half-hearted attempt to include a group of Inuit in Treaty 11, but when they refused this offer it was abandoned. At that time the Arctic barrens seemed empty, limitless and worthless. There was no need for the land, and thus no need to consider who actually might have owned it.

The establishment of RCMP posts in the Arctic in the early 1900s had solidified Canada's jurisdiction over the Inuit, but the government had not accomplished this out of any coherent policy towards the land and its people. It did so because it was forced to, and carried out its duties as minimally and as reluctantly as possible. It left the educa-tion of Inuit to the missionaries and their social welfare to the traders.

Governmental interest in the Arctic until the 1950s can best be summed up by a comment made by Louis St Laurent, Prime Minister of Canada from 1948 to 1957: 'Apparently we have administered the vast territories of the north in a continuous state of absence of mind.' This was all the more negligent when contrasted with the Danish government's enlightened and comprehensive policy towards Greenland, developed in the 1780s.

By the late 1940s many Inuit had reached a desperate state. Epidemics had periodically swept through their camps. The collapse of the fur trade had devalued their furs. As trade decreased, they had to turn back to the old ways of living on the land. Then in the early 1950s, changing caribou migration patterns in the central Arctic district led to a widespread shortage of game, and to starvation among Inuit.

Public accounts of the starvation finally pushed the government to action. It airdropped supplies of food to the starving, and started moving Inuit groups away from their camps to places (usually trading posts) where they could be properly administered. Some hunters remembered that at this time the Royal Canadian Mounted Police shot the dog teams they used for transport, ostensibly to control rabies, but also to stop the Inuit from moving back to their camps. This period saw the end of the nomadic way of life of the Inuit.

The government embarked on an energetic programme of building houses and schools, improving health care and setting up local Eskimo Councils in order to encourage the growth of local government. The results were dramatic. From 1941 to 1971 the infant mortality rate dropped from 208.9 to 49.9 per thousand, the death rate fell from 25.6 to 6.6, and the rate of natural increase rose from 0.8 to 30.4. In one generation, the living conditions of the Inuit improved substantially.

The move off the land changed their lives even more dramatically than the fur trade had done. They settled in permanent communities, living in houses with amenities they had never known. They went from camps of two to three families to settlements of families and they sent their children to schools run by southern teachers. Many Inuit entered the wage economy for the first time. They were also exposed to the social ills that other native people had already experienced.

The decade of the 1960s was a period of adjustment to new circumstances. They had to get used to the idea that somehow their freedom had been curtailed. They had become wards of the federal government, and found that their new material comfort had been achieved at the expense of their self-confidence.

Authority over the Territories had always been exercised from Ottawa, first by an appointed Council and Commissioner, then with the addition to the Council of several elected members. In 1967, the seat of government was moved to Yellowknife by relocating the Commissioner and Council, and by establishing a Territorial Civil Service. One of the first tasks of the new Territorial government was to develop local government in the newly created settlements across the Arctic.

The Territorial government established settlement councils, to which it delegated limited responsibility. Their main function was to advise the government on existing and proposed policies for the running of the settlements, but they had no real power. Having very recently come from a tradition of governing themselves in almost all respects, the Inuit had trouble adjusting to this loss of control over their own lives.

The intent behind the establishment of settlement councils was gradually to assimilate Inuit and northern Indians into the greater Canadian culture. Policy followed the colonial model of development so often used in other parts of the world. It had the same consequences.

Settlement councils could not really understand what was expected of them. They would try to exercise influence over aspects of settlement administration, only to find that power lay with the administrators. Advice that was acceptable was acted upon; otherwise it was ignored. The initial result was that Inuit leaders became frustrated. Faced with a seemingly impenetrable wall of government authority, many of them just let the white people have their way. This confirmed the impressions of white civil servants that the Inuit had become a dependent people who had lost control of their lives. They argued that it was necessary for the white man and his administrators to step into the breach and take responsibility for their 'wards' – and the circle was complete.

The experience of the Inuit paralleled that of other colonized peoples. As they lost control over significant aspects of their lives, so they experienced a diminished sense of responsibility. There was one mitigating factor, however. So far, the Inuit had not experienced an influx of large numbers of southerners, who would have overwhelmed their society with alien southern values and customs. This protected the social fabric of Inuit culture from the kind of disintegration seen in other colonized cultures.

Then, in 1968, oil was discovered in Prudhoe Bay, Alaska, and there was a great flurry of speculation in Canada that the Beaufort Sea in the western Arctic, and other parts of the high Arctic, held important reserves of oil and natural gas as well. Suddenly, Inuit land was worth money. As the developers mobilized for wholesale development of the Arctic oil and gas fields, the Inuit realized that greater changes to their lives lay ahead.

Growth of Inuit political consciousness

It would still be some time before the government and the Inuit came into direct conflict, but by the late 1960s many Inuit were awakening to the fact that important decisions were being made which would affect their future. The western Arctic had already had more experience of this than the east. Development of natural resources had moved down the natural corridor of the Mackenzie Valley to the delta giving onto the Beaufort Sea. White men had already reached this part of the Inuit homeland in great numbers, and the Alaskan oil discoveries stimulated exploration in the Beaufort Sea. In 1969, the Inuit of the area formed a political organization, the first of its kind in the Arctic, to defend their rights before they were swamped in the rush of development. It was called COPE – the Committee for Original People's Entitlement. COPE was followed in 1971 by the formation of a national Inuit organization, called the Inuit Tapirisat of Canada or the ITC, and meaning 'Inuit Brotherhood'.

The Inuit who formed these organizations did so out of goodwill, out of a conviction that the government just needed sound advice from them to rectify some of the mistakes that had already been made. However, the federal government department responsible for all Inuit and Indians in Canada, the Department of Indian Affairs and Northern Development, or DIAND, had been created during the days when no coordinated northern policy existed, and it did not seem possible that Indian and Inuit interests would become an obstacle to the development of natural resources. DIAND had always taken seriously its mandate to regulate the development of northern resources, but had virtually ignored its responsibility to represent the native people. This attitude was still prevalent when the Inuit Tapirisat of Canada was formed. In fact, the ITC found the Department more of an adversary than an ally in its struggle for recognition.

The Inuit based their arguments for recognition on the concept of aboriginal rights. They considered that their aboriginal rights and their right to self-determination had never been surrendered, by treaty or otherwise. However, in 1969 Pierre Trudeau, then Prime Minister of Canada, had said that his government would not recognize aboriginal rights. In that same year, the Nisga'a Indians of British Columbia took their provincial government to court, suing for recognition of these rights. The case eventually reached the Supreme Court of Canada. The decision was split 3-3 and the case was dismissed on a technicality, but the point had been made. The federal government was forced to reconsider its policy, and admitted that 'perhaps' aboriginal rights did exist. However unwillingly, it did commit itself to settling outstanding claims.

COPE and the ITC wasted no time in formulating a land claims proposal. They started from the position that their rights had never been surrendered by conquest or by treaty, and that in exchange for giving them up, they were entitled to compensation of various kinds – land grants, money, hunting and certain other limited rights – but they stopped short of demanding rights to self-government.

In some ways the proposal was similar to the Alaska Native Claims Settlement Act of 1971, which was generous in its economic provisions, but had as its ultimate purpose the assimilation of native people into the mainstream economy. The ITC/COPE document failed to consider who would exercise political control in the Inuit homeland. The proposal was presented to the Canadian government for negotiation in February of 1976. By this time many Inuit were voicing doubts about its contents, because of several related happenings in other parts of the north.

James Bay

In April 1971, the Premier of Quebec, Robert Bourassa, announced the James Bay hydro-electric project, which would generate 30 per cent of Canada's current power production by damming all the major rivers flowing into James Bay from the eastern (Quebec) side, in three phases. Phase 1 alone, to dam the La Grande river, was estimated to cost $5.8 billion, and the series of reservoirs would stretch for almost 500 miles.

The land of the Cree Indians and Inuit had been ceded to Quebec from the Northwest Territories in 1912, but the province did not want responsibility for the Inuit. In the 1930s Quebec took the federal government to court, claiming that the Inuit should be classed as Indians and were therefore a federal responsibility. The court agreed, and so the native people were administered entirely from Ottawa. Finally, in 1963 the Quebec government took up its provincial responsibilities in the north, and the native people now had to deal with two governments instead of one.

The Quebec Inuit were hunters like their relatives in the NWT, and had experienced the same difficulties in giving up their nomadic life to settle in communities. They faced the added burden of coping with a development which would bring enormous changes – some of their ancestral hunting and trapping grounds would be flooded, there would be other serious environmental consequences, and an army of foreign workers would occupy their land. And yet the provincial government had not consulted them about these plans, and had done very little work on assessing the environmental impact of such a gigantic scheme.

In May of 1972 the province approved the project, and work started almost immediately. The Cree and the Inuit, having failed to stop it politically, applied in December 1972 for a court injunction to temporarily halt work on the dams while the courts decided on the nature of their rights. On 15 November 1973 the injunction was granted, but eight days later it was overturned by the Appeals Court. The government was now worried that the work would be stopped by further appeals; the Cree and Inuit were desperate because the project was already far advanced, and court costs were astronomical. The two sides agreed to negotiate, and in a year of hard bargaining came to an agreement in principle. The Inuit were unhappy with the compromise, but the only alternative was to be given nothing. The James Bay and Northern Quebec Agreement was signed a year later.

The agreement was similar to the Alaska Native Claims Act in that it was concerned with making a once-and-for-all deal that would exchange aboriginal rights for a package of benefits, thus freeing up the land for development. The package of benefits included $90 million in cash, title to 5,250 square miles of hunting grounds, exclusive hunting and fishing rights on a further 60,000 square miles and various social programmes. The agreement also allowed for a regional government and a regional school board to be set up.

Two factors created difficulties for the Inuit and Cree of James Bay as the agreement came into force. First, it had been negotiated in extreme haste, as negotiators worked to deadlines imposed by the hydro-electric companies and the courts. The result was that many sections of the agreement were vague, and left enormous latitude for interpretation as to how they would be implemented. Second, the Inuit and Cree were caught in the middle of bureaucratic wrangling between the federal and Quebec governments over who had responsibility for certain provisions of the agreement.

The Quebec Inuit spent the first few years after the signing of the agreement in selecting land for Inuit ownership, and in setting up structures such as the regional government and school board. The implementation process took place against a backdrop of growing nationalism in Quebec.

In November 1976 a nationalist government, the Parti Québecois, was elected in Quebec, and soon clashed with the Inuit. The Parti Québecois advocated a new constitutional relationship with the rest of Canada, called sovereignty-association, which came close to demanding outright separation from Canada. The government maintained the right of Quebeckers to self-determination, which is interpreted as making Quebec completely French-speaking, and it passed Bill 101 to restrict the use of English in the province. The Inuit had been educated in English in federal schools, and were alarmed by the effect Bill 101 would have on their society. They protested massively, forcing the closure of numerous schools and government offices in northern Quebec. The Quebec government responded by sending riot police into several communities. Although no clashes developed, it was a clear warning that Quebec self-determination was not Inuit self-determination.

In areas of the agreement where the Inuit had most responsibility, they made more rapid progress. For instance, they set up Makivik Development Corporation, which was soon successfully running an airline in northern Quebec, called Air Inuit, and a shrimp fishery employing Inuit trained by Greenlanders.

In areas of joint Inuit–government responsibility, particularly involving Quebec, implementation of the agreement was slowed down and in some cases halted. One of the problems was that the agreement had not guaranteed funding levels for organizations like the regional school board, which had to compete with other Quebec school boards for its budget from the Quebec government.

A big problem arose from the feeling in government circles that it had made the native peoples rich, and they no longer needed programmes and services to which they were still in fact entitled. Notably in health care, standards actually dropped after the signing of the agreement, and are only now recovering. In addition, the $225 million cash payment to be shared between the Cree and the Inuit was to be paid out in instalments until 1977, rendering its actual value between $86.8 and $171.9 million due to inflation and various other factors.

The Inuit eventually took their grievances to a committee of the Canadian Parliament in March 1981. The evidence they gave so embarrassed the federal government that it immediately ordered a review of its responsibilities in the implementation of the agreement. The review committee agreed that there were serious problems, notably in areas that had been hastily and vaguely drafted. The federal government committed some funds to improving its own performance, and agreed to honour the spirit of the agreement in a more constructive way. The Quebec government also made efforts to work out appropriate implementation strategies.

One other consequence of the speed with which the James Bay Agreement was drawn up was that Inuit in many communities were not fully consulted by their negotiators. After the signing of the agreement, Inuit in three settlements rebelled because their aboriginal rights had been given up in exchange for the benefit package, and rejected the agreement. This led to demands for a new form of regional government which would work better than the existing Kativik government set up under the agreement. In 1989 a committee was established to devise an effective form of self-government. In 1991, Inuit and non-Inuit in northern Quebec voted in a referendum for the establishment of a regional assembly and a Constitution.

Many Quebec Inuit are bitter about the way the agreement was forced on them, and feel that they got a poor deal, that it is in fact a modern-day 'beads and blankets' treaty. Its eventual success will depend on who wins the battles over implementation, which will continue for some time. In the meantime, the northern Quebec Inuit contribute to the national Inuit movement, where their political experience has made them tough negotiators on the Canadian constitutional issues that have occupied Inuit leaders for the past several years.

The Mackenzie Valley pipeline

Shortly after the discovery of oil and gas in Alaska, the Canadian government offered to permit the building of a pipeline through the Mackenzie Valley in the NWT to carry oil to United States markets. The American government declined the offer, and so the Canadians decided that perhaps a gas pipeline would be a more attractive proposition. This would transport both American and Canadian Arctic gas through the valley, and an oil pipeline could also be added if enough reserves of Canadian oil were discovered. In March 1974, a consortium of energy companies called Canadian Arctic Gas announced its proposal: a pipeline stretching 2,625 miles from the Mackenzie Delta to southern Canada, at an estimated cost of $10 billion. The National Energy Board of Canada was given the task of evaluating the proposal.

Like the Cree and Inuit of James Bay, the Dene (Indians) of the Mackenzie Valley felt threatened by such an overwhelming project. They had already experienced the cultural dislocation brought on by the influx of great numbers of foreigners from the times of the Yukon gold rush. They formed their own political organization, the Indian Brotherhood, to represent them. The Brotherhood quickly absorbed the lessons in decolonization being offered in parts of the Third World, and attracted radical young Dene, who embarked on a programme of consciousness-raising inspired by liberation movements in South America and Africa.

The Brotherhood was concerned that the National Energy Board only had the mandate to consider physical questions related to the building of the pipeline – economic, technical, environmental – and could not examine its social impact. It lobbied forcefully with the federal government to allow the Dene and Inuit to express their views about the pipeline. In March 1974, the government appointed the widely respected Justice Thomas Berger of the Supreme Court of British Columbia to inquire into the effects of a pipeline on the people of the valley and, if necessary, to suggest conditions under which it should be built.

The Berger Inquiry held exhaustive hearings in the north, travelling to every community and sitting through long hours of testimony by the Mackenzie Valley Dene. The hearings acted as a catalyst for the developing political views of the Dene, who spoke unanimously against the pipeline. Justice Berger eventually recommended to the federal government that the pipeline be delayed for ten years to allow the Dene to settle land claims and to prepare for the project.

As Dene politicians became more radical, they changed the name of their organization from the Indian Brotherhood to the Dene Nation. They withdrew an earlier land claims proposal based on the Alaskan real-estate-transaction model, and stated that they would never give up aboriginal rights in exchange for land. They expressed their political creed in the Dene Declaration of 1975, which said among other things:

'We the Dene of the NWT insist on the right to be regarded by ourselves and the world as a nation. And while there are realities we are forced to submit to, such as the existence of a country called Canada, we insist on the right to self-determination as a distinct people and the recognition of the Dene Nation.'

The Dene Declaration changed the nature of the Dene's relationship with the Government of Canada. The Dene Nation drew up a different proposal for the settlement of rights, with a focus on self-government rather than on land and money deals. It is still being negotiated.

The Inuit of NWT had observed the negotiation of the James Bay Agreement and the Dene struggle against the Mackenzie Valley pipeline, and now had to choose between two kinds of negotiation of their own claims with the federal government. The first type would extinguish aboriginal rights in return for a negotiated package of benefits, such as land, money, hunting rights and some social programmes. The underlying assumption was that aboriginal rights were limited, involving rights to hunting and perhaps some property, but not to any political powers. It was assumed that the fundamental basis of the relationship between the government and the native people had already been established, and it was just a matter of settling some outstanding claims. This kind of agreement has been called a 'real-estate deal'. The Alaska Native Claims Act and the James Bay Agreement are of this type.

The second type would re-examine the relationship between the government and the native people, starting from the premise that the right to self-determination had never been surrendered. This would serve as the basis for an agreement which would specify the political rights native people could exercise, and would also include some compensation for past wrongs. It would initiate a process by which the native people would maintain (in some cases recover) control over their lives, while giving up sovereignty over their lands. The Dene Declaration was a start in this direction.

The federal government, however, held that the James Bay Agreement in Quebec was 'historical' and would serve as a precedent for the settlement of all other land claims. It wanted to maintain political control, and would not allow the subject of the sharing of political power to come up within the framework of claims negotiations.

The Inuit of COPE and the ITC realized that the proposal they were about to negotiate with the government was of the 'real-estate' variety. They had time to analyse the James Bay Agreement, and saw how inadequate it was to their needs. They decided to withdraw the proposal and to start work on another. This time, the Inuit decided, the proposal would come out of community discussions rather than from legal consultants. The document, simply called 'Nunavut' ('Our Land'), that was ratified at a general assembly in Frobisher Bay (since renamed Iqaluit) in October 1977 was a simple one that went back to first principles. It also bore the influence of the Dene Declaration. Two pages long, it started off: 'Whereas Inuit and the Government of Canada have never had an agreement with regard to the constitutional relationship between the Inuit and Canada...'

The most important feature of the document was that the Inuit wanted to negotiate 'the formation of a new territory and government within Canada Confederation along the lines of Inuit political institutions'.

The road to Nunavut

The idea of dividing the Northwest Territories into two new territories had been proposed in 1962, but the federal government had not thought that the Inuit in the eastern part of the NWT were ready for it. Leaders in the western NWT wanted to push for provincehood, and felt the eastern Arctic was holding them back. Fifteen years later, the Inuit themselves brought the idea up again. This time it was the eastern Arctic which had definite political aspirations, and the western NWT which was disorganized.

Inuit argued that there was a natural division in the NWT anyway, along the treeline which ran from the Mackenzie Delta diagonally to the NWT–Manitoba border. It separated the tundra, land of the Inuit, from the forests that were the home of the Dene. The climates of the two regions were different; their peoples had different histories, cultures and languages. The Inuit argued that the NWT included two regions and people who would always remain different. The capital of the NWT, Yellowknife, lay south of the treeline and was run by white civil servants who had no comprehension of the Inuit and their land. The Inuit saw the land claims negotiation with the federal government as an opportunity to push for more representative government closer to home. Accordingly, they proposed a division along the treeline, with a new government in the eastern territory, which would be called Nunavut – 'our land'.

The Inuit knew that their population majority of about 75 per cent in Nunavut would ensure that the new government would represent them, but more importantly they could also negotiate new powers not presently held by the NWT government. They denied strenuously that they were proposing an ethnic state; the new system would be public government within the limits defined by the Canadian Constitution. The only safeguard of Inuit rights was the proposal that the normal residency requirement of one year for participating in Territorial and municipal elections be raised to three years. The Inuit said this would limit the ability of the north's large transient white population (average length of stay perhaps two years) to exercise undue influence.

The ITC embarked on a campaign to publicize its proposals. Most people canvassed, including many white civil servants who had to deal with Yellowknife daily, agreed that the NWT government was remote and unresponsive to their needs. They accepted the idea of a division along the treeline, and welcomed the opportunity for reform of the system of government at the same time. The Inuit saw a clear need for the protection offered by a three-year residency requirement before voting, and some long-term white residents agreed. Others were quick to call the proposal unconstitutional, and it remains the most controversial aspect of the Nunavut plan.

The federal government responded to the proposed creation of Nunavut by reiterating that political development was not a subject that could be included in land claims negotiations. It stuck firmly by its original position that the James Bay approach would be followed. However, the Canadian Prime Minister, Pierre Trudeau, recognized that native groups would not agree to abandon their ideas of negotiating political rights. Accordingly, he appointed an inquiry into constitutional development in the north, under the Hon. C.M. Drury, a former cabinet minister.

Drury tried to find a way of addressing native political concerns outside the claims process. However, the ITC still wanted to negotiate its proposals through land claims, and refused any compromise. Inuit in Canada were greatly encouraged when, in 1979, Greenland was granted Home Rule by Denmark. The new form of government would give Greenlanders much increased autonomy, with the Inuit majority exercising democratic control, just as they would in the proposed territory of Nunavut.

In the NWT, the political ferment was creating changes in the old forms of colonial government. Native groups had always seen the NWT Council as nothing more than an arm of federal government policy. Now, the Council began to involve itself in questions of land claims. In October 1979, a native majority was elected to the Council. Its first act was to reverse the pro-development, anti-native rights stance of the previous Council. It then set up a Unity Committee which held hearings across the north to evaluate the depth of feeling for division of the NWT into two new territories.

The Committee reported back to the Council that the evidence was overwhelmingly in favour of a split. The Council endorsed the principle of division, and held a plebiscite of all residents of the NWT on the question. Most Inuit communities voted 80 per cent in favour of division, although support was lower in some settlements in the western Arctic. South of the treeline the result was mixed, with a small majority in favour. The overall result was that 60 per cent wanted the NWT to be divided. The Council and the native groups, now working close together, pressed for an early federal government decision on the matter. In November of 1982 John Munro, then Minister of Indian and Northern Affairs, announced that, subject to certain conditions, the NWT would indeed be divided.

Labrador

The course of development in Labrador in the east of Canada and also in the western Arctic has been different to that in the more central areas of Inuit population in Canada. These two regions have always been more appealing to white men than the rest of the Arctic: they were closest to the advancing population of settlers and, occupying the transitional zone between tundra and forest, their climates and topography were more familiar to settlers than the true Arctic. It was also easier to make a living there, fishing for cod in Labrador, and whaling and trapping in the Mackenzie Delta. The impact on Inuit populations there was correspondingly greater than in other regions.

Labrador was colonized in 1770 by the Moravian missionaries, who had already established a presence in Greenland. They converted the Inuit, and traded with them to pay for the expense of running the missions. According to northern historian Keith Crowe[5], they used their missions to change Inuit ways so they could survive in a European society. They traded only essential goods, kept liquor out of the territory and encouraged the Inuit to fish in a European style. By 1840, their educational efforts had resulted in almost all of the Inuit being able to read and write the roman script of the Moravians. The missionaries also trained teachers, and right up to 1949, when Newfoundland and Labrador joined Canada, the language of instruction in the schools was Inuktitut.

In the 1800s, white settlers had already begun to make their homes in Labrador, and by 1900 there were 3,000 fishermen, most of them settlers. The newcomers were by and large not converted by the Moravians, and as a result could not attend their schools, the only ones on the coast.

The protective influence of the missionaries waned as the southern ways of the settlers took hold. There was some intermarriage between Inuit and settlers, but both groups retained a sense of pride in their origins and identity. They both lived from the resources of the land and so had similar economic systems, but each group had its special methods, technology and knowledge of the land. According to a contributing article in a study of Labrador land use by Hugh Brody, Inuit and settlers maintained distinct hunting and trapping areas, with minimal overlapping. Although of different races, they respected each other, as befitting people who knew the difficulties of survival on the coast. Life had always been hard, and the Labrador Inuit had experienced their share of disease and starvation. Their inclusion in Canada as a part of Newfoundland did not help much. Newfoundland was a poor province with a disinclination to spend any of its money on Labrador. Its people were denied the quality of housing, health care and municipal services that, for instance, the Inuit of the NWT were receiving. What little assistance there was had to come from the federal government: until 1947 at least, it had provided 90 per cent of all the money spent on native people in Labrador.

The Newfoundland government was also reluctant to consider the question of aboriginal rights: long after the federal government had admitted these rights existed in 1973, Newfoundland refused to admit that the native people could have special status. The Labrador Inuit Association was formed, and in 1978 submitted a proposal for the settlement of claims to the federal government, demanding rights to land, compensation and management powers over resources and for regional government. The claim was held up until 1990, when the Newfoundland and federal governments worked out an agreement on how to handle the claim. Since then, negotiations have proceeded slowly.

The western Arctic

Although white men came later to the western Arctic than to the east coast, their advent brought rapid and devastating change to the Inuit. By 1890, the whaling industry was bringing in large numbers of white men, as well as Alaskan Inuit who had learned the whaling trade. Winter camps were set up around the Beaufort Sea. Before long, death from disease as well as liquor-influenced killings were seriously affecting the Inuit. By 1910, the population of 2,000 Mackenzie Inuit had been reduced to approximately 130.

The fur boom of the 1920s attracted many trappers of all races from the south, and there was some intermarriage. Fur prices brought great affluence to the west, even during the 1930s and 1940s, years that were disastrous for Inuit in other areas. The western Arctic was spared the worst, because of an abundance of several kinds of fur that still sold well. Cultural pressure from the large white population accelerated the change in Inuit society, and many Inuit became fluent in English. It was the threat of massive oil and gas development that prompted the Inuit to form the Committee for Original People's Entitlement in 1969 to fight for their claims.

COPE was a major force in the national Inuit organization, the Inuit Tapirisat of Canada, and strongly supported the first ITC land claims proposal. However, COPE did not agree with ITC radicals who began to see the proposal as a sellout, and finally split with the ITC over its decision to withdraw the document from negotiations with the federal government. COPE then tailored the rejected proposal to suit the western Arctic, and submitted it to the government on its own in 1977. A final agreement was signed in 1984.

The deal gave the Inuvialuit title to 91,000 sq. km. of land, and mineral rights in one-seventh of that area. In addition, they were given $152 million in compensation for other land.

They also received $10 million for economic development initiatives, and $7.5 million for various social programmes, such as housing and health. In return, Inuvialuit had to surrender all rights to traditional land. COPE re-created itself as the Inuvialuit Regional Corporation (IRC), which established a corporate structure to administer the benefits of the agreement. The IRC created many subsidiaries – one to control the land from the agreement, another to invest the cash compensation, another to engage in business activities. Today Inuit money is the most significant player in the regional economy.

Although the agreement also gave the Inuit joint power with the government to approve development in the region, it did little to establish local government. This remains a problem area, which other claims do not share.

The Inuit of the west have not had the same protection as those in other regions, and accordingly their culture has suffered greatly. However, the general renaissance of Inuit cultural pride has caught on in the west, and efforts are under way to reverse the trend towards assimilation with southern society. Inuit society as a whole is strong, so there is every reason to believe these efforts will succeed.

The economy

The traditional economy of the Inuit was organized around camps, where a few related families produced and circulated amongst themselves all they needed for survival. The harshness of the environment was a factor in the egalitarian character of the society: if anyone had accumulated wealth at the expense of others this would have threatened the whole group.

This way of life started to change with the influence of the whalers in the 19th Century. Anthropologist Hugh Brody remarks that what Inuit today call their traditional economy was actually a mixed economy, involving some hunting, some trapping, occasional work for wages with white people, and trading for such staple goods as guns, flour and tea. These activities did not force great changes on Inuit society, because they were land-based and allowed the camps to function as they always had done. However, trade led to an improvement in the standard of living and a greater dependency on southern goods. The dramatic drop in fur prices in the 1940s, which created much hardship, was in itself not critical. However, prices of trade goods had continued to rise, and the Inuit had no other source of income to pay for them. The crisis occurred when the animals they hunted for food temporarily disappeared. The resulting starvation forced the Inuit to move off the land into settlements.

The move away from hunting grounds further weakened the land-based economy, by increasing the distance the hunters had to travel to find game. The advent of the snowmobile in the 1960s pushed up the cost of hunting. The introduction of government assistance in the form of old-age pensions, child allowances and welfare started to weaken social bonds. These welfare payments were made to individual families, thus creating disparities in wealth and undermining the tradition of sharing. Anthropologist Michael Asch has called this process the individualization of poverty, and yet Inuit cultural values have mitigated against the entrenchment of poverty.

Although welfare payments have represented a significant source of income for some Inuit, their main function has been to subsidize hunting and trapping. The problem is that welfare has not been designed to do this, and hunters are now demanding a direct subsidy of their activities that would avoid the traps inherent in welfare.

The Canadian government's answer to these problems has been to emphasize the role of the wage economy, largely through the extraction of non-renewable resources. Historically, the exploitation of frontier resources provided the foundation for growth of the Canadian economy. Canada is still dependent on resources to some degree, and the need to exploit the frontier remains. The extraction of Arctic resources, oil, gas and minerals, relies on a core of skilled workers and experts who travel the country from project to project, aided by cheap unskilled labour hired for the backbreaking job of actually extracting the resource.

At first, the lack of education of the Inuit made them unsuitable for all but the most unskilled jobs. The companies did not want to pay enormous training costs for people who could not move to projects in other parts of the country, as experience has already shown. Thus wage labour took Inuit away from hunting and discouraged the learning of land-based skills, but did not replace them with industrial skills. Rather than creating 'development', this process was leading to underdevelopment.

The federal government attempted to improve the situation by starting its own industrial training schemes for the Inuit, most notably in the operation of heavy industrial equipment. It also tried to educate the resource companies to deal with cross-cultural problems that had made them unwilling to hire Inuit workers. It induced the companies to set up job rotation plans so that native workers could visit their families frequently. The government also attempted to maximize the benefits of development to northerners. For instance, it only agreed to the opening of the Nanisivik lead-zinc mine on Baffin Island on condition that the company slow down production to increase the life of the ore body from six to twelve years. It also set a quota for the Inuit workers that the company should aim to achieve. In spite of all these efforts, numbers of Inuit employed in the resource industries have remained small and benefits have not been great.

The government itself has been the main source of employment for Inuit. The extension of services to the north has brought with it a bureaucracy which provides a large percentage of the income in many settlements. The government has been determined to 'Inuitize' the bureaucracy, and this has been possible in the smaller settlements where the workers have remained a part of a strong Inuit society. In regional centres the influence of southern culture is still strong, and the Inuit perceive the administration to be owned by whites. The improving quality of education, and the revitalizing of Inuit society, will eventually result in native bureaucracy here too. For instance, the NWT government has made efforts to train Inuit managers in recent years.

However, government cannot hope to employ everyone. The federal government projects that the Inuit population of the NWT will almost double in the next 25 years from 20,860 in 1991 to 40,770 in 2016. And as the 'Inuit baby-boomers' grow up, the number of employable adults will grow even faster. Thousands of new jobs will have to be created just to keep the current high rate of unemployment from going even higher. It is very unlikely that the non-renewable resource sector will expand at a rate that would allow it to absorb these new job-seekers (or that northerners would want to see it grow that quickly, for environmental reasons), so new sources of employment must be developed.

In spite of government efforts to involve them in wage labour, Inuit have stubbornly refused to give up their feeling for the land and for the land-based, renewable resources economy. In looking into the impact of the Mackenzie Valley pipeline, Justice Berger acknowledged this: 'Native people consider renewable resources, particularly fur, fish, game and timber, to be essential to their way of life. These resources must be the cornerstone of native economic development, and neither the initiatives nor the benefits can be appropriated by others.'[6]

The federal government has never made a serious attempt to shape the renewable resource economy into a viable operation. Various efforts were made to domesticate caribou, to herd reindeer, even to raise southern farm animals such as pigs and chickens, in the Arctic. The results were often hilarious but nearly always disastrous. The marketing of Inuit crafts has been strikingly successful, and soapstone carving and printmaking have become an increasingly good source of income for some. However, the government has done very little to organize and support hunting and trapping, which are fundamental to a successful land-based way of life.

Seal hunting provides a good example of an activity which was traditionally important for survival, but which is now being threatened by changing economic circumstances. In the old days the hunter's ability to kill seals at the breathing-hole in the winter was often the only protection against starvation, and the carcasses were utilized down to the last scraps of fat and fur. The Inuit hunted seals in all seasons, and had a precise understanding of their habits and biology. As the commercial seal fur market developed in the 1940s, the hunters began to sell sealskins to help pay for their equipment. However, the income from this activity has only served to subsidize the harvesting of the seal meat which is still a staple in the diet of many communities, and has rarely provided any profit. In most areas, hunting and trapping do not pay their way: social scientist Bill Kemp studied one community where the sale of furs only accounted for one-third of the cash needed for hunting equipment.

Because there is no commercial market for seal meat, hunters have had to rely increasingly on the sale of skins to keep pace with rising costs. They have always had to sell them to southern Canadian companies, to meet the demand created in North America and Europe by consumers far from Inuit homes. Hunters have thus been vulnerable to changes in the market caused by consumer pressure, such as the anti-seal-hunt campaign in Europe.

Inuit have relied on the seal hunt to generate the cash needed to continue hunting. They have not pursued the seal in the same way as the much-publicized commercial seal-pup harvest in other parts of Canada. Inuit hunters disagree with commercial culling methods, and have felt victimized by the European sealskin ban. The economic consequences of the ban have been drastic – the loss of income has forced some Inuit to give up hunting.

It is possible to create a local and regional economy based on the products of the hunt, which would allow the hunters greater self-sufficiency. The Inuit are now urging the government to consider ways of doing this: to support the land-based economy in a systematic way. Greenland has done just that, instituting a system of distribution and secondary processing of the products of the hunt to provide many jobs. It is unrealistic to expect renewable resources to provide total employment. However, a mixed economy founded on land-based activities, which are supplemented by wage labour and occasional subsidies, would serve the Inuit well. They know their survival as a people depends on maintaining their relationship with the land, and so government support of the mixed economy would not only provide employment, but would also relieve the social problems which a reliance on industrial labour merely exacerbates.

The late 1980s and early 1990s have seen Inuit organizations becoming increasingly involved in northern economic development. The Makivik Corporation and the Inuvialuit Regional Corporation have used the capital they obtained from settling their land claims to become major players in their regional economies. Their strategies range from investing in existing businesses (Makivik has purchased the airline First Air, which provides scheduled and charter service to northern Quebec and across the NWT), developing expertise in potential growth areas (the Inuvialuit Regional Corporation has established an Inuvialuit Petroleum Corporation), to operating construction companies and regional airlines and building commercial office complexes. Makivik is also implementing an ambitious project to develop inter-settlement trade in a range of 'country food'.

Inuit organizations also have a track record of making the most of the range of economic development initiatives sponsored by governments. Under the current federal government's Canadian Aboriginal Economic Development Strategy, for example, the ITC and its regional affiliates are developing regional economic development institutions designed to deliver business development, human resource development and financial services identified by the Inuit themselves. An early result of this strategy is that federal dollars which used to be sent to the Territorial government's economic development channels are now flowing directly to these Inuit-controlled groups.

The quiet revolution

Since their move off the land into settlements, the Inuit have come to understand the Canadian political system. They have shown themselves to be tough, capable politicians, as the success of the campaign for the new Nunavut territory demonstrates.

Much has been written about the destructive effects of colonialism on aboriginal societies, and the Inuit have experienced many problems: the breakdown of social and family bonds, the loss of culture, alcoholism and suicide. However, these problems have not been as severe as in other parts of the world for at least two reasons.

First, the Inuit have been spared a massive influx of southerners, because their land has proved so inhospitable to most whites. They have remained greatly in the majority, and have been able to control southern influence to some degree.

Second, the Inuit have been resourceful, and determined to attack these problems before they become unmanageable. For instance, they have followed a quiet programme of using institutions to achieve their own purposes. John Amagoalik, the President of the Inuit Tapirisat of Canada, remarked to the NWT Council in 1980 that it was naive to pin all hopes of social change on a land claims settlement, when many changes should be accomplished through the present government as a matter of fundamental right. In three related areas – education, language and communications – the Inuit have been pushing government institutions into serving rather than dominating them, with fair success.

Education

Historically, the government's attitude to education was characterized by the same reluctance to make a policy that informed its other dealings with the Inuit. It did not start building schools in the NWT until the late 1940s. Before that time it was happy to turn over the responsibility for education to the various missions, mainly Anglican and Catholic, which got a government subsidy for building schools and residences. The missions did not reach many of the Inuit (in 1944 it was established that over 80 per cent of Inuit children were not being taught in schools), and were a mixed blessing for those whom they did reach.

The mission schools were lonely and terrifying places for native children. They took the children away from their families, taught them in foreign ways and in foreign languages, and in many cases forbade them to speak their mother tongue. Much evidence has come to light in the past five years of the brutality with which native children were treated at these schools. Severe corporal punishment was accepted as normal and sexual abuse by priests and teachers occurred regularly in some places.

When the government started to build its own schools, the situation did not improve much for the children. Because many families still lived on the land, the schools were of necessity residential. The children would be collected from the scattered camps by aeroplane in the autumn, spend the winter in school and be delivered back to their parents in the spring. The government schools were more moderate than those run by the missionaries, but their policies were cut from the same cloth. Their intent was to assimilate Inuit into the mainstream culture, to prepare these children to play a part in a foreign world. They assumed that the Arctic was an inhospitable land that could not support a growing population, and that the only hope for the Inuit lay in migrating to the south. To this end, instruction in the schools was in English or French, and the curricula were imported wholesale from the southern provinces. No teaching was done in native languages.

The system had two effects. First, it drew the Inuit away from their camps towards the newly established settlements, to be near their children. (The Inuit were still too much in awe of the authority of the white man to refuse to allow their children to be taken from them.) The second effect was to accelerate the breakdown of traditional Inuit family life and values.

The children sent away to school were drawn increasingly towards the white world. They learned a new language, new habits of diet and hygiene, new attitudes. They became caught in the disorienting trap of the colonial system: the only hope of adaptation lay in trying to become white, and yet they were continually being measured and coming up short of this goal. They were taught that to be native was bad. Some children came to occupy a tragic no-man's-land between the white culture which would never fully accept them, and their parents' culture which was no longer appealing. At the time when the government was finally reconsidering this policy, a parent remarked: 'It was far too late when they did start asking Eskimo parents to become involved in teaching, so the present young people have only learnt some white ways. Now they are like lost people.'

The policy of assimilation only started to change after the NWT government was established in Yellowknife in 1967. In the early 1970s, individuals in the Department of Education pressed for the teaching of native languages in schools, and for the inclusion in the curriculum of materials relevant to the Inuit culture. Some halting steps were taken in this direction: the first Inuit teacher graduated in 1972, and a 'cultural inclusion' programme was set up in some schools. This meant the older Inuit would come into the schools regularly to teach the boys how to build *qamutit* (wooden sleds), and the girls how to sew *kamit* (sealskin boots). This programme had only limited success, because it was not associated with a systematic attempt to rework the approach to education. The Department of Education resisted further changes, because it feared that overall standards of education, measured against southern standards, would fall.

Right from the beginning, Inuit parents had seen the schools as white institutions over which they could have no control. As the schools' influence spread, parents gradually relinquished the task of bringing up their children, thus increasing the sense of dislocation in the family. However, the awakening of political consciousness in the mid-1970s brought the problems with the educational system into focus. Pressure began to mount for real changes. In the late 1970s the NWT Council, now with a native majority, set up a Special Committee to undertake a systematic review and analysis of the educational system.

The Special Committee recommended: a) that control of education be decentralized to allow local school committees a greater say, through the creation of regional elected boards of education; b) that the government support the use of native languages in the schools through a stepped-up programme of training native teachers, and the development of relevant curricula in the native languages; and c) that the system of adult education be vastly improved.

The Special Committee report encouraged schools in many areas to respond to local wishes. For instance, it had long been the case that in the lengthy days of spring, children would spend most of their time outdoors and would also go camping on the land with their parents. Attendance at school would drop by 10 per cent or more every spring. Some schools recognized the value of an education on the land, and incorporated the camp cycle into the last two weeks of school, allowing pupils and teachers to go out on the land to learn from the older Inuit.

There are other signs that the educational system is returning to health. Since 1980, a teacher education programme in Frobisher Bay has been training Inuit to be teachers. Thirty-seven of the 359 teachers in Inuit schools have graduated from the programme. In addition the Department of Education now allows classroom assistants, whose work with teachers from the south was never given due credit, to obtain a teaching diploma by doing most of the course work in their home communities.

The number of native students going on to post-secondary education has jumped from 16 in 1978–9 to 154 in 1983–4. There has also been a tremendous upsurge of interest in adult education programmes, which have been redesigned and given increased funding to provide training for employment as well as academic upgrading. A $1 million Indigenous Languages Development Fund was created in 1983, and education committees throughout the NWT are using the money to develop language teaching programmes in the schools, and to design curricula for their region.

In the 1970s many Inuit parents had come to believe government assertions that only through an education in English could their sons and daughters fit into the new society. Now that Inuit teachers have shown them that it is possible to learn such subjects as mathematics or history in Inuktitut without any drop in academic standards they hope that an innovative educational system can be developed to function in native languages as well as English.

Communications

The spread of broadcast communications to the Arctic has always had the potential to be the most destructive force acting on Inuit culture. Again, the Inuit have been quick to realize this, and have struggled both to stem the tide of proliferation of radio and television in the north and, wherever possible, to appropriate the airwaves for their own uses.

The Canadian Broadcasting Corporation (CBC), Canada's national system, took an interest in the north at the same time as many government departments, and in 1958 set up its Northern Service, broadcasting on short-wave radio. Right from the beginning, it made efforts to generate as much native language programming as possible. CBC stations were set up in the north in the 1960s. In 1972, Canada's first domestic communications satellite went into operation. It was called Anik A, from the Inuit word for 'brother', and was followed by Anik B in 1978 and C and D in 1982. The satellites gave good quality AM radio reception to the smallest settlements, and most places were provided with the equipment to receive the signals.

Suddenly Inuit across the north were linked by radio, and they asked for more Inuktitut programmes from the Northern Service. Today CBC stations at Inuvik, Rankin Inlet, Kuujjuaq and Iqaluit produce Inuktitut and bilingual English–Inuktitut programmes for their listeners, as well as relaying national CBC English-language programming. For example, the Iqaluit and Rankin Inlet stations combine to produce over 60 hours of Inuktitut or bilingual programmes per week, or about 45 per cent of the total hours broadcast.

This was not achieved without a struggle. At first, the Northern Service was staffed by well-meaning southerners who did not understand Inuit reality. They tended to assume that Inuit just wanted southern programming translated into Inuktitut. Rosemarie Kuptana, an Inuk announcer with CBC Inuvik, commented in 1980: 'the native broadcaster merely becomes a clone of the English Language Announcer, spreading news written by and for the already dominating southern culture...what actually is practised is a kind of colonialism.'

Later, the CBC developed its northern radio programming to reflect more of what Inuit wanted to hear. It trained Inuit producers, who now generate more and more original Inuktitut-language material, covering current affairs, cultural activities and sports.

A more serious threat to Inuit language and culture came with the extension of southern television service to the north in the early 1970s. By 1982, the national CBC television service was broadcasting over 100 hours a week to Inuit homes across the Arctic. The programmes were entirely in English, although over half of those Inuit could not understand English.

The Inuit reacted strongly to the divisive effects of TV on their families and on their society. They petitioned the Canadian Radio, Television and Telecommunications Commission (CRTC), the national regulatory body, asking for more control of the medium and for Inuktitut programming to be made available. In 1975 the Inuit Tapirisat of Canada proposed the Inukshuk project, to make Inuktitut TV programmes for satellite distribution, and to experiment with two-way inter-settlement communication via TV. The project led to the creation of the Inuit Broadcasting Corporation, which has been in production since 1981.

Inuit life in Greenland used to be organized around kinship and other networks of close social association. THE HULTON-DEUTSCH COLLECTION

A settlement in Scoresby sund, East Greenland. B&C ALEXANDER

Inuit schoolgirls in Savissivik, NW Greenland. B&C ALEXANDER

Eskimo walrus hunt in Siberia. ALEXANDER MILOVSKY/REX FEATURES

Nenet children with a reindeer calf in Siberia. B&C ALEXANDER

Chukotka schoolboy at his lessons. ALEXANDER MILOVSKY

A Nenet family in front of a gas rig at Bovanenkovo, Siberia.
B&C ALEXANDER

Endicott Oil Production Island at Prudhoe Bay on the North Slope,
Alaska. B&C ALEXANDER

Hunting and fishing rights continue to be important to Alaska Natives.

Rosemarie Kuptana and John Amagoalik, two of the principal Inuit lobbyists for Nunavut. CANAPRESS/PHOTO SERVICE

The Inuit Broadcasting Corporation of Canada began in 1981.
CANAPRESS/PHOTO SERVICE

Inuit boys outside their modern school in Iquluit, NWT, Canada.
B&C ALEXANDER

Saami wedding in Finland in 1954. HULTON DEUTSCH COLLECTION

Reindeer herding is the source of Saami culture.

The IBC's goal was to produce original Inuktitut-language programmes that would be relevant to their Inuit audience. It trained Inuit production crews to make programmes about contemporary Inuit life which would counterbalance the influence of southern programming. By the mid-1980s IBC was producing five hours a week of current affairs and children's programming out of five production centres across the north, running on government funding of over $1 million a year. (Its current budget is over $3 million a year.)

One problem was that IBC had to find limited space on the CBC satellite channel to distribute its programming, so most of its programmes were aired late at night or in the morning – well away from 'prime time'. In the late 1980s, IBC and other native broadcasters lobbied the federal government for the funding of an all-northern channel, to be called TV Northern Canada (TVNC), which could resolve their programme distribution problems. TVNC went on the air in January 1992, and now broadcasts northern and native programmes across the north.

Language
It should be stated first that, although the Inuit population is not large, Inuit languages have never been in danger of disappearing. Some dialects have been weakened considerably, but a regenerative movement in recent years has halted this erosion, and in some areas the languages are making a comeback.

One main language, Yupik, is spoken in southwest Alaska by about 18,000 Inuit, and also in Chukotka. The other, Inupiaq (called Inuktitut in Canada), is spoken from northern Alaska right across to Greenland by about 66,000 Inuit. Yupik and Inupiaq speakers recognize the common origins of their languages, but cannot understand each other. There are many dialects of Inupiaq, reducible to perhaps ten main ones. Comprehension of other dialects diminishes the further a speaker moves from his or her dialect area but, for example, Canadian Inuit from the Beaufort Sea can communicate with Greenlanders.

Inuktitut did not have a written form until the arrival of southerners. The colonization of the circumpolar Arctic at different times and by different peoples is reflected in the history of the development of writing systems. The Greenlanders were writing a romanized script by the middle of the 18th Century, whereas Canadian Inuit were not writing until the end of the 19th Century. That is when the Reverend Peck, an Anglican missionary, transported a syllabic writing system originally developed for the Ojibway Indians to the eastern Arctic. The syllabic system used characters to represent whole syllables.

In the western Arctic, other missionaries developed their own roman scripts for the language. The various systems were used to translate the Bible, and they made literate virtually a whole population in a fairly short time. It is interesting to note that the native population was then more literate than most of the white men who arrived in the north. It is curious, however, that the missionaries who taught the Inuit to read and write, and so played an important part in strengthening the language for the modern world, were the same individuals who forbade Inuit children to speak their language in the mission schools.

The advent of the governmental residential school system further contributed to the weakening of the Inuit language. Since the pupils were taught in English or French, by the 1970s in certain areas there had grown up a population of children who could not speak their mother tongue well enough to communicate with their parents.

Inuit knew they had to protect their language from the extinction that has been the fate of many Canadian Indian languages. In order to do so, they faced a double challenge: could they successfully make the transition from an oral culture to a literate one, with the standardization of script and the creation of a literature that this implied; and could they strengthen and standardize the dialects of Inuktitut to move towards a stronger pan-Canadian Inuit language (and perhaps ultimately a circumpolar Inuktitut)?

The first goal was to develop a uniform writing system. In 1960 the government hired a linguist, Raymond Gagne, to create a standard orthography. He recommended dropping the syllabic system, and instead devised a roman orthography which was logical and easy to learn, but the scheme was not implemented. Many of the Inuit using syllabics had been taught to read by the Church, and interpreted Gagne's recommendation as an attempt to undermine its influence. They had grown attached to syllabics and considered it a true Inuit form of writing. There were also fears that the proposal for change was an attempt to change the language itself, so Gagne's work did not take hold.

The next attempt came in 1974, when the Inuit Tapirisat of Canada set up the Inuit Language Commission, headed by Jose Kusugak from Rankin Inlet. The Commission consulted Inuit in most communities, asking all the questions that Gagne had not asked. The message came back that the Inuit did not want to abandon the system they were familiar with, whether roman or syllabics. The Commission's answer was to develop a dual orthography by reforming and matching up the roman and syllabics systems so they could be used interchangeably.

The reforms to the two systems are gaining gradual acceptance, aided by their adoption for writing Inuktitut curriculum materials in the schools.

The dual orthography has made possible the development of an Inuit literature, but it is hard to say how long that will take. All early writing in Inuktitut was religious, and to date very few books of a non-religious character have been written. However, government publications in Inuktitut and Inuit cultural and news reports, along with translations of Greenlandic Inuktitut as well as of English literature, are gradually increasing the amount of material available. Most effort is taking place in the school system, which has its own publishing unit to print native-language material.

At the international level, Inuit have expressed the hope that a pan-Inuit writing system and language could be developed, but that does not seem possible as yet. Inuit groups in Canada, at least, are determined to retain the dialects that preserve their identity, and so far no agreement on which dialect would become the base for a 'standard Inuktitut' has emerged. However, people speaking different dialects are starting to understand each other better, because of the spread of Inuit radio and the great number of meetings to which Inuit travel in different areas each year. In Canada the success of Inuit TV will encourage this trend, and in the future the creation of a 'standard Inuktitut' should be possible.

In Canada, the Inuit language is evolving rapidly. Prior to Inuit efforts to reform and protect their language, it was being steadily eroded by the influx of southerners, and by the teaching of English in the schools. The move off the land into the settlements and the change in hunting technology rendered obsolete many old technical terms. More importantly, however, the new rhythm of life and changing relationships in Inuit society forced the old language to adapt to keep up. Today, the young do not understand elderly Inuit when they revert to the old Inuktitut. And yet, the language is not withering. Old hunting terms are being replaced with Inuktitut words invented to describe the new technology. For instance, 'satellite' is 'qangattaqtitausimajuq', meaning 'it has been made to fly'. Inuit concerned with the language, educators, interpreters and cultural workers, meet regularly to standardize the new terminology, and the results are stored in computers. The old language has not been forgotten, and is often drawn on to provide new words. In areas where Inuktitut has come under serious attack, such as the western Arctic, Inuit organizations have started programmes to rebuild the language and to entrench its use in the schools and in the media.

The future

Older Inuit have said that the move into settlements deceived them into thinking their troubles were over. Life on the land had been a constant struggle for survival in one of the world's more inhospitable environments. The new towns made the conditions of life much more pleasant; the houses were always heated, and no one lacked food. In fact, the Inuit came to realize that the struggle for survival was to continue as a fight to maintain their identity and values.

At the heart of that struggle have been differing views of the relationship between native people and government. The Canadian government has always seen native people as *de facto* Canadian citizens, albeit with limited rights to the use of land for subsistence. Government efforts have concentrated on bargaining away a certain amount of land, money and power in exchange for the extinguishment of aboriginal rights, in an effort to arrive at a once-and-for-all deal. Native people have considered aboriginal rights the cornerstone of their relationship with Canada. To give up those rights would be to alter irrevocably their relationship with the government in ways they might not be able to accept.

For the Inuit, the struggle over which interpretation would take effect has been carried out on two fronts: land claims and constitutional negotiations.

Land claims
Inuit leaders in the three Eastern Arctic regions – Baffin, Keewatin and Kitikmeot – eventually decided to establish a separate organization, the Tungavik Federation of Nunavut, to negotiate their land claim. Over the years, their negotiating positions have remained consistent:

a) Inuit wanted the creation of a new territory, Nunavut (which was originally conceived to stretch north from the treeline to include all above it, but which was later reduced in scale to the three eastern Arctic regions covered by the TFN land claim). In the vital area of development, Nunavut would press for greater responsibility in land and offshore management, to balance the interests of development companies against the interest of those favouring a renewable-resource economy. The territory would also take a share of the federal government's royalties on oil, gas and mineral production. Inuit proposed provincial-type responsibilities in the areas of social policy, health, housing and the control of labour to avoid social problems caused by the influx of large numbers of transient workers. Nunavut would be a public government, with Inuit guaranteed control through their majority of 80 per cent of the population.

b) In addition to the powers that public government would provide, Inuit requested a direct share, through Inuit-controlled organizations, of management powers over wildlife and land, including marine areas important for subsistence hunting.

c) Inuit wanted to be granted outright ownership of some land, including ownership of the resources on and under the land.

d) Inuit sought compensation for past wrongs through royalties on resource development and sought payments from the government to allow them to participate in the economic future of the new territory.

It is to the credit of the Canadian government that it embarked on a negotiated process of settling claims at all, since this represents a commitment that many governments with aboriginal populations are still not ready to make. Of course it has been in its own interest to do so, but it could have adopted a more heavy-handed approach to solving the problem. It has funded native groups with many millions of dollars to develop their proposals, although much of this money must be repaid when a settlement is reached. However, it has on occasion manipulated the direction some native groups were taking by withholding these funds – a tactic that has earned it criticism.

From the perspective of government and industry in Canada and the United States, land claims were a concession required to allow access to the non-renewable resources – North Slope and Beaufort Sea oil, hydro-electric power in northern Quebec – situated on or under land claimed by aboriginal people. However, the implications of landmark court decisions in the late 1960s and throughout the 1970s induced the federal government to develop the process of 'comprehensive claims', to address the claims of all aboriginal people who had never signed treaties. ('Specific claims' became the vehicle for addressing the government's failure to live up to the obligations it made in the treaties.)

One of the most controversial aspects of the federal government's land claims policy has been its insistence on 'extinguishment'. Beginning with the James Bay Agreement, the Inuit (along with the Indian First Nations) have been forced to extinguish their aboriginal rights related to the use and management of land as a precondition to settling their land claims with the federal government.

As historian Keith Crowe has noted:

'The extinguishment controversy arises from the need of government to conclude settlement of claims in which it is clear who owns what, with no fear of future claims and confusion. From the native perspective, the settlements should confirm aboriginal title, at least to the lands

assigned by legislation, and should not prejudice general aboriginal rights as guaranteed by the 1982 constitution and amendments. The word "extinguishment" is absent from government policy and the settlement agreements, but synonyms such as "surrender", "release" and "convey" describe the same process with less emotional effect.[7]

In a submission to the 1985 federal government Task Force to Review Comprehensive Claims Policy, the Tungavik Federation of Nunavut stated that:

'TFN rejects the concepts of certainty and finality on several grounds. Even if it is to be admitted, for the sake of argument, that Inuit territorial rights are vague and uncertain because their precise incidence cannot be exhaustively defined, that is the best reason for not having them extinguished. Inuit would not know what they were giving up if they agreed to extinguishment... Further, the federal government policy on finality goes only one way. A once-and-for-all settlement means that it is the Inuit who have to take all of the risks. The James Bay settlement is a good example. Defective drafting, important omissions, and hostile administrative and political policies on the part of the federal and provincial governments have all undermined the Inuit's efforts to make that settlement work...

'...for the federal government to insist on extinguishment of the Inuit's aboriginal title as a pre-condition to a land claims settlement is to load the dice against the Inuit, and to rob the negotiating process of the flexibility that is necessary to arrive at a settlement that properly protects the legitimate interests of the Inuit.[8]

But when forced to choose between signing an agreement-in-principle and walking away from the negotiating table, the leadership of TFN (like the Inuit leaders in northern Quebec and the western Arctic before them) decided it was worth it:

'Surrendering to government our aboriginal title to land, water, and the offshore, as is required in the federal land claim policy, is not something that we want to do, nor is it something that we take lightly. It is quite rightly a controversial issue.

'Surrendering aboriginal title is a bitter pill for Inuit to swallow, but it is not hemlock.

'The question that has to be explored in the months ahead is whether the rights and benefits to be provided to Inuit through the prospective land claim settlement outweigh the rights and benefits being delivered now and in the foreseeable future to Inuit through aboriginal title.[9]

And so, after many years of negotiations, in 1989 TFN leaders signed an agreement-in-principle for a land claim in the eastern Arctic. Inuit leaders had no option but to 'surrender' on the issue of extinguishment, and they were unable to obtain support from either the federal or territorial government for a wildlife harvester income support programme similar to the one obtained by the Crees of northern Quebec in the James Bay Agreement.

They had rather more success in circumventing the Conservative government's refusal to include self-government provisions in a land claim package: TFN insisted on signing a political accord committing the federal and territorial governments to the creation of a Nunavut territory to come into existence in 1999.

On 3, 4 and 5 November 1992, a ratification vote was held in all three regions of the proposed Nunavut. Sixty-nine per cent of the eligible voters (the Inuit who would be beneficiaries of the claim) approved the Final Agreement, the provisions of which include:

- title to approx. 136,000 square miles (350,000 sq. km.) of land, of which 14,000 square miles (36,300 sq. km.) will include mineral rights. Access by non-Inuit to settlement lands is governed by provisions in the Final Agreement;
- $580 million (in 1989 dollars) to be paid to a Nunavut Trust (established by TFN) over 14 years;
- annual receipt of 50 per cent of the first $2 million of non-renewable resource royalty received by government, and 5 per cent of additional non-renewable resource royalties;
- increased Inuit participation in government employment and contracting in the settlement area;
- a $13 million Training Trust Fund;
- a Nunavut Wildlife Management Board with equal Inuit and public membership to oversee wildlife harvesting, and specific wildlife harvesting rights and economic opportunities related to guiding, sports lodges and commercial marketing of wildlife products;
- compensation where developers cause provable damage to property or equipment used in harvesting wildlife, or for loss of income from wildlife harvesting. A surface rights tribunal will be set up to determine liability when claims are not settled; three national parks to be established within the settlement area;
- detailed provisions ensuring equal Inuit representation on boards with responsibility for land use planning, wildlife management, environmental and socio-economic reviews of development proposals, and water management;

● following negotiation of an accord dealing with political powers, financing and timing, the introduction of legislation in Parliament to establish a Nunavut territory.

The Constitution

In the area of constitutional negotiations, the Inuit have played an important part in fighting for the entrenchment of aboriginal rights in the new Canadian Constitution. The then Prime Minister of Canada, Pierre Trudeau, had been determined to patriate Canada's Constitution from Great Britain and to add a charter of rights, during his time in office. After having tried repeatedly to obtain agreement from Canada's provinces to do this without success, he finally decided to do so unilaterally. Native leaders demanded that the proposed charter of rights contain protection of aboriginal rights, knowing that it would be next to impossible to amend the charter to include such a provision once the Constitution had been adopted. After extensive lobbying by native organizations, the federal government agreed to insert a clause protecting 'Existing' rights, only to drop it again in federal-provincial negotiations to make the proposed Constitution acceptable to the provinces. The native people were infuriated, and mounted a strong campaign to have it reinserted that gained much public support. On this issue, the Inuit occupied a middle ground between the federal government and many Indian groups whose demands were more extreme. They were instrumental in reaching a compromise that led to the clause being reinstated into the Constitution, along with a guarantee to hold a conference to define aboriginal rights.

In March 1983 the federal government convened such a conference with the provinces and native leaders, at which the participants could only agree to meet again to continue discussions. The difficulty had been provincial fears that attempts to specify aboriginal rights would involve them in added responsibilities, and would change the balance of power between themselves and the federal government. Native leaders were disappointed at the failure of the conference, but saw the educational value of having had it televised nationally. They had secured a government commitment to continue negotiations from a basis of equality, and understood that the process had the potential to satisfy their demands.

Sociologists Augie Fleras and Jean Leonard Elliott have summed up the 1983 constitutional conference, and the three that followed it, by noting that:

'in the end [the] emphasis on self-government, with its implied recognition of aboriginal peoples as "nations within", was rebuffed, and Canada lost its chance to entrench aboriginal self-governing rights as part of the national constitution. Federal and provincial leaders rejected what appeared to be a nebulous concept with potentially undesirable implications for the existing division of power and wealth. This rejection left current government–aboriginal relations in disarray...'[10]

The role of aboriginal peoples in defeating the Meech Lake Accord[11] and the Mohawk barricades at Oka and Kahnawake helped ensure that aboriginal concerns were at the forefront during the most recent attempt, in 1991–2, to reform the Canadian Constitution. ITC – now under the leadership of President Rosemarie Kuptana – played a prominent role throughout this process, with media commentators calling the Inuit the 'biggest winners'.

The 1991–2 process resulted in the Charlottetown Accord signed by the Prime Minister, the ten provincial premiers, the two territorial government leaders, and the leaders of the four national aboriginal organizations. Among many other provisions, the Accord recognized the 'inherent right of self-government' of the aboriginal peoples of Canada. While opinion polls showed a high degree of public support for the 'aboriginal package', the Charlottetown Accord as a whole proved unpopular with most Canadians and was rejected in a national referendum in November 1992. The considerable gains made by aboriginal leaders at the negotiating table were lost.

It is not clear how the inherently constitutional question of aboriginal rights can be addressed during a period when leading southern politicians are calling for a moratorium on constitutional negotiations. One option for Inuit was hinted at on the day after the defeat of the Charlottetown Accord by former Makivik Corporation and Inuit Circumpolar Conference President Mary Simon – a key adviser to ITC President Rosemarie Kuptana – who noted that just as the provinces entered the Canadian Confederation at different times, and under different terms, so might aboriginal peoples.

The circumpolar movement

At the national level, the Inuit revival is leading to a re-definition of their place in Canadian society. At the international level, the creation of the Inuit Circumpolar Conference (ICC) has given the Inuit much to hope for.

The ICC was inaugurated in Barrow, Alaska, in 1977 by Inuit from

Alaska, Canada and Greenland, initially to represent the concerns of Alaskan and Canadian Inuit about oil and gas development in the Beaufort Sea. It has met every three years since then. At the first three ICC General Assemblies an empty chair was placed at the head table to signify the absence of Inuit in the former Soviet Union. A delegation of Inuit from the Chukotka region of Siberia attended the 1989 General Assembly, and the Inuit residing in the Russian Republic were accepted as full members of the ICC at the 1992 meeting.

In 1981, the ICC decided to help Canadian Inuit in their struggle against the Arctic Pilot Project (APP), a proposal to ship liquefied natural gas from the Canadian high Arctic to southern Canada through Davis Strait in icebreaking tankers. The Inuit feared the environmental consequences of the APP, and were concerned that the Canadian government's lack of a comprehensive northern policy would open the door to such projects to the detriment of Inuit. The ICC testified at the Canadian National Energy Board hearings into the APP, and succeeded in persuading the Board to postpone the hearings indefinitely, until the project was modified.

In May 1983, the ICC was granted Non-Governmental Organization status at the United Nations, thus obtaining a great opportunity to influence world opinion on the Arctic. (One forum where it could participate in the future is at the hearings of the new Working Group on Indigenous Peoples' Rights which has been established by the UN Human Rights Sub-Commission.)

The ICC has already undertaken many initiatives to link Inuit communities through economic and social programmes, and has prepared a comprehensive Arctic Policy. Links are being forged between broadcasting networks in three countries, and at the Iqaluit meeting the Inuit Broadcasting Corporation of Canada aired 17 hours of coverage, part of which was transmitted by satellite to Alaska and Greenland. In addition, the ICC has encouraged business initiatives between Inuit organizations in Canada and their counterparts in Greenland, Alaska and Chukotka.

The ICC maintains that it does not intend to threaten the sovereignty of any government over the Arctic, but the united voice of circumpolar Inuit has the potential to greatly influence national policy in the Arctic regions.

Conclusion

Anthropologist Colin Irwin recently concluded an idiosyncratic but insightful study of the Inuit with the following projection:

> *'The reality emergent in the Arctic is a reality in which a growing Inuit population will come to live in larger, and possibly more regionalized, communities and towns. If current trends continue, rates of unemployment will not improve, even though the number of job opportunities may rise. Although Inuit families may decline in size, they will probably be more numerous, requiring expanded housing and social services. Should migration remain a socially undesirable and economically high-risk strategy for members of this poorly-educated population, then most of the Inuit can be expected to remain in the Arctic, even though they will probably have lost most of their language, culture and land-based skills.*[^42]

This pessimistic view contains some elements of truth. The main problem facing the Inuit is how to develop an economy which will provide jobs for the rapidly growing population. There are not enough jobs available now. Where will additional jobs come from?

One answer is that the land claim and the setting up of the new territory Nunavut will provide many opportunities. The catch here is that most of those jobs will be political or administrative, requiring a higher education than most young Inuit possess. There has been much talk about training in preparation for the coming of Nunavut, but not enough has been done. The result is that there are few Inuit qualified today to take jobs in the new Nunavut administration, particularly in management positions. Training funds made available through the land claim will gradually improve this picture.

On the positive side, Inuit have been determined to protect their language and culture as much as possible. Educators have made steady progress in incorporating the teaching of Inuktitut into the schools. Inuktitut is one of three Canadian aboriginal languages (of a total of 53) thought by linguists to be capable of long-term survival.

At the national political level, Inuit have achieved what many thought they could not: the creation of a new territory to be called Nunavut. The administration of Nunavut and the recently-signed land claim will keep Inuit busy for years to come. There will be immense problems; but at least the successes and failures will be theirs, and not somebody else's.

The battle to entrench aboriginal self-government in the Canadian Constitution has been temporarily suspended. Canadian public opinion is still in favour of self-government, but this will not last forever. Canadian Inuit and Indians probably do not have much time to make a deal. However, it is difficult to see how they could do this without re-opening the constitutional negotiations of which most Canadians are so tired.

The Inuit survived for many generations by skilful adaptation to a harsh world. Although their material circumstances have improved, the struggle for survival of their culture and way of life is no less real than that of their forefathers. Their relative isolation from Euro-Canadian culture has allowed them time to prepare for further changes to come. They are also aided by the fact that their relations with the Government of Canada are at a high point. They now have some time, but not too long, to consolidate the political gains they have made, and to evolve a modern Inuit culture based on traditional values but coexisting with the larger Canadian culture.

A few final words from John Amagoalik, former President of ITC and negotiator of the Inuit land claim for Nunavut:

'Will the Inuit disappear from the face of the earth? Will we become extinct? Will our culture, our language and our attachment to nature be remembered only in history books?...To realize that our people can be classified as an endangered species is very disturbing...If we are to survive as a race, we must have the understanding and patience of the dominant cultures of this country...We must teach our children their mother tongue. We must teach them what they are and where they come from. We must teach them the values which have guided our society over the thousands of years...It is this spirit we must keep alive so that it may guide us again in a new life in a changed world.'[13]

5

THE SAAMI OF LAPLAND

by Hugh Beach

Introduction

The Saami, or Lapps, are the native people of the area in north-ernmost Europe known as Lapland. The land of the Saami is a land of extremes: the midnight sun can circle the horizon without ever descending below it during the summer, while in winter there are short, pale 'days' when the sun never rises above the horizon at all. A hike from the high mountains to the lowland forests can resemble a journey in time through three different seasons. In early June the high mountain lakes are often still frozen over. Snow is still abundant, and will never fully disappear from the mountain slopes before winter replenishes the supply. Further down the mountains, birches show the first light green foliage of spring, while down in the deep evergreen forest valleys, summer is in full bloom.

Due to the national borders forced upon them, the Saami have been parcelled into four separate countries: Norway, Sweden, Finland and Russia. The description of this part of the world by the 10th Century Viking poet Egill Skallagrimsson can hardly be bettered:

'In northern Norway one finds the wide flat tundra land called the "vidda", and along the Norwegian coast there are deep fjords that penetrate into the heart of the mountains. Finland's broad forests are broken by innumerable lakes and waterways. All along the western frontier of Sweden there is a massive mountain chain. These mountains continue into and cover most of northern Norway, but in Sweden the land drops into a broad lowland forest district of pine and fir before meeting the Baltic Sea.'

Barents
Sea

North
Sea

Arctic Circle

White Sea

Tromsø
Karasjok
Masi
Kautokeino
Inari
Utsjoki
Murmansk

Kiruna

6
7
8
9
5
4
3
2
1

Gulf of Bothnia

FINLAND

RUSSIA

NORWAY

Oslo

Helsinki

SWEDEN

Stockholm

Baltic Sea

☐ Saami Core Areas

The Saami Dialects

SYDSAMISKA
1. Sydsamiska
2. Umesamiska
CENTRALSAMISKA
3. Pitesamiska
4. Lulesamiska
5. Nordsamiska
ÖSTSAMISKA
6. Enaresamiska
7. Skoltsamiska
8. Akkala- och Kildinsamiska
9. Tersamiska

0   400km

Credit: Svenska Samernas Riksförbund, (1987). Samer: informationsskrift.

There were social, economic and linguistic differences within the general Saami population before the division into separate states, but these were and largely still are subordinated to the overall unity of Saami ethnic identity. Unlike many other ethnic minorities, the Saami maintain access to much of *their* land, despite ongoing debates concerning questions of legal ownership. Yet, in spite of the fundamental differences between the Saami minority and other non-indigenous minorities in these countries, the Saami have been treated in many respects like immigrants, to the extent of being subjected to powerful assimilation policies. (In fact, in some respects it is only thanks to policies forged to support the cultures and languages of immigrant groups that the Saami too have gained similar support.)

The last ten years have been momentous for the Saami. Norway and Sweden have established democratically elected Saami Parliaments (*Sametings*) and altered significant aspects of governmental Saami policy following upon the extensive work of Saami Rights Commissions in both of these countries. Although Finland has had a Saami Parliament since 1973, well in advance of both Norway and Sweden, here too significant policy changes have been enacted largely in the light of important new findings from research into Saami resource rights and because of efforts to harmonize Saami policies within the Nordic countries. The dissolution of the Soviet Union has had a profound effect on the Saami of the Kola Peninsula. With the economy in shambles, the Russian government has terminated the old state-owned farms, *sovkhozes* – including the reindeer *sovkhozes* in which many of Russia's Saami were employed. Farm capital (reindeer stock) has been thrown on to the open market for purchase by the highest bidder. Yet this economic turmoil is accompanied by new freedoms, and the Kola Saami have in record time organized themselves politically, made firm connections with their Saami neighbours to the west (cultural and educational exchange programmes, for example) and even joined the Nordic Saami Council (*Sámiráddi*), first as observers, but by 1992 as full voting members (causing the modifier 'Nordic' to be omitted from the name of the organization).

Accurate demographic statistics on Saami population size and distribution are largely lacking. Much depends, of course, on the operational definition of 'Saami', and this presents a difficult problem. Ruong's standard work on the Saami from 1975 claims there to be a total of 35,000 Saami, of whom 20,000 are in Norway, 10,000 in Sweden, 3,000 in Finland and 2,000 in Russia. The 1982 revised edition of this work, however, gives considerably higher numbers: a total of 60,000 Saami, of whom 40,000 are in Norway, 15,000 in Sweden,

4,000 in Finland and 1,500 to 2,000 in Russia. Obviously this rise of over 58 per cent in seven years reflects more than a growing birth rate; it reflects various definitions of Saamihood based largely on criteria of language and individual self-ascriptions (criteria still debated but commonly accepted by the Saami themselves and formalized in the definition of those eligible to participate in the election of representatives to their respective Saami Parliaments in Norway, Sweden and Finland). Finnish figures from 1991 indicate that there are 4,000 Saami living in northern Finland and 2,000 Saami living in other parts of Finland. There is furthermore a growing tendency for those Saami who earlier sought to avoid public admission of their ethnic roots for fear of stigmatization to take new pride in their ethnic membership.

Saami political organizations have demanded for a long time that government census record their ethnicity. Knowledge of Saami numbers would indicate potential Saami political strength. Later, while legislation for the establishment of Saami Parliaments (see pp. 197-202) in Norway and Sweden was under formulation, the issue of a Saami registry was again actualized in order to define the Saami electorate for these new democratically elected assemblies. Finland, however, has kept a voluntary Saami registry for over 30 years. Just who is to be recognized as a Saami for voting purposes in the officially recognized Saami electorates in the election of their representatives to the Saami Parliaments has only recently been finalized and 'harmonized' within the Fennoscandia nations (with the construction of the Swedish Saami Parliament). It has been a major concern of the Saami that someone recognized as such in one of the countries with a Saami indigenous population should also be recognized as such in the others.

In Russia, ethnic registration is involuntary and depends upon the ethnicity of one's parents, children of mixed marriages being given the option to choose registration with the ethnic group of one or the other parent at the age of 16. Such registration in Russia, however, does not entail eligibility for Saami to vote for any kind of special Saami representation.

In the spirit of Nordic harmonization of Saami policies, the governments of Norway and Sweden (following the Finnish precedent) have instituted a combination of subjective and objective criteria defining those Saami who, if they so desire, can register themselves to vote in their respective Saami Parliament elections. In order to join the Saami electorate, one must feel oneself to be a Saami (subjective criterion), and one must have used the Saami language in the home or had a parent or grandparent for whom Saami was a home language (objective criterion). The Saami Parliaments of Norway and Sweden are composed of Saami representatives elected by freely registered Saami, as is already the case in the existing Finnish Saami Parliament. However, some Saami are anxious that apathy causes many Saami to refrain from joining the Saami electorate, and if Saami language skills decline further over the generations, the potential electorate, not to mention those who actually register, will decrease severely. Sweden, unlike Norway, has therefore added a further clause to the objective criteria: if someone of Saami descent is not eligible to join the Saami electorate in Sweden according to the language criterion, this person might still register simply if his or her parents or grandparents have been registered.

Continuity of registration can in effect substitute for language continuity; yet, nonetheless, if both registration and language continuity lapse for more than two generations, eligibility to join the electorate under this legally constructed Saami definition is lost. While there are proponents among the Saami for a mandatory, objectively determined Saami census, most agree that ethnic registration should only occur voluntarily. Critics of the Saami voting definitions point out that the reliance on language for those eligible to vote is extremely narrow compared to the provisions in international texts for the definition of both minorities and indigenous peoples.

The Saami call themselves *saemie*, *sápmi*, *saa'm* or similar dialectical variations. For many years Saami spokesmen in Norway, Sweden and Finland have campaigned to substitute 'Saami' for 'Lapp' (considered by many Saami to be a derogatory term). In Russia, 'Saami' is already the accepted usage. During the 1960s and 1970s 'Saami' (in Swedish and Norwegian 'Same') has come to replace 'Lapp' in all official texts. Similar replacement has gained momentum internationally. For a small minority people, threatened with assimilation, the destruction of their resource base and deterioration of their language, gaining authentication for their own name for themselves by others is a symbolically significant step towards international recognition of their cultural needs and rights to self-determination.

Few groups have had so much written about them as have the Saami, and in this short space it is impossible to do this material justice. My purpose, therefore, will be to provide basic information about the situation of the Saami and to contribute a much-needed analytical update in view of recent and highly significant developments.

The Saami people

In the capital cities of the Fennoscandian countries (Norway, Sweden and Finland), where many Saami have settled, it is generally impossible to distinguish a Saami who is not traditionally dressed from any other

Swede, Norwegian or Finn. In fact, Saami representatives have been known to cause consternation at international congresses among their aboriginal brethren who have never imagined that indigenous peoples could be 'white'. A common stereotype of the Saami is that they are short, with dark hair and eyes, high cheek bones and narrow nose bones; yet, there are many tall, blond-haired and blue-eyed Saami.

Despite a broad range of traditional subsistence lifestyles and adopted modern livelihoods, the Saami are best known to the world for their reindeer herding. Nonetheless, one cannot take for granted that in Fennoscandia all reindeer *owners* are reindeer *herders*, that all herders are owners, or even that all herders are Saami. While in Sweden and most but not all of Norway, reindeer herders are of Saami origin, this is not necessarily the case in Finland at all. In Sweden, even though Saami origin is not a criterion to *own* reindeer, any non-Saami owner must employ the services of a Saami herder to herd his or her deer.

Characteristic of Saami, however, whether herders or non-herders is that they regard the reindeer as a basic guardian of their culture, their language and identity. It is true that the policies of their encompassing nation states have commonly interpreted Saami resource rights as privileges (which can be revoked as a simple policy adjustment without due process of law or just compensation) and conferred these exclusively upon the reindeer-herding Saami, but the Saami preoccupation with reindeer stretches far beyond the resource rights practised by the herders alone. Reindeer-herding Saami are a small minority of the entire Saami population (in Sweden, for example, only about 10–15 per cent, in Norway 5–8 per cent), but the herding livelihood is something all Saami will fight to protect. It is regarded as the source of their culture and the flame which keeps their identity as Saami alive.

Of course, reindeer herding is a broad term for a livelihood which has undergone tremendous development. Besides keeping deer for decoy (see p. 170) and transport purposes, one can base one's herding economy upon the use of the deer primarily for milk or meat, and whichever one practises the manner of utilization determines largely the kind of herding one pursues. Before modern transportation linked the herders to a broader, non-Saami market and also provided them the means to meet commercial demands, herding was basically a subsistence livelihood with few external transactions. Herding families kept tight control of their deer (continually guarding them and preventing them from straying or mixing with other herds) and for a large part of the year milked them daily. The milk was usually made into cheese, and it was an old saying that the last cheese of one year should 'see' the first cheese of the next.

When a reindeer was slaughtered, there was little which was not used. Early texts recording meetings with Saami generally comment upon the herders' knowledge of each individual deer and of their great usefulness for the Saami, providing everything in the way of food and clothing. Later, when new foodstuffs and materials could be purchased, and when the sale of meat could provide the funds for such purchases, milking gradually disappeared, and the herds were used basically as a meat resource. This change was accompanied by pressures for changes in herd size and methods of herding. However, the seasonal cycle of herding work today is still regulated by the reindeer's natural rhythm and by the availability of grazing.

In early spring the reindeer herds migrate to the calving grounds, in Sweden in the mountainous area near the Norwegian border and in Norway along the coast or on the many offshore islands. The herders follow to guard against predators and in the summer to round up the herd for the marking of the calves. Then, as the autumn approaches, the herds begin to pull towards new grazing lands and the rutting season begins. The herders are engaged in dividing the herds and in slaughtering. Later still, the reindeer move on to the winter, lichen grazing lands, and the herders must perform further herd divisions and slaughtering, all the while guarding against predators. Herders often split into their smallest groups (commonly just the nuclear family) in order to best utilize the scarce winter pastures, and it is therefore necessary to divide the reindeer according to owner.

During the winter, each owner prefers to guard his own animals against predators (not always four-footed), and he naturally wants ready access to his own animals for slaughter. An ill-timed thaw can 'lock' the lichen, that is, coat it with a hard layer of ice rendering it inedible for the reindeer. Or else the snow cover can freeze into such a hard surface that the deer cannot break through it to dig down to the lichen. In such cases, which in the past would have been disastrous (but even today can be still prove devastating), the herders must try to feed their deer expensive artificial fodder twice a day. Should the greenhouse effect cause milder winters and more frequent oscillations between warmer and cooler periods, lichens might be 'locked' more often, causing regular use of artificial fodder and threatening the entire Saami pastoral pattern.

In many Saami summer camps the traditional dome-shaped Saami hut, built with a log frame, waterproofed by birch bark and insulated by a final cover of turf, is still in use. In the centre is an open hearth (sometimes replaced by a wood stove), and if someone is at home, a column of smoke usually rises from a smoke hole directly overhead. In the past, when herding was more intensive, for example during the days when the deer were milked regularly and the herders' camp moved frequently, mobile tent *goattiehs* were used. Some Saami families, especially on the Norwegian *vidda*, still use a tent during migrations, but on the whole, camps have become more permanent, and the turf-covered frame has seen increased use, although it in turn has now frequently been replaced by a wooden cabin. During the winters, when the herders are generally no longer in the high mountains but dwelling in smaller, often mixed Saami and non-Saami settlements, or at least enjoying access to the road network, they commonly live in regular houses with modern facilities.

Active herders relish the free life it affords them in one of the world's most beautiful regions. It is a tough existence of frequent moves, physical risk (Swedish statistics based on proportion of work-related fatalities and serious injuries show reindeer herding to be the country's most dangerous job) and long separations of family members. While there are a few so-called big herders with many head of reindeer, most have only enough to get by when the family income is supplemented by other part-time jobs. Yet reindeer herding itself is precisely a life within a Saami community, as a Saami, and not just a job. Those who are used to it are not at all necessarily inclined to leave it for higher paying employment and better living standards in the south. Nonetheless, be it by carrot or stick, many Saami have left their traditional core geographical areas and moved to the cities.

Reindeer herding has spread widely outside of its traditional borders. Saami have often been contracted as herding teachers among distant Inuit groups. At the end of the 19th Century, for example, approximately 70 Saami from northern Norway (in two waves) were imported to Alaska to help build a strong herding industry and, so it was planned, to seed a permanent Saami colony there for the supply of future herding instructors. As it turned out, many of the would-be instructors were swept up into the Alaskan Gold Rush instead. Some did indeed teach herding to the Inuit and with the termination of their contracts stayed on to tend their own private herds, but most returned to Norway after only a few years. When in 1937 new American legislation prohibited reindeer ownership to anyone but a Native Alaskan Inuit, Indian or Aleut, the few remaining Saami herders were forced to sell out.

Similar programmes where Saami were brought over to care for fledgling domesticated reindeer enterprises occurred in Canada. In Greenland too, where herding has not been confined to native Greenlanders, Saami established herds. A Swedish Saami who married a

British anthropologist moved with his reindeer over to Scotland in the early 1950s, and individual Saami also immigrated to other countries along with the great waves of other Scandinavians in the 1800s without necessarily any connection to reindeer herding. While permanent Saami colonies were not founded in any of these instances, Saami descendants have been spread far and wide. There has recently been a revival of interest in Saami heritage in North America. *Baiki*, the North American Journal of Saami Living (quarterly) based in Duluth, Minnesota, was launched in 1991 and has elicited enthusiastic response. The Saami have regular and increasing communication with a wide variety of indigenous peoples' organizations. Pursuant to the inauguration of the Swedish *Sameting* in August 1993, communication and organization within the national Saami communities will take a major step forward with the founding of a Nordic Saami Parliament with representatives from the national Saami *Sametings*, a development firmly on the agenda.

Origins

Tacitus wrote in AD 98 wrote of the *fenni*, north of the Germanic tribes. According to his description, these *fenni* had no horses, no weapons and no houses. They dressed in hides and slept on the ground. Women as well as men joined in the hunt. In AD 550, Prokopios described what he termed the *skrithiphinoi* in much the same way. The prefix *skriti-* used by Prokopios is an Old Norse word meaning 'to ski'. The Saami have been referred to as *scrirdifiner*, *scirdifriner*, *rerefenar*, *scricfinner* or simply *finner* and *finnar*. *Finner* is an old Nordic name for the Saami which is still used at times in Norway and evident in the name of Norway's northernmost region, Finnmarken. The Finns, inhabitants of Finland, were then known as *kväner*.[1]

Around AD 1200, Saxo Grammaticus described the Saami as moving with their houses and was the first to use the term *Lappia* for Lappland. Gradually it became common to speak of Lappia inhabitants as Lapps, usually together with the modifier 'wild'. Thus the term 'Lapp' is a relatively recent name for the Saami which spread via Swedish to the rest of the world. (Another, probably mistaken derivation of the term 'Lapp' claims it to come from the word *lapp* used to signify a piece of cloth, a rag[2] or a triangular cloth piece used in sewing clothes.)[3]

Early researchers into Saami racial traits were largely preoccupied with measuring Saami skulls, and have presented a range of hypotheses claiming almost every conceivable origin for the Saami. Guerault (1860–3) and Nilsson (1866) considered the Saami to be mongoloid.

Schefferus (1673) grouped the Saami with the Finns. Giuffrida-Ruggeri (1913) placed them with the Samoyeds. Wiklund conceived of the Saami as the remnants of the root race for both yellow and white races. The Saami have even been called the lost tribe of Israel. The confidence with which these theories are presented must be weighed against the enormous range of their variability. We simply do not really know where the Saami originated or even if this is the proper question. Poul Simonsen (1959) suggests that the appropriate question to ask is not where the Saami came from, but rather when the various peoples in the north coalesced into Saami with a Saami identity.

From the mid-1800s to the mid-1900s, it seems that many scholars wished to isolate the characteristics of their own 'civilized race' by making crude comparisons with other peoples. Social or 'vulgar' Darwinism was in vogue. So-called racial hygiene, condemning intermarriage between races seen to be of different order, was a respectable topic. As a result, descriptions of the Saami race from this period are often hard-drawn, absolute and derogatory. In any case, scholars have been convinced that Saami traits bespeak long isolation. For example, *as a population*, Saami demonstrate some special physical characteristics, such as an extremely high frequency of the A-2 blood type.[4] New forms of research using so-called genetic markers may well alter greatly our understanding of Saami origins. According to Professor Pekka Sammallahti from Oulu University in Finland, Indo-European genes prevail over Finno-Ugric genes in Finland as a whole, whereas the situation is clearly reversed among the Saami. He views the Finns as Indo-Europeanized Saami to a large extent.[5]

The often-encountered debate over who was 'first in the mountains', Saami or Scandinavians, as linked to the question of who should therefore be given special resource rights, is misguided. The fact is that the Saami as a fully developed ethnic group held the area and had held it past the brink of human memory when the nations to the south took the first steps to colonize it. New evidence presents itself continually on this topic. The recent archaeological finds of Dr Inger Zachrisson, for instance, indicate that Saami already inhabited the Härjedalen area of Sweden in the year AD 1000, a postulate casting strong doubt on one of the main pillars of argument in the Swedish Supreme Court's 1981 ruling in the famous Skattefjäll or Tax Mountain Case (see p.190) in which Saami land rights were tested.

Language

The Saami language belongs to the western division of the Finno-Ugric branch of the Uralic family. Finnish, Estonian, Livonian, Votic, Vepsian, Mordvin, Mari and Permian (Udmurt and Komi) belong to this same western group.[6] Although it is undergoing change, Saami is basically a so-called agglutinated language, meaning that the function of a word in a sentence is decided by building prefixes and suffixes onto a root. Additions can be pasted on to the root in long chains.[7] The root is often characterized by internal consonant value changes according to the form of the agglutinating syllables.

Saami is characterized by as many as 7–8 noun cases and numerous diminutives. Its personal pronouns exhibit the dual as well as singular and plural forms. As a language, it is equipped to deal with the ecology of the far North and especially with the reindeer-herding livelihood. For example, Saami terminology distinguishes reindeer according to a three- or four-category nomenclature based on: 1) sex and age, 2) colour and 3) the form or absence of horns.[8] By combining the distinctions of each category in different permutations, hundreds of descriptive terms can be generated and used to pinpoint accurately each particular reindeer in an entire herd. The herder who does not speak Saami is at a distinct disadvantage.

The Saami language is divided into a number of major dialects with variations so marked that a Northern Saami and a Southern Saami in Sweden might resort to Swedish in order to communicate. In fact, Hansegård (1974) claims that these major variations can be considered different languages.[9] Marjut Aikio (1991) corroborates this view, claiming it more appropriate to speak of seven Saami languages.[10] The major languages/dialects encompass sub-dialects so that the trained ear can pinpoint quite accurately the original home area of a speaker.

The Saami dialects are: Skolt, Kildin and Ter Saami, spoken on the Kola Peninsula of Russia; Enare Saami, spoken around Enare Lake in Finland; Northern Saami, spoken in northern Norway, Torne Lappmark in Sweden and neighbouring zones in Finland; Lule Saami, spoken in Lule Lappmark; Pite Saami, spoken in Pite Lappmark; Ume Saami, spoken in the southern Arvidsjaur region and in northern Västerbotten; Southern Saami, spoken in most of Västerbotten and in Jämtland, Härjedalen, the Idre region in Dalecarlia and nearby areas in Norway.[11] These can be grouped into three major categories: Eastern, Central and Southern Saami.[12] However, because of border disputes constraining the traditionally free flow of nomadic Saami across the Nordic countries and the Kola Peninsula, and in particular the enforced relocation of many Northern Saami families southwards during the first half of the 1900s (to be discussed later), the Northern Saami dialect is now widely spread to the more southerly areas as well.

Saami contains many borrowed words from Finnish, indicating Saami–Finnish relations for at least 2,000 years, and also from Old Norse, going back at least 1,300 years.[13] Even in recent times, large parts of northern Sweden and Norway have been bilingual in Saami and Finnish, although Swedish and Norwegian have increasingly pushed out Finnish in these areas. Yet, in certain areas it is not uncommon to find trilingual populations, speaking Saami, Finnish, and Swedish or Norwegian.[14] On the Kola Peninsula it is the rule that all Saami can speak Russian. However, of the 1,615 Saami registered on the Kola Peninsula in 1989 (about 200 live off the peninsula), 707 could speak both Russian and Saami (Afanasjeva and Rantala).

The colonizing powers have had fluctuating attitudes towards the Saami language. On the one hand, Saami has been suppressed as a language unfit to carry the weight of higher civilization or to convey the glories of Christianity: some churchmen even considered the Saami language to be the Devil's tongue. On the other hand, more enlightened churchmen understood that the most effective way to spread the gospel to the Saami was through the Saami language.

In the early 1700s, Thomas von Westen led the Saami Mission in northern Norway. He saw the use of Saami as essential for missionary work, and the Saami Mission continued in this spirit for many years after his death. By the late 1700s, however, the tide had changed in Norway. The Saami language did not receive renewed support until around the 1820s, but then enjoyed a comeback largely due to the work of the priests Deinboll and Stockfleth. With the rise of Norwegian nationalism around the mid-1850s, the Saami language was once again suppressed. Apparently, large-scale immigration of Finns to northern Norway at this time fanned the flames of a one-state-one-culture ideology, and in many ways, the Saami suffered from the Norwegian fear of 'Finnicization'. For example, a ruling in 1902 forbad the sale of land to citizens who had not mastered Norwegian and used it daily.[15] This bleak period for Saami language and schooling in Norway continued until the close of the Second World War, when human rights issues re-emerged. During the war Norwegian Saami and non-Saami fought side by side against the German occupants and saw their homes destroyed. The war was a watershed in the relations between Saami and non-Saami in Norway; the most severe discrimination ceased.

Similar shifts between the poles of Saami language support and suppression have occurred in Sweden and Finland. During the worst periods, Saami children received instruction only in the Nordic language of their encompassing state and were often not permitted to speak Saami together in school. Saami speakers were stigmatized in general, with the result that this stigma frequently became internalized by the Saami themselves.

Under the Soviet regime in Russia, while the study of the Russian language was compulsory for all schoolchildren, considerable support was given to the language maintenance of the northern indigenous peoples. Orthographies were developed, and native language instruction was provided. Nonetheless, on the Kola Peninsula among the non-herding Saami population, Saami language loss is a serious problem causing much concern. There are few school texts for teaching Kildin Saami, the main Saami dialect spoken there, and these are the focus of heated debate. The one side claims that the only way to preserve the Kola Saami language is to join with the standardized Saami orthography based on the Latin alphabet used in Fennoscandia. In this way, the Kola Saami children will be able to utilize school texts from the West and to enjoy the far larger body of Saami publications. The other side maintains that the Kola Saami children should have their Saami school texts in the Cyrillic alphabet, an alphabet they already know through Russian. If they are required to learn an entirely new orthography to preserve their Saami language, it will disappear all the faster. They argue that once Saami has been mastered, there is time enough to learn the Latin alphabet and to link with the Western Saami literature if one so desires.

The Saami language was first put into writing by missionaries of the colonizing powers in the 1600s. In 1755 the New Testament was translated into Saami, and the whole Bible followed in 1811.[16] In fact, the use of written Saami in Finland was mainly confined to religious texts up until the 1970s.[17] Naturally the various churchmen wrote the Saami dialect they had learned from their mission station, and as there was no standard orthography, they devised their own systems. Dialectal variation was thereby compounded by orthographic variation. In the interests of maintaining a strong, living Saami language, it has been important to try to achieve a standardized orthography. Professor Knut Bergsland from Norway together with the Saami professor Israel Ruong from Sweden composed a standard Saami orthography which was used by many dialect groups from 1951 to 1979. Later, some adjustments were made so that now the major Saami dialect groups in Norway, Sweden and Finland have agreed upon a standard.

Language loss and lack of reading and writing skills have been pressing problems for the Saami. The research of Henning Johansson for the non-herding Saami population in Sweden showed alarming results: 20 per cent cannot understand Saami; 40 per cent cannot speak Saami; 65 per cent cannot read Saami; 85 per cent cannot write Saami.[18] In Finland, the outlook for maintaining the Saami language is not good. Measures to teach reading and writing skills in Saami through the schools have been focused upon children alone.[19] While figures demonstrating Saami linguistic competence give cause for alarm, the situation is far worse when it comes to actual language use. Individual linguistic competence has been found to persist far longer than actual usage, but it is the latter which keeps a language alive through generations, breeding new competence. Aikio has pointed out that in Finland, shortage of teaching material, shortage of Saami-speaking teachers, little media exposure and lack of official recognition even within the realm of the reindeer-herding administration have all inhibited the use of the Saami language even by those competent to do so. Recent research by Guttorm[20] found that Saami-speaking children often spoke Finnish outside the home even when speaking to each other.

Now, with increasing pride in Saami identity, the rise of Saami political and cultural organizations and support from state governments, this situation can be improved. Largely due to laws designed to cope with the great influx of immigrants to Sweden, the Saami have been given increased support for the maintenance of their language. Saami children have the right to mother-tongue training within the Swedish schools. In the so-called Saami schools, of which there remain only six in Sweden, elementary Saami schoolchildren now receive much of their instruction in Saami.

Earlier, children of reindeer herders had to attend so-called Nomad Schools, but after 1962 these schools for nomad children were opened to all Saami. Nonetheless, of the 2,500 or so Saami children of school age in Sweden, only about 5 per cent attend the Saami schools. In these schools, instruction is given in both Swedish and Saami. In some areas, Saami kindergartens have been started where the children receive language training and also contact with Saami culture. However, home language support for children of kindergarten age in Sweden is not strictly commanded by law as is that of older children.

There is a Saami Folk High School for older children and adults in Jokkmokk, Sweden, but after 1968 financial difficulties forced the school to open itself to non-Saami students as well. This school maintains a strong Saami profile, with courses in Saami language, handicraft and reindeer herding. A Saami School Board was established in 1980, also in Jokkmokk.

In 1975 a Saami department was founded at the University of Umeå, Sweden. This department has a professor and a lecturer; it provides courses in Northern, Southern and Lule Saami dialects for both beginners and mother-tongue speakers. Saami language courses are also available at Uppsala University and at the Teacher Training College in Luleå.[21]

In Norway, the Primary School Act of 1969 and its later revisions assure the Saami children in the Saami areas the right to Saami language lessons through the first six school years (until they are about 13 years old) upon parental request. With the 1985 revision, these children could also obtain Saami as a language of instruction (at least until they were about nine years old). Older children, from about 13 to 15 years of age, make their own decisions about language classes in school. Saami is a school subject taught to children 16 through 18 years of age in Saami centres such as Kautokeino, Karasjok and Hamarøy. Even outside the traditional Saami areas, such as in Oslo, Saami immigration has occasioned Saami language instruction in schools. Alta, Bodø and Levanger host teacher training colleges with Saami courses, and advanced language studies can be followed at Oslo and Tromsø universities. A professor's chair in Saami was established in 1986 in Tromsø, while a chair in Finno-Ugrian languages has existed in Oslo since 1866.[22]

In Finland, with but minor exceptions, the Saami language was not taught at all to Saami children in school prior to 1970. Since then, it is permitted to instruct Saami students in their own language dialects, thanks to the efforts of a Planning Committee for Instruction in Saami.[23] Nonetheless, in Finland, Saami children do not have special Saami schools, and it has not always been possible to offer them all instruction in Saami. The obligation for the municipalities to provide Saami instruction in the so-called Saami Homeland has been especially stressed in recent legislation. Gains have been considerable, if uneven. During the 1992–3 school year, instruction in Northern Saami was given at 20 lower classes of the comprehensive school, 6 upper classes of the comprehensive school and 4 senior secondary schools. Inari Saami was taught in 5 lower classes and 2 upper classes, while Skolt Saami was taught in 3 lower and 2 upper classes.

In Finland as in Norway and Sweden, one of the main stumbling blocks to Saami language instruction until recently has been the lack of appropriate teaching material. Teachers in Finland since 1975 have been able to take a leave of absence in order to study the Saami language, and since 1981 paid leaves of absence have been provided for those who wish to prepare educational materials in Saami.[24] A standardized orthography has meant much in overcoming the lack of

Saami teaching material, as Saami texts produced in any one of the Nordic countries can be used in the others.

At university level in Finland, there are presently three lecturers' chairs: one at the University of Lapland, founded in 1979; one at the University of Oulu; and one at the University of Helsinki. A professor's chair in Saami language and culture has existed since 1982 at the University of Oulu. Saami language courses are regularly offered at Oulu and Helsinki. It is also possible to find courses in Saami ethnography offered at the major universities of the north.

Inter-Nordic cooperation took a major step forward with the founding of the Nordic Saami Institute (NSI) in 1973 in Kautokeino, Norway, whose goals are to further the social, cultural, legal and economic situation of all the Saami in the Nordic countries. Among other things, the NSI supports research in Saami linguistics and history and also arranges language courses.

An excellent example of cooperation among the Nordic nations is the production of the Saami language course, *Davvin*, through both textbooks and radio broadcasts. This cooperation has involved the national radio networks of Norway, Sweden and Finland. *Davvin* is designed for those who do not already have Saami as their first language. Another radio course, *Samas*, has been produced to teach reading and writing skills to those with Saami as mother tongue. This course has also been broadcast on TV.

Saami representation on the Nordic TV networks has otherwise been weak but is growing slowly. Swedish television broadcasts 4–7 hours of Saami programmes per year, reports and documentaries in the Saami language. These two kinds of programme are produced by the Swedish Saami TV department in Kiruna, and others are bought in from Norway. In Norway there is now a permanent Saami TV department, also with its own programme production, transmitting 10–15 hours per year. There is as yet no Saami TV department in Finland to produce its own Saami programmes, but Saami-related ones are bought in from Sweden and Norway and shown for approximately 4–6 hours per year.

There are, however, regular radio programmes and news broadcasts for the Saami, both in their own language and in that of the majority. In Norway, Saami Radio broadcasts from Karasjok three times daily in the Northern Saami dialect for a total of about ten hours a week. There is also a small programme in the Southern Saami dialect sent from Trondheim. In Sweden there is a national Saami programme (in Swedish) 30 minutes a week and national programmes in the Northern dialect $3\frac{1}{2}$ hours a week, and in the Southern dialect for 30 minutes a week. In Sweden, the regional radio station of the Norrbotten province also broadcasts programmes in the Northern dialect for one hour a week. Unfortunately, broadcasts in the Lule dialect are absent for the time being in both Norway and Sweden. It has proven difficult to find trained radio personnel in the various dialects. However, it is a top priority to establish a position for Lule Saami broadcasts with a broadcasting time of 30 minutes a week.

In 1986, Aikio listed for Finland only about 3½ hours of radio broadcasts per week in the Saami language. Today in Finland, however, the Saami have their own special radio channel, broadcasting Saami-related programmes all day using the Northern, Enare and Skolt Saami dialects, and Finnish, and covering the so-called Saami Homeland. Except for the summer months and on weekends when reductions occur, approximately 5 hours of broadcast time per day is in the Saami language. It is plain that Saami radio broadcasting in Finland has made major progress. Finland is the first country to establish a radio channel entirely in Saami control.

The Saami Radio departments of Norway, Sweden and Finland have themselves organized a cooperative news team with combined broadcasts in the three countries. For example, from 8:00 to 8:10 each morning each of these three countries transmits the same Saami news. Sweden's morning Saami programme continues for another 20 minutes and Finland carries the full half hour as well three days a week. The team hopes to expand its combined broadcasts.

Along with reindeer herding and Saami handicrafts, the Saami language stands as a major feature of Saami identity. Understandably, those Saami in groups which have been most severely weakened by language loss and assimilation, while attributing significance to the ability to speak Saami, may consider other aspects of Saami identity more important.[25] Nonetheless, all Saami would agree on the vital importance of maintaining and developing the Saami language for the continuation of Saami culture and collective identity.

As noted, the Saami Parliaments in both Norway and Sweden implement a language criterion to define their Saami electorates, and if those Saami who do not speak the language have a parent or a grandparent who speaks or spoke Saami, then the non-Saami speaker can still register as a Saami for voting purposes. Not so long ago, the overlap of Saami ethnicity and language was much more complete. Language loss on a large scale has been a more recent if frighteningly rapid development, and it is thought that the extended language criterion should cast a net broad enough to capture all those Saami who wish to vote.

While an official Saami electorate can probably be maintained despite language erosion, it is doubtful if the very content of the term Saami as an identity and culture marker can survive the death of the Saami language. Helander (1986) lists four major conditions essential for the maintenance and development of the Saami language: official status; institutional support; experienced need and interest; and actual use of a language in daily life.

In order to strengthen the Saami language, an Act of the Saami Language was introduced in Finland in 1991. It entered into force on 1 January 1992. A person who fulfills the criteria for a Saami may use the Saami language in matters regarding him- or herself or in which he or she is heard before courts of law, regional or local state authorities, whose jurisdiction covers all or parts of the Saami Homeland (Section 6) and the authorities of the municipalities of Enontekiö, Inari, Utsjoki and Sodankylä (Section 14). Such a right exists also with respect to the Saami Parliament, the Advisory Board on Saami Affairs, the Chancellor of Justice and some other officials. When cases are dealt with on the initiative of an authority in the Saami Homeland, a civil servant shall use the Saami language if a Saami party so requests. Acts and government decrees and decisions which especially relate to the Saami shall also be published in Saami translation (Section 12). The problem with implementing this Saami Language Act stems from the scant efforts to educate civil servants in the Saami language.

In Norway, a new chapter (Chapter 3) on Saami language use was inserted into the Saami legislation from 1987. This chapter applies to the municipalities of Karasjok, Kautokeino, Nesseby, Porsanger, Tana and Kåfjord. As in Finland, acts and decrees of special concern to the Saami shall be translated into the Saami language. A person who addresses in writing a local or regional public body in Saami has the right to a written answer in Saami. A party may use Saami orally and in writing before courts with jurisdiction in the six Saami municipalities. A person also has the right to be served in the Saami language by institutions in the fields of health care and social service. Like Finnish colleagues in the Finnish Saami Homeland, Norwegian civil servants in the six municipalities are entitled to paid leave of absence in order to study the Saami language.

In Sweden, a similar proposal pertaining to the municipalities of Kiruna and Gällivare was put forward by the Swedish Saami Rights Commission, but it was ignored by Proposition 1992/93:32 and has not been acted upon.

Cultural expression

Traditionally, the Saami have been a sparsely spread hunting and pastoral people whose cultural activities have not been directed towards grand exhibition or material permanency. Saami creative genius has instead been concentrated in the improvised and the transient. Utilitarian articles, such as wooden reindeer milking bowls and knives sheathed in reindeer antler, demonstrate excellent craftsmanship and individual variation within a traditional framework of form and function. After the colonial encounter, to be sure, Saami forms of expression developed considerably, but within this development there has always been a continuity, a basic Saami sense of pattern and design. For those acquainted with it, the Saami touch is unmistakable.

Perhaps the most unique and characteristic art form is the *yoik*. The Saami Johan Turi has called such singing 'a way to remember'. To describe it as a song is to indicate its outer mode of expression only. It is vocal, melodic and rhythmic, and yet its original purpose was not simply to entertain. In fact, yoiks were and still are often improvised on the spot, not repeated and not meant for any ears except those of their creator. It was the expression of the yoik which was its essence. By conceptualizing in sound the characteristics of a person, animal or place, the yoiker could feel himself close to his object, he could 'remember' it.

People have personal yoiks which somehow describe them in sound even though the yoik is often totally lacking in words. A bear yoik cannot be mistaken for the yoik of a reindeer calf. The yoik has roots deep in the shamanistic past, and it is probable that once the yoik was not only a means to remember, but also a means to become. With the yoik a shaman might transpose his spirit into the shape of an animal or travel to far-off places. It has been said that the yoiker 'imitates' its subject, but this word does not convey its spirit, for the yoiker is not striving for some external accuracy (even if he can achieve it to a great degree). He is opening himself to his subject, filling himself with it; in a sense he remembers by becoming.

The yoik is often a very emotional experience for the yoiker. Should a listener be present who shares the yoiker's vocal grammar and who can feel with him the object of the experience, a good yoik will be equally moving. Of course there are yoiks which have become true songs – that is, they have become standardized in music and text and are now in the public domain. Today one can hear yoiks accompanied by guitar and accordion, and they can be performed in front of a large crowd or bought on a record. Yoiks can indeed be beautiful songs. But the proper criteria for appreciating a yoik are quite different from those appropriate to the rhythms and melodies of standard European folk music. For a Saami a yoik can be a yoik, while to an outsider the same yoik can only be heard as a song. To hear a yoik spring unannounced from the lips of a herder in the context which inspired it and to share its feeling as a yoik is an unforgettable experience.

Saami handicrafts are now famous in Scandinavia and are becoming increasingly known throughout the world. Men commonly work in horn and wood, while women work with leather, pewter thread, roots and fabrics. Traditionally each family produced its own utensils. Someone especially skilled at a certain form of handicraft might make things for a wider circle, but there was no large, external cash market as there is today. With the introduction of modern materials and the transition to more settled lifestyle, many of the old handicraft skills began to disappear. Basketry weaving with roots, for example, has only barely been rescued from oblivion through the efforts of Asa Kitok and her daughters.[26] The art of pewter thread embroidery has been revived largely through the interest of Andreas Wilks.

Saami handicraft work has become of considerable economic importance, not only to those few who have become full-time Saami handicraft artists, but also to reindeer herders, for whom it can afford seasonal work and much-needed supplementary income. Now, in Sweden, after much lobbying, Saami access to the raw materials necessary for traditional handicraft work finally has been secured. Before the changes enacted in 1993 in Sweden, non-herding Saami did not share with herding Saami the uncontested right to take raw traditional materials from the *sameby* territory. The production of traditional Saami handicrafts, *duodji*, is now supported by various grants and taught in a number of forums like the Saami Folk High School in Jokkmokk, Sweden, and the centre for Saami arts and crafts, the Norwegian National Saami Crafts Organization, *Sámiid Duodji*, centred in Kautokeino.

A major threat to Saami handicraft is the production of cheap simulations of Saami handicraft. Imitation Saami handicraft has been produced as far away as Asia and sold in Saamiland to unknowing tourists. The Handicraft Commission of *Same-Ätnam* in Sweden, the Norwegian organization *Sámiid Duodji* and the Finnish organization *Sápmelas Duodjárat* have established quality control checks, so that today most real Saami handicraft will be marked as such with a special label. Tourists who learn something about the methods of manufacture of Saami handicraft and who gain an eye for its quality should have no difficulty in spotting counterfeit handicraft.

The Saami language has only recently been used as a literary means for the Saami to express themselves. The Saami preacher Lars Levi Laestadius, mentioned later, was the first to write Saami prose with a literary style.[27] There has been much debate as to whether the epic poems related by Anders Fjellner in the Saami language in the mid-1800s were entirely his own creation, but in any case they show genuine poetic merit. Johan Turi's *Muittalus Samid Birra* came into print in 1910; Nils Nilsson Skum's *Same sita, Lappbyn*, in both Saami and Swedish, was issued in 1938; Anta Pirak's *Jahttee Saamee Viessoom* (dictated to Harald Grundström) appeared in 1937. Each of these works provides detailed and often fascinating accounts of the older Saami lifestyle, as well as their folklore and general world view. These books are all classics for those interested in the Saami and have been published in different languages.

The first novel published in the Saami language was *Baeivve-Alggo* by Anders Larsen which appeared in 1912. Pedar Jalvi published his novel *Muottacalmit* (Snowflake) in 1915. The poet, Paulus Utsi, has produced a collection of poems in *Giela giela*. Saami authors, for example Erik Nilsson Mankok, have also written novels in Swedish dramatizing the Saami situation in modern European society. Currently there are many active Saami authors appearing in print, some writing in Saami and some in Swedish, Norwegian or Finnish. Nils-Aslak Valkeapää, a Saami author, recently received the Nordic Prize Literature. A few internationally renowned books have also been translated into Saami.

In Norway, Saami literary activity has increased greatly since 1971 due to the support of the Culture Board of Norway. Approximately 5–10 Saami books are published per year in Norway, many of them by the Saami publishing company Jår'galaed'dji.

The oral literature of the Saami is vast, and much of it has been collected and put into written form. These stories demonstrate a wide influence from traditions far afield. The so-called Stallo legends of the Saami contain a number of motifs reminiscent of Homer's *Odyssey*, but other thematic elements are found nowhere else. The Stallo is a giant figure who seeks to capture and eat the smaller Saami. Luckily, Stallo is quite stupid, and the clever Saami is usually able to trick him. Stallo legend motifs and even the name 'Stallo' indicate a Scandinavian identity to this dangerous story figure.

A number of Saami have worked in the less-traditional media of drawing and painting. Johan Turi illustrated his book with his own highly original drawings. So detailed, informative, colourful and artistic are the famous pictures by Nils Nilsson Skum that they often assume the dominant position in much of his published work describing the life of the herder and hunter. Skum was a stickler for accurate detail, and his beautiful pictures are also of great ethnographic value. The woodcuts of John Savio depict wonderfully the life of a herder on the *vidda*. The works of Iver Jåks and Lars Pirak exemplify the marriage of the traditional Saami handicraftsman and the modern creative artist. They work both with the old materials and forms and with the new. Their etchings, watercolours, sculptures and oil canvases depict with feeling the nature of Saamiland, the Saami way of life and their ancient spirit world. In 1979 a Nordic artists' union for Saami, *Sámi Dáiddacehpiid Searvi (SDS)*, was established, and in 1981 Saami artists gained entrance to the Nordic artists' association.

The Norwegian National Theatre Centre toured the country in the 1960s with puppet shows in the Saami language. Now in Norway there are several Saami theatre groups. One such group, *Beaivvas*, has become quite famous. Since 1990 there is also a permanent touring Saami theatre in Norway, based in Kautokeino. The *Dálvadis* theatre group was started in Sweden in 1971 and for approximately 20 years produced dramatizations of the Saami predicament and stories from Saami mythology. This theatre group had close contact with other Native theatre groups and played a part in the development of international Native theatre. A South Saami theatre group, *Åarjel Saemien Teatere*, has started in Sweden, and some of the forces behind the *Dálvadis* group, together with others, founded in 1982 a new Saami Theatre Association (*Sámi Teahter Searvi*) which in 1993 led a project, *Lama-Hado*, featuring a nomadic theatre troop, travelling by reindeer caravan. Finnish Saami and Finns together formed the *Rávgos* theatre group in 1981. In 1986 a joint secretariat (*Cálli*) for associations of Saami artists was formed.

Besides those organizations already mentioned, there is in Norway a Saami studies association; an association for Saami sportsmen; an association for Saami authors; a Saami youth society and a Saami music society. Two Saami newspapers appear in Norway, *Nuorttanaste*, weekly, and *Sámi Áigi*, twice weekly. *Ságat*, a newspaper which was supported by the Norwegian state to distribute news to the Saami population, has almost completely ceased using the Saami language.[28]

In Sweden there is a National Saami Museum in Jokkmokk (Ájtte), and a monthly Saami newspaper, *Samefolket*. The Saami youth organization, SSR-U, also produces a quarterly newspaper, *Sáminuorra*. In Finland, the magazine *Sápmelas* is published monthly and is distributed free of charge to each Saami household. A small number of Saami language articles also appears in the Finnish newspaper *Lapin Kansa*.[29]

Much more could be said about Saami cultural expression. Even the method of butchering a reindeer is extremely complex and sophistica-

ted, varying within the different Saami groups. The colourful traditional Saami clothing reveals the origin of the wearer just as does the
dialect he or she speaks. The incredible engraved designs on Saami
antler work and the patterns of woven bands are not only beautiful,
but they have a complex history of their own. Likewise, the construction of the Saami mobile tent or the permanent turf dwelling contains
many traditional and specifically local refinements. Indeed, the greatly
detailed and refined character of all these traditional crafts constitutes
a general context of highly developed skill which provides the foundation for much individual creativity and genuine art.

History

The history of the Saami can be discussed according to three phases or
major forms of influence: 1) the early centuries and initial colonization; 2) a policing period to regulate Saami-settler relations and 3) a
rationalization period with increasing focus on meat production and
welfare norms at the expense of ethnic land rights and cultural elements. Of course the characterizations of these periods are to some
extent arbitrary, and aspects of one period can be found to persist in
later periods without clear-cut time divisions. Nonetheless, I believe
they will be helpful in organizing this historical sketch and will eluci-
date the essential facets of Saami relations with nation states. This
sketch cannot strive for completeness. It is designed rather as background for an appreciation of current affairs.

The reader might feel that this background material is overly concerned with developments in Saami reindeer herding when, as noted,
reindeer herders are but a minority within the Saami minority. The
Saami were hunters and fishermen long before some of them became
pastoralists, and, for many, fishing is still the dominant economic
activity. They have also herded and farmed in combination, but access
to resources and their utilization have been heavily regulated by the
nation states, which have not necessarily followed similar policies. In
Sweden, the integration of reindeer herding and agriculture would
have been far more prevalent had it not been for laws insisting on
their separation. This policy (together with a shortage of labour experienced by many households) led to the collapse of many Saami combined economies, and those who were not able to sustain themselves
on herding alone had to give it up altogether to join what became
known as the 'poor Saami proletariat'. Nonetheless, as mentioned previously, despite an economic tradition based on non-herding as well as
herding, and despite regulations driving many Saami from herding,

reindeer management is still of enormous weight for the legal status and culture of all Saami.

Early centuries and initial colonization

According to the earliest written sources the Saami were hunters and fishermen living in a winter village form referred to by scholars as the old *sita* or old *Lappby* organization, which they relate to that *sita* organization most preserved today among the Skolt Saami (a Saami group with their original homeland in the border area of Finland and Russia) and once believed to be the basic pan-Saami form of social structure. The origin, distribution and character of the old *sita*, however, have not been adequately researched. We do not know, for instance, to what extent the winter villages may have been influenced in their concentration and localization by outside trade relations.

The 9th Century Norwegian chieftain Ottar, in his account recorded by Alfred the Great, mentions that he possessed 600 unbought reindeer of which 6 were trained decoy deer used in the hunt of their wild brothers. A female deer might be staked out during the mating season to lure an unwary buck within range of the hunter's bow and, later, rifle. Or a buck with a tangle of ropes or thongs in his antlers was staked out. Other rutting bucks, interested in defending their breeding zones or their harems, might seek to drive away the intruder and end up caught in his antlers.

A number of scholars have jumped to the conclusion that Ottar's account substantiates the existence of full-fledged reindeer pastoralism at this early date. However, it is impossible to know from the text alone how he obtained these deer, if they constituted a breeding unit or were even assembled in a herd. Most evidence indicates that the pastoral economy in Lapland did not develop for another seven centuries. Olaus Magnus (1555) makes it quite plain that some reindeer pastoralism was practised by the beginning of the 1500s at least.[30] This is not to say, however, that deer were not tamed for decoy purposes and for transport much earlier.

There has also been disagreement as to whether the development of pastoralism grew from domestic stock used for decoy purposes, or from stock used for transport – or whether it owes its origins to the taming of entire wild herds. However, it is known that trading relations were well developed before the creation of official markets at fixed locations and times. East–west trade among different peoples across the top of Lapland was well established by the time the interests of the emerging nations started trade moving also in a north-south direction.

Long before the Danish, Swedish and Russian Crowns became entities to reckon with, various peoples from Russia, Finland, Sweden and

Norway made raiding and trading forays into Saamiland to extract what they could of her riches, for example, in foodstuffs and furs. With the rise of the governments to the south, certain 'traders' of this sort, called *birkarlar*, received royal sanction and support for their trading activities and were granted judicial competence in specific areas claimed by a king, in return for which a certain percentage of the goods was to go to the royal coffers. These traders are thought to have come from Finland and to have held these privileges from the mid-1300s to the early 1500s. As the Crown increased in power, as the riches from Saamiland became more desirable, as the licensed 'third party' traders proved dishonest in supplying the Crown's share, and as Saamiland gained in geo-political importance, it became all the more logical for the different royal powers to take over and to assert their own taxation administrations.

Wiklund (1918) and Hultblad (1968)[31] both hypothesize that with the gradual decrease of hunting and increase of the importance of herding, the Saami were pushed towards so-called whole-nomadism (characterized by long and frequent migrations and a livelihood totally integrated with, and dependent upon, reindeer herds), and the collective winter village had to split up. The argument for this supposition is that big herds cannot be concentrated around a single camp for a long time, for the grazing will run out. For similar reasons, it became increasingly necessary in certain parts of Saamiland to begin using the mountain grazing lands in the summer and to scatter widely throughout the forest lands in the winter.

Information concerning the further evolution of herd forms before the 18th Century is scant. Before that time, Hultblad (1968)[32] suggests that there was little ground for separating herders into mountain-Saami and forest-Saami categories. The national borders were not fixed at this time, and the herders migrated through different spheres of influence. Some Saami paid tax to three courts at the same time (in the 14th Century, even to the Republic of Novgorod), even if they were registered under the protection of one authority. Should this authority prove too demanding, a nomad might well shift his allegiance to another. The kings who laid claim to regions in Lapland often followed a rather Saami-friendly course, for they could ill afford to estrange 'their' Saami. Not only did the Saami supply valuable goods in the form of tax, but their allegiance to a particular king helped him to motivate a claim on the territory used by them.

The Norwegian–Swedish border was not specified in the northern districts until 1751. Saami had migrated across what was to become the border between Norway and Sweden for centuries without hindrance and were guaranteed the right to continue to do so in a codicil to the boundary agreement. Immemorial territories (the old *Lappbys*) of the different Saami groups were crosscut by the national border. Swedish Saami traditional grazing rights were respected in Norway, and the traditional grazing rights of Norwegian Saami were respected in Sweden. (Of course, this does not mean that different Saami groups have not had internal conflicts due to competition over grazing resources.) This 1751 codicil has been termed the Saami Magna Carta, as it grants the old *Lappbys* a central position. It has never been cancelled, but its implementation has been regulated by bilateral commissions, the last and presently operative one from 1972 – as a result of which Swedish Saami access to Norwegian grazing is now tightly constrained. While some penetration across the border is allowed for some *samebys* (the approximately fifty defined social and territorial herding units of Sweden, before 1971 called *Lappbys*), the time of stay in Norway and the distance of penetration permitted are highly controlled. Renewed implementation of the agreement regulating this reindeer traffic must be in place by 2002.

Throughout the north, it was common to specify so-called Lappmarks, wilderness areas supposedly reserved for hunting, fishing and herding by the Saami, as opposed to the coastal and most heavily colonized zones suitable for agriculture and the primary use of settlers. Farming continued its spread, however, so that Lappmark borders, while limiting Saami rights beyond them, lost power to protect Saami rights within them. Nevertheless, these lines (and others of a similar nature such as the Agriculture Line in Sweden) have been incorporated into various administrative grids.

Parallel to the gradual administrative encapsulation of the Saami came missionary activity. The previous religion of the Saami, a form of animism, had used shamanistic techniques and ecstatic trances to contact and negotiate with the spirit world. The Saami shaman, or *noaide*, was similar to that of many other circumpolar peoples. He could beat on his magic drum and in a condition of trance release his spirit to travel to other worlds, for example in the form of a bird or a fish. Through consort with spirits, the shaman could cure the sick or tell of events in far-off places. They were known to be able to tie the winds in knots or to unleash them in full fury. The warring powers to the south even employed Saami shaman in their military exploits.

The first attempt to Christianize the Saami was by the 'Apostle of the North', Stenfi, in 1050. In the mid-1300s the archbishop of Uppsala, Hemming Nilsson, made a missionary trip to Torneå. In 1313, the Norwegian king proclaimed a 20-year tax reduction for the Saami upon conversion to Christianity. In Sweden, permanent preachers settled first among the pioneers along the northwestern coast of the Baltic Sea, and in the mid-1500s they began to preach among the inland Saami. Norsemen founded a church at Tromsø in 1252 and one at Vardø in 1307. The Skolt and Kola Saami to the east came under the religious sphere of the Greek Orthodox Church. In the mid-1500s, Trifan the Holy built a Greek Orthodox church at Boris-Gleb and a monastery in Petsjenga which became an important centre for the eastern Saami.[33] The major transition of the Saami to Christianity, however, occurred in the 1600s, even if shamanism was to persist in places hundreds of years later.[34]

The communication of the Saami shaman with helper spirits was seen by these early missionaries to be discourse with the Devil. Shamans were killed and their drums were burnt. Fascinating accounts of the Saami pre-Christian religion have come to us largely by way of these early missionaries, but they must be read very critically. It is significant that these missionaries did not conceive of themselves as merely spreading light among superstitious people. In their accounts, the missionaries frequently marvel at the supernatural powers of the Saami shamans, powers which the missionaries experienced as no mere sleight of hand. Instead they saw themselves as doing battle with a real and powerful devil with whom the shamans consorted.[35]

The Church played a prominent role in Saami education. The early markets, to be held once a year in fixed places, usually at churches and on religious holidays, were also occasions when the Saami registered themselves and paid taxes to the Crown. It is also evident that much of the colonial administration was facilitated by the Church. At this time, missionary activity was also a means for a kingdom to establish political control (with tax rights) over a territory. Swedish church constructions in the 1500s and 1600s on what has since become Norwegian land, for example, spurred the Danish–Norwegian Crown to increased missionary zeal.

Much later, in the 1830s a fundamentalist movement started by Lars Levi Laestadius in Karesuando gained a strong following in Saamiland. This puritanical movement did much to overcome the terrible social problems in the north caused by alcohol. However, it also played a part in the 'revolt' and killing of officials by some Saami in Kautokeino, in 1852. While these officials may have been oppressive, there is no denying that the responsible Saami had become religious fanatics who claimed God had given them the moral right to take life as they (with God's blessing) saw fit. This is a far cry from orthodox Laestadianism, which is still a vital force today among Saami and non-Saami alike and has also spread to other countries such as the United States.

Policing Saami–settler relations

The transformation of the administration dedicated to the levying of taxes was largely a result of the spread of farming and of the inevitable conflicts between farmers and herders. The old system of administration had been devised basically to ensure the even distribution and efficiency of tax-producing operations. Later legislation, however, became increasingly devoted to the strict regulation and inspection of herding in order to smooth herder–settler relations.

It was generally believed that conflicts could be avoided by geographically separating the herding and farming systems as much as possible. In Sweden, grazing areas were to be contained in newly specified *Lappbys* (after 1886 these territories were imbued with new legal significance) whose members would collectively be responsible for the damage caused farmers by the reindeer. Anything (such as a commitment to farming and a permanent house) which might cause the herder to leave the nomadic life or neglect his reindeer – allowing them to spread unattended and cause damage – was frowned upon by the authorities. By the late 19th Century, the Saami were often considered beings of a lower order, who should not be given the same legal status as the Nordic peoples, nor stand in the way of higher civilization.

The well-defined territorial herding zones existing today in Fennoscandia, so-called *districts* in Norway, *samebys* in Sweden and *paliskuntas* in Finland, define social units as well: those people whose reindeer are permitted to graze these zones. The evolution of these herding zones has been heavily influenced by legislation and administrative policy in each of these countries.[36] For example, in Sweden, although the *Lappbys* were designated in 1886 with many accompanying regulations, they were basically composed of the old Saami *sita* entities, old *Lappbys*, determined by natural environment and traditional social groupings. The Swedish *samebys*, which in 1971 replaced the *Lappbys* as designated in 1886, brought some new regulations and a collectivized work model besides a new name to these entities, but did not change their physical or social borders.

The territorial and social units recognized and confirmed in legislation by the governments of the Nordic countries for the reindeer-herding Saami are derived to a great extent from original Saami patterns. Beneath these defined units and externally imposed constraints there still exist previous layers of individual and group associations to land and resources recognized by the Saami. These herding groups are often seasonal in composition, so that the name used to describe them frequently has a temporal and spatial as well as a social meaning. In Sweden, for example, *sameby* reindeer can run mixed and quite unattended for most of the summer, but by early autumn they may be gathered together for herd separations before being released on the less plentiful autumn grazing. Come the winter, herd separations will become more frequent, and the reindeer separated into smaller and smaller entities, controlled by smaller and smaller herding groups, commonly at the nuclear family level, as the deer move eastwards and use the scarce winter lichen grazing resources.

The issue of damage by Saami reindeer to the settlers' property was a dominating theme in herding law until the conflicts diminished, particularly in Sweden, with the reduction of northern farming after the Second World War. Herding law during this interval (from 1886 to 1971) was most detailed about taking due consideration of farmers. Officials of the administration in Sweden were to be informed of all herding movements and even to direct them within bounds. (In Finland, developments have followed a somewhat different course, as here the policy of strictly forbidding the combination of herding and agriculture within the same family has not been pursued. In Finland, one need not be a Saami to be a reindeer herder; one need only be a resident – and therefore very likely a farmer – within a designated herding district.)

The Swedish case will serve to illustrate a common Nordic pattern: the transformation of Saami *rights* into Saami *privileges* granted by the Crown/state. A noteworthy feature of the Swedish Reindeer Act of 1886 was the beginning of a series of fractional divisions of the Saami category. For example, this act demanded that all reindeer herders register themselves as such with their *Lappbys*. Yet there is nothing in the Act which says that only herders have Saami hunting and fishing rights. The Act says simply that all *herders* should belong to a *Lappby*; not that hunters and fishermen did not belong to *Lappbys*, or that these had no immemorial rights in their *Lappbys*. The goal was to have the herders registered to a *Lappby* so that they would be collectively responsible for damage caused by reindeer to farmland, when it was often impossible to specify the exact owner of those miscreant reindeer.

It is one thing to say that only *Lappby* members can herd, and quite another to say that only herders are *Lappby* members. It was the Act of 1928 which brought together for the first time both of these regulations. In effect, while all Saami were free to devote themselves to reindeer herding, hunting and fishing under the Acts of 1886 and the following Act of 1898, these immemorial rights were heavily restricted under the Act of 1928 to apply only to *Lappby* members, now only herders.

The prevalent attitude of the times was that 'a Lapp should be a Lapp', that is, a true nomad. Herding families were not to build chimneys in their houses lest the herders become too comfortable and less inclined to brave the elements in the care of their reindeer. Saami nomad schoolchildren were to lead a spartan existence so as to foster the lifestyle 'for which they were most fit'.[37] Sweden's attitude seems to be that the Saami should be able to keep their exotic culture and enjoy certain *privileges* (as opposed to *rights*) of access to resources as long as they keep to the reindeer-herding niche and do not disturb the pace of 'progress'. A Saami who leaves the herding occupation loses his privileges and has no more resource rights than any other Swede.

Norway's attitude was somewhat different. Norway had been annexed by the Danes for centuries, only to be forced into union with the Swedes. This historical heritage, combined with the fear of 'Finnicization', brought about a surge of Norwegian nationalistic fervour towards the turn of the century. All official posts were given to Norwegians, and the Norwegian language experienced a renaissance – all, unfortunately, to the detriment of the Saami who became severely stigmatized. The Saami soon learned that worldly advancement was open to those who 'went Norwegian'.

In 1905, the Norwegian–Swedish union (established by the Treaty of Kiel in 1814) was dissolved. Norwegian settlers expanding north, according to the wishes and stimulation of their government, wanted to restrict access of Swedish Saami to the Norwegian grazing lands they had used since time immemorial, an access confirmed and protected in the bilateral codicil of 1751. Sweden chose to ignore Saami rights in favour of accommodating Norwegian demands. In the following decades, many Swedish Northern Saami were forcibly displaced from their summer lands in Norway and relocated to grazing areas in the south of Sweden. Here was a double affront to Saami civil rights. The forcible relocation of Northern Saami to points south was a direct violation of their immemorial rights as defined by Swedish and Norwegian law. It was equally a violation to force the Southern Saami to accept them on their territory.

Cramér ascribes the stipulation in the Swedish Reindeer Act of 1928 – that Saami herders must become officially registered members of the *Lappbys* in order to herd, hunt and fish – to the state's need to override Saami immemorial rights and enforce the relocation.[38] Under the new Swedish Act of 1928, the state authorities could legitimize the transfer of Northern Saami herding rights much further south by registering them as members in the Southern *Lappbys*. The same law also provided authorities with a means to exclude 'degenerated' Southern Saami (for example, those who might herd and farm in combination) from their *Lappbys* by omitting them from the membership lists.

State stimulation and direction of agricultural settlement in the north, with resulting conflicts with settled farmers, this time in Sweden, caused further constraints in the Act of 1928. New methods were sought to reduce the number of reindeer herders. According to paragraph 1 of this Act, those of Saami heritage are eligible to be herders *if* they have a parent or grandparent who has had herding as a steady occupation. As a result of this law, Saami were divided into those who were eligible to herd and those who were not. Moreover, still today, despite the changes introduced in 1993 which opened herding eligibility to all Saami, there are those (eligible to herd) who do not or cannot herd because they have not acquired *Lappby* (now *sameby*) membership. Since 1928, they no longer have the *right* to exercise their rights.

The rationalization period
As the 20th Century progressed, farming declined drastically in the north of Sweden. Sweden made a major transition from a country dominated by a rural, farming economy to one of large-scale industry. Small-scale farmers had little choice but to move south or find some other employment. Job opportunities came to be scarce, and large rural areas were gradually depopulated. The conflicts between herders and farmers, which had once preoccupied the authorities, subsided and the emerging welfare states turned their attention to maximizing profits for the sake of higher living standards. This was the policy of 'rationalization'. Rationalization policy has not been implemented with the same rigour or speed throughout Fennoscandia. In Norway, for example, the state has supported the maintenance of farming in its northern regions. Nonetheless, here too the ideals of rationalization have been felt among the Saami, even if conflicts between herders and farmers have not declined.

Some of the motivations that prompted the programme of rationalization were based on humane values of caring and compassion. Medical surveys showed the 'vital statistics' of the Saami to be comparable with those of people in underdeveloped countries,[39] despite the fact that the Saami in principle shared with their non-Saami neighbours the benefits of the national health programmes. Shocked by the poor living standards (usually calculated only in monetary terms) and high infant mortality rates among their herding populations, the Nordic states sought to raise the living standards of the Saami and considered that in doing so one would automatically help preserve Saami culture. These two goals, however, do not necessarily integrate without difficulty.

In Sweden, a two-pronged plan was adopted, so-called structure rationalization and production rationalization. The ideals of the former advocated a 30 per cent reduction of the herding labour force on the grounds that there were currently more herders than necessary to do the job. Moreover, the fewer the herders, the more reindeer each might own. The ideals of the latter, production rationalization, advocated modern ranching methods, with calf slaughter, to maximize the amount of meat produced per grazing unit – methods quite counter to Saami traditions and not always rational by the state's own definition.[40]

Of course, the Saami too were in favour of an updated legal herding framework and actively campaigned for it. With the end of the demand for constant policing by a Swedish Saami-sheriff, herders saw the opportunity to gain more autonomy within their herding territories. By the Act of 1971,[41] the old Saami administration was dissolved in Sweden, and the new administrative offices were established under the Department of Agriculture. The *Lappbys* were renamed *samebys* and reorganized as a hybrid form of economic corporation. The *sameby* collective was to be responsible for the herding on its territory. (However, the members as individuals are still responsible for any eventual *sameby* debt.) The *samebys* became emancipated from the rule of the Swedish Saami-sheriffs and were encouraged to establish a rotating labour force funded by a herding fee paid by the reindeer owner per reindeer to the *sameby*'s communal treasury. Certain premises derived from earlier laws continue to persist, however. Just as herders are not supposed to acquire the major part of their income from a source other than herding, so are the *samebys* not permitted to engage in any economic activity other than herding.

Each *sameby* has a specific rational herd number, that is, the total number of reindeer maximally allowed to be herded by the *sameby*'s members on the *sameby*'s grazing territory. Such numbers have been calculated so as to avoid overgrazing, and should the reindeer population come to rise above this limit, the *sameby* is responsible for enforced slaughters. Figures given for the number of reindeer needed today to support a normal family vary from around 300 to 500 head, and it is this figure (assuming for the moment that all reindeer within a *sameby* are distributed equally among its herders) divided into the rational herd number which indicates the maximum number of herding families supportable (according to the authorities) in a given *sameby*. Reindeer ownership, however, is private and unequal. Moreover, herders and their wives do not necessarily subsist on reindeer herding alone, so any calculation of this sort is hopelessly more complex than outlined here. Nonetheless, the *sameby* herd limit does put a ceiling upon the number of herders likely to be members of the *sameby*.

Unfortunately the number of reindeer needed to achieve a certain living standard rises steadily, thereby causing the number of herding families supportable by the *sameby* according to this standard to decline. Many Saami point out that a living standard in line with that of a Swedish industrial worker is less important to them than a life in the north within the traditional herding livelihood. Of course, there are ecological reasons which can also decrease the supportive capacity of a grazing territory for both reindeer and reindeer herders. Disregard of rational herd numbers can cause overgrazing and eventual herd decline, and diminished grazing resources due to extractive industries decrease the capacity of a *sameby* to support herders.

Throughout Saamiland, the group of herding Saami forms a small minority within the Saami minority. For example, today there are only approximately 900 active reindeer herders in Sweden and, with their family members, this means there are at most about 3,000 persons economically dependent upon reindeer herding. There comes a point when the improvement of living standards for reindeer herders at the expense of intensified curtailment of their numbers cannot lead to improved cultural maintenance of the Saami as a whole. The problem stems from the inability of the Nordic states to integrate their strictly economic herding policies with their native minority policies, or to realize that reindeer laws cannot adequately substitute for such native policy.

Current herding structures

Saami reindeer herding in Norway can be found in the regions of Finnmark, Troms, Nordland, Nord-Trøndelag, Sør-Trøndelag and northernmost Hedmark. Non-Saami can practise herding outside of these areas. The Department of Agriculture administers reindeer herding centrally, but each region has its own local administration (Finnmark actually has two local herding administrations). Herding is regulated by the Reindeer Act of 1978. Reindeer-herding Saami are represented in both the local and the central levels of administration.[42]

Currently there are 52 *samebys* in Sweden divided into three basic types: 1) mountain *samebys* with long, narrow grazing lands running from the Norwegian–Swedish border towards the southeast; 2) forest *samebys*, with a territory smaller and rounder in shape, situated in the lowlands and mainly east of the Agriculture Line but west of the Lappmark Line; and 3) 'concession *samebys*' in the Torneå area and east of the Lappmark Line. These concession *samebys* are similar to the forest *samebys* but are operative only on a ten-year, renewable lease from the state. Despite certain changes introduced by Proposition 1992–93:32 which gained effect on 1 July 1993, reindeer herding is still regulated by the Reindeer Act of 1971. The total area of land open to reindeer herding in Sweden is technically about 240,000 sq. km., but because of the natural impediments, lakes, high mountains and other areas without pastures for grazing, the net area of usable pastureland for herding has been estimated at 137,000 sq. km.

As noted, in Finland, non-Saami can own and herd reindeer as long as they live within the reindeer-herding area. This area is divided into 58 herding districts (*paliskuntas*), and covers most of the Lapland province and the northern part of Oulu province. The Finnish Reindeer Act stems from 1932, although it has been revised a number of times since. The *paliskunta* is a type of economic cooperative which served in part as a model for the Swedish *samebys'* reorganization in 1971. A *paliskunta* has a communal treasury to which members pay according to their reindeer stock. Finnish law does not seek to stop herders from receiving the main part of their income from sources other than herding, as is the case in Sweden. Each *paliskunta* is a member of the central organization, *Paliskuntain Yhdistys*, formed in 1948, which is responsible for reindeer administration, development and research.

Until a few years ago, the herders were members of their own organization, *Poro ja Riisto Oy*, for the distribution of their reindeer products. This organization was forced into bankruptcy, largely it seems because of mismanagement and a mild winter, causing some reindeer meat in storage to go bad and damage sales when it reached consumers. Some say the bankruptcy was occasioned by the financial crisis in the reindeer-meat business following the Chernobyl nuclear disaster, but while this may have played a part, it was apparently not the main reason.

Unlike the other three nations encompassing the Saami, Russia contains many traditional reindeer-herding peoples. According to Marxist-Leninist ideology, the so-called Small Peoples of the North, including many reindeer-herding and hunting peoples, were at a pre-capitalist stage of socio-economic development at the time of the Russian Revolution. The Soviet government sought to foster in these peoples a society of socialistic content while at the same time allowing for the continuation of their cultural forms. The capitalist stage of development was to be leap-frogged.[43]

The means of production, among them the reindeer, were collectivized. Under the Soviet regime, native struggle in opposition to the state was muffled under the banner of building the Soviet culture. A programme of forced centralization was imposed whereby many Saami were relocated to larger towns (such as Lovozero); their traditional villages were often bulldozed to prevent their return. Private ownership of reindeer was basically abolished, and the state was therefore able to promote both structural and production rational procedures unhindered. Some private ownership on a small scale was permitted, mainly to keep up customs and allow for private transportation.[44] Reindeer-herding *kolkhozes* were established where the workers themselves owned the means of production collectively, worked collectively on large farms and shared their produce. Later, many reindeer-herding farms in the Soviet Union were reorganized under the *sovkhoz* form. In this form, the state owned the reindeer, and workers were wage earners paid by the state. Increasingly the *sovkhozes* grew to encompass more than one type of production, even if one main form of economic pursuit was usually dominant. The *sovkhozes* were also multi-ethnic. The Saami in the Kola Peninsula, for example, herded reindeer along with Komi and Nentsi peoples within the *sovkhozes* there.

In the wake of *glasnost* and *perestroika*, the Saami in the Soviet Union organized their own, ethnically-defined political organizations, notably the Kola Saami Association (*Associacija Kolskih Saamov*), based in Murmansk. Reindeer herding in the Soviet Union was not a privilege bestowed as a concession to the cause of cultural preservation; under Russian administration it is still unclear how the priorities of upholding native culture and the surge towards a market economy will be balanced. President Yeltsin announced that come 1 January 1993 all the former *sovkhozes* would be dissolved. While the herders might now gain the right to own unlimited numbers of deer, they can scarcely afford to buy any. And who controls the grazing rights? To whom will they sell their meat produce now that the *sovkhoz* and the state-run slaughter company are no longer part of the same centrally programmed economy? The old system was beset by many problems, but the transition to a new one will not simply be one of painless liberation.

According to Andrejev,[45] 77 per cent of the world's tame reindeer stock (2,400,000 head) was to be found in the former Soviet Union. Reindeer herders in the former Soviet Union were among the highest paid workers in the country. The Kola Saami herders were mainly employed by Sovkhoz Tundra, centred in Lovozero, where, along with the other workers, they were provided with schools, housing, a clinic, club-house and child care facilities. In the current political and economic turmoil, it is unclear what the employment situation is for the Kola Saami herders. At one point a Swedish concern began working with the Kola Saami herders, and Fennoscandian Saami herders became fearful that should the meat produced by Russian slaughter-houses come to meet Western hygenic standards, the low price of Russian reindeer meat (due to the poor economy and desire for Western currencies) would force prices down drastically for the Fennoscandian Saami. However, cooperation with the Swedish business had apparently ceased in the spring of 1993, and the old Sovkhoz Tundra is now privatized, that is, converted into a shareholding company, Tundra Inc., led by the Saami Olga Anufrieva and a board of 12 members with Saami majority. Contacts between the Saami of the Fennoscandian countries and those in Russia have increased markedly during the past eight years. Initially such contact was on a cultural or practical herding plane, but today discourse and exchange encompass political and organizational goals as well.

Ecology

Colonization of Saamiland has had grave effect on its ecology. Not only has the fur-bearing fauna been decimated by early forms of taxation (tax was paid by the northern inhabitants in the form of natural produce: for example, furs and barrels of fish), but in modern times, even after the fixing of national borders, the northern regions have served the southern metropolises as internal colonies. Saami reindeer herding is seriously threatened by the ever increasing encroachments of extractive industries, notably the timber, mining, hydro-electric power and even tourist industries. Each industry has its own history, and yet none can be grasped in isolation from the others. Much of the labour force brought north by the hydro-electric power industry, for instance, has shifted to the timber industry. The road cut through the wilderness to transport a huge generator and other building materials to a dam site can later open the nearby forests to logging by the timber industry.[46] The mines have often established large cities around them with a wide transportation system and populations which demand recreation facilities. The various extractive industries have together created populations in the north which dwarf the local Saami into a minority position (with proportionately reduced political power) in most of the municipalities of their own core regions.

Conflicts are inevitable and focus upon not only the loss of total grazing area, but also the loss of strategically important pasturage, natural land formations, calving lands and even the hanging beard moss growing on old trees, an important emergency food for reindeer during bad winters. The combined resistance of the Saami and conservationists to the construction of the Alta hydro-electric dam in Norway was a significant factor in the institution of Saami Rights Commissions in Norway and Sweden. On the other hand, there are communities of mixed Saami and non-Saami habitation where both groups share the same livelihoods and ecological adaptations and hence are spared local ethno-political conflicts.

With its world-famous production of steel and timber and its position as Scandinavia's main producer of hydro-electric power, Sweden demonstrates all the problems caused to herders. Currently in Sweden it is the timber industry which poses the severest problems for reindeer herding. Because of difficulties with expensive transportation and with competition from abroad, Swedish mining in the north is no longer so expansive as it once was. The hydro-electric power industry is in painful retreat, and threatens the few remaining untouched waters in order to give its employees jobs.

The timber industry has reached a point where irreplaceable, virgin forests in the mountain regions are sacrificed in order to supply raw material to the over-dimensioned timber plants for finished products along the coast and to the south. Here again employment opportunities are frequently given as the justification for permanent environmental damage. Yet the timber industry, almost more than any other, has rationalized its labour structure and developed its technology to the extent that one man operating a modern timber machine replaces scores of workers. The large-scale penetration of the timber industry for the first time into mountainous forest zones, thus far spared, leads to the loss of beard moss, and the soil preparation necessary for replanting efforts destroys ground lichens, the reindeer's main winter food.

Tourism is widely acclaimed as the 'solution' to the unemployment problems of the north. It is hoped that tourism will give new jobs without destroying the necessary land base for old jobs. For Saami pastoralists, however, tourism is a mixed blessing, for while it depends largely upon the maintenance of an unspoiled natural environment, it does not always seek to maintain Saami herding within this environment.

The tourist whose greatest challenge is to experience 'Europe's last wilderness', rather than to understand an indigenous people, does not always appreciate the knowledge that this wilderness is in fact the immemorial homeland of Saami and the stamping grounds for a highly developed traditional reindeer herding. The Saami have in fact been instrumental in creating the environment which some conservationists wish to label as purely natural. As the conceptualization of Nature comes to exclude humankind, the Saami herders will find themselves increasingly hampered in their traditional lifestyles.

Ironically, the Saami herders and their reindeer are advertised as major tourist attractions. The tourist who desires a wilderness challenge is often willing to accept a leather-clad herder living in an old traditional tent, tending his herd on foot, but should the herder, garbed in synthetic materials, fly to his modern cabin by helicopter, the tourist can become indignant and demand restrictions. He argues (and not without grounds) that if there are rules protecting the environment which apply to him, they should also apply to the Saami herder. Of course, most tourists will recognize the right for herders to use, for example, snowmobiles in their herding work within national parks, even if tourists are not allowed to drive there for fun, but many question if even Saami herders should be permitted to use motorbikes and other 'high-tech' equipment without limits, if the environment will be injured.

Tourism has in places grown to grotesque proportions, but it should be noted that tourism in reasonable proportion and considerate of the environment is also of some benefit to Saami herders. Contacts lead to mutual understanding which can lead to strong friendships and alliance in the face of threat from extractive industries. The herders gain the ability to supplement their economy by offering seasonal services to tourists (boat transport, for example) or by selling handicrafts and provisions.

Naturally, one cannot take the position that traditional cultures should be frozen in time and that all modern developments are deleterious. It cannot be denied, however, that northern industrialization has decreased the ability of reindeer herding to serve as a livelihood. Herding can support fewer active herding families, and rationalization efforts generally support the survival of large-scale herding enterprises only. While some argue that industrialization offers new job opportunities to those who might otherwise have commenced a herding career, thereby luring them away from their traditional livelihood, others argue that these same jobs provide those Saami who would leave the herding livelihood anyway with a means to stay within their home districts. Herders themselves often take part-time, non-herding jobs during slumps in the seasonal herding work schedule, and in many ways modern developments aid the herder in his herding work.

The spread of nuclear fallout across Lapland from the Chernobyl disaster in the former Soviet Union has had a profound effect on the Saami. The lichen which the reindeer eat during the winter has absorbed large doses of cesium 134 and 137. In fact, the lichen, the reindeer and many northern inhabitants were already contaminated by nuclear fallout before the Chernobyl disaster due to atmospheric atomic bomb testing in the Soviet Union especially during the 1960s.

The distribution of the new fallout on the grazing lands was highly patchy depending upon the course of wind and rain in late April 1986 when the Chernobyl explosion occurred. The limits set by the Nordic governments for cesium concentration in foodstuffs to determine their marketability have also been highly variable. In Norway the limit rose quickly from 600 becquerels Cs 134 and 137 per kg. meat to 6,000 Bq/kg., while in Sweden the initial limit of 300 Bq/kg. (for Cs 137 only) was raised to 1,500 Bq/kg. in May 1987 (for reindeer meat, wild game, and inland fish only).

In the 1960s, however, cesium concentrations in Swedish reindeer meat reached values of 3,000 Bq/kg., that is, above the limit which today has been declared unfit for human consumption. Why were no limits set then? Understandably many Saami suspect that the precautions taken today stem from the fact that the fallout from Chernobyl was not confined to Lapland and did not affect only basic foodstuffs of the Saami population. Because of the absorption properties of the lichen and the grazing habits of the reindeer, it is now mainly the reindeer herders (but also inland freshwater fishermen) in certain areas who must continue to deal with the problem. The cost of compensating herders for their confiscated reindeer after Chernobyl has been high, and it is also understandable if herders regard this as the main reason behind the raising of the contamination limit for marketability of reindeer meat in Sweden.

Thousands of reindeer from the usual autumn and winter slaughters were confiscated after the Chernobyl disaster, their meat declared unfit for human consumption and their bodies dumped in pits or ground into fodder for fur farms. Although the governments of Norway and Sweden, those herding countries hardest hit by the fallout, have paid compensation for confiscated reindeer, many herders have still suffered financial losses and had to change their dietary habits and work schedules. In the worst hit areas, the problems the Chernobyl disaster caused for the Saami will surely continue for many years to come. Even in the more lightly affected areas, herders suffer deteriorating prices for their reindeer meat, at least in part certainly a consequence of consumers' fears about contamination. Reduced sales may in turn result in an overpopulation of reindeer. The repercussions are endless and hard to track.

For many, the psychological effects have been every bit as great as the practical ones. Herders tried to work as before, only to see the fruits of their labour thrown away. A small minority, living a traditional life close to nature, has suffered one of the worst blows of pollution created by industrialized humankind. There is no escaping the irony of the situation, and news of the destruction of Saami society and culture became not only a media scoop, but also a hot issue in nuclear power debates. Frequently the mythic qualities of the story far outgrew the facts. Undoubtedly harm to the environment and to the people has been done, and this should not be belittled because of the demands of controlled verification and measurement. Nonetheless, the Saami are not suddenly vanishing from the earth because of the Chernobyl disaster. The lives of the herders are back to normal in most of Lapland; their reindeer are marketable. In the hardest-hit areas new methods are used to decontaminate the reindeer with good success. Families have changed their eating habits, even if their network of friends and relatives helps to supply them with 'clean' products. It is far from over, but life goes on.[47]

Ethnic mobilization

In Norway today there are three main Saami political organizations: the Confederation of Norwegian Reindeer Herders (NRL), founded in 1948; the Norwegian Saami National Union (NSR), founded in 1968; and the Saami Confederation (SLF), founded in 1979. Besides these, there are other, much smaller organizations.

The first Swedish Saami local organization was founded in 1904, and in 1918 the first Saami national conference was held in Östersund. Another major national conference took place in 1937 in Arvidsjaur. In 1950 the Swedish Saami National Union (SSR) was founded at a national conference in Jokkmokk. SSR is composed of representatives from all the *samebys* and Saami local organizations. At the outset, SSR was mainly active in building public opinion, but in 1962, with its employment of the jurist Tomas Cramér, SSR entered into a phase of legal confrontation with the Swedish state.

Another Saami organization, *Same-Ätnam* (RSÄ), is primarily concerned with Saami cultural activities. *Same-Ätnam* has established a number of committees, such as the committee on Saami handicraft, and works in support of Saami language, art, literature and music. It also works for inter-Nordic Saami cooperation and cooperation with other native peoples throughout the world.

The Confederation of Swedish Saami (LSS) is composed primarily of non-herding Saami. This organization campaigns for the rights of Saami on a broad, ethnic basis. There are many other Saami organizations of different types, among them a Saami youth group, *Sáminuorra* (SSR-U).

The Swedish Saami political organizations receive financial aid from the Saami Fund. This fund comprises money received from the government in support of Saami social and cultural activities through compensation payments for *sameby* lands which have been taken for other, non-herding purposes. Of course, the support of Saami cultural activities and organizational forms by the Saami Fund is welcome, but at the same time the recipients are ever conscious that such support is paid for by money amassed from the destruction of *sameby* grazing territory.

During the last few decades, representatives from the Norwegian Saami organizations NRL and NSR (but not the younger SLF) together with representatives from the Swedish Saami organizations, SSR and RSÄ, and the Saami Parliament of Finland have cooperated within the framework of the Nordic Saami Council. Saami representation from Norway and Sweden to the Nordic Saami Council has now been assumed by the new *Sametings* (Saami Parliaments) in these countries. The Nordic Saami Council (now termed simply the Saami Council following upon full membership of the Kola Saami) was founded in 1956 during a Nordic Saami Conference meeting in Karasjok, Norway, and meets now every second year. Its purpose is to promote Saami economic, social and cultural interests.

In 1973, upon the recommendation of another Nordic Saami Conference, a Nordic Saami Institute was founded in Kautokeino, Norway. This Institute promotes research into Saami traditions, language, values, economic situation and legal rights. It plays a dominant role in the spread of Saami information and coordination of Nordic Saami activities. The Saami Council now acts as the Institute's advisory organization.

The Finnish Saami organizations acting on a regional basis are *Johtti Sápmelaccat* in Enontekiö, *Sámi Siida* in Utsjoki, *Anára Sámisearvi* in Inari and *Soadekili Sámi Searvi* in Sodankylä. Saami living in the Helsinki metropolitan area have founded *City Sámi*.

The Saami of Norway, Sweden and Finland have become members of the World Council of Indigenous Peoples (WCIP). The Saami also keep close contact with the United Nations Working Group for Indigenous Populations in Geneva, the UN Conference on Environment and Development as well as other international bodies. The Saami Council has NGO status within the UN, and Saami representatives frequently serve as experts on the national delegations from Norway, Sweden and Finland to the UN. The Saami have therefore become quite experienced at lobbying for indigenous peoples in general and have also been instrumental in the building of institutions and the writing of official texts for other indigenous peoples. The Saami Council has been in a position to advise the national development agencies of the Fennoscandian countries and the foreign ministries in the application of funds dedicated to the promotion of indigenous causes and development projects abroad.

Native status, immemorial rights and land claims

In 1980, during (and largely as a result of) the major conflict over the damming of the Norwegian Kautokeino–Alta waterway, a Saami Rights Commission was initiated in Norway. Eighteen representatives from different regions and interest groups, including NRL, NSR and SLF, have worked together on this Commission. This Commission has had a broader mandate than that given later to its 'twin', the Swedish Saami Rights Commission. The Norwegian Commission was to deal with issues of a general political character, with the issue of a Norwegian Saami Parliament and also with economic issues. It was to investigate questions about Saami rights to natural resources and make recommendations towards new legislation. Because of its mandate to analyse Saami resource rights in Norway, thereby necessitating a thorough historical study, the Norwegian Saami Rights Commission has not confined its legal perspective on Saami rights mainly to the requirements of international law, as has the Swedish Commission.

From 1980 to 1985 Professor Carsten Smith led the Norwegian Saami Rights Commission and presented its first partial report, *On the Legal Position of the Saami*,[48] a work of enormous breadth and solid scholarship. This report marks a new era in Norway's Saami policy. The Swedish Saami Rights Commission followed largely in its wake. It was as a result of the recommendation of this Norwegian Saami Rights Commission, that the Norwegian Parliament voted to establish a Norwegian Saami Parliament.[49]

Still, despite the gains made, there are many points on which Saami demands were not met by the Commission. Many Saami demanded that this Saami Parliament be empowered with a veto on land encroachments injurious to Saami land usage – at least that it have the ability to cast a kind of delaying veto until the government has passed its judgement. No such veto rights were granted. Instead, however, the Saami Parliament is able to force issues before the government and the public authorities on its own initiative: any issues which the *Sameting* itself considers pertinent to the Saami people.

In the realm of international law, the Norwegian Saami Rights Commission has stated that the Saami cannot be considered a 'people' according to the meaning of the term in the UN's 1966 International Covenant on Civil and Political Rights and its 1966 International Covenant on Economic, Social and Cultural Rights. Without this recognition, the Saami are not considered to possess the right of self-determination. Instead, the Commission argues that the Saami come under the safeguards of Article 27 of the Covenant on Civil and Political Rights and interprets this article to require positive discrimination for minorities and indigenous populations.

The combined effect of extractive industries on Swedish Saami grazing lands which had alarmed herders for many years was finally recognized as an issue for the national political agenda. By a directive of the government,[50] the Swedish Saami Rights Commission was instructed to consider: 1) the advisability of strengthening the Saami legal position with regard to reindeer herding; 2) the question whether a democratically elected Saami organization should be established; and 3) the need for measures to strengthen the position of the Saami language. Later the Commission's directives were broadened to encompass the situation of the Saami as an indigenous people.

The Commission's first partial report leaves aside the important questions of the historical rights of the Saami and instead concerns itself solely with comparing the situation of the Saami in Sweden to the minimal requirements of international conventions on human rights. Yet, essential to any Swedish commission on Saami involving resource rights, culture and political organization is a thorough analysis of immemorial rights. The Commission has been set up to investigate whether contemporary pressures from extractive industries have threatened herding to the point that protective measures should be taken to maintain Saami culture. If so, the Commission is to make concrete proposals for such protective measures. This manner of framing the issues constitutes an implicit acceptance of the supposedly pro-Saami premise that herding is something to be supported (or perhaps not) as a kind of sympathy action for the Saami. In short, the legal rights of the Saami to herd, and their rights to shield their herding from extractive industries, are here treated merely as a special privilege which the state can give or withhold depending upon its own perception of Saami needs. The legal issues of land ownership and resource rights remain ignored in favour of a new slight adjustment of welfare.[51]

The same attitude of privilege and welfare outlined above with respect to herding and Saami resource rights in general finds a distinct echo in the Swedish state's approach to Saami political organization as well. The state may allow the Saami the privilege of advising state authorities, but it will not imbue Saami organized on ethnic grounds with real power. Nowhere, even in the Saami core area of Sweden, do Saami form a majority of voters, and no political party finds much motivation to support Saami demands. The directive of the Commission states from the start that any eventual Saami Parliament should not be given constitutional authority or veto rights. Although established with only an advisory capacity, the resulting Swedish Saami Parliament, cutting across the herder/non-herder Saami split, is of major importance for the Saami.

The Swedish government does not recognize any general Saami ownership of land, but according to the Swedish Supreme Court's verdict in the Skattefjäll (Tax Mountain) Case 1981, Saami reindeer herding rights constitute a special form of property right based upon immemorial ancestral use. This viewpoint was hardly enshrined in the Reindeer Act of 1971 which was enacted while the Skattefjäll Case was ongoing, and even after the verdict, the government insists that all Saami immemorial rights are completely regulated in the Herding Act. Of course, this Herding Act has now been given a face lift by the Swedish Government Bill, Proposition 1992–93:32, but its real character, assigning the practice of Saami rights to Saami herders alone, has hardly been altered. Sweden's revised Herding Act now states that all Saami possess the reindeer-herding right because of the Saami people's collective immemorial rights (no longer linked to the herding occupation of a parent or grandparent), but as before (since 1928), whatever Saami rights are considered to be or however they are derived, they cannot be practised unless one is a *sameby* member.

According to the Norwegian Altevatn verdict, however, it is the *samebys* (stretching back to the old *Lappbys*), as collective entities, besides Saami individuals, which are the proper subject of Saami immemorial rights. To be sure, the Swedish Supreme Court in its 1981 verdict in the Skattefjäll Case did confirm Saami immemorial rights in principle,[52] but in fact Swedish legislation continues to ignore that ruling. The closed shop ruling whereby only *sameby* members (the herders – a limited group not open to free access by any Saami) can practise Saami rights, first demanded in the Act of 1928 and continued in the current Act of 1971, is incompatible with the existence of Saami immemorial rights far prior to these Acts. By implication of the Skattefjäll decision, the right of a Saami to hunt, fish and herd on land to which he or she can demonstrate immemorial ancestral ties (without major discontinuity in active usage) supersedes any prerequisite of *sameby* membership. However, this concept of immemorial rights is generally ignored. It is ironic that through the Norwegian court's Altevatn verdict in 1968, the rights of Swedish *samebys/Lappbys* to continue their immemorial utilization of areas in Norway have been upheld. Yet their immemorial rights in their own country are not properly acknowledged.

What then are the immemorial rights confirmed for the Saami by the Swedish Supreme Court? A description of immemorial rights can be found in the 15th chapter of the old Swedish Code of Land Laws (*Jordabalken*) from 1734, now retained in point 6 in the promulgation to the new *Jordabalken*:

> 'It is immemorial right, when one has had some real estate or right for such a long time in undisputed possession and drawn benefit and utilized it that no one remembers or can in truth know how his forefathers or he from whom the rights were acquired first came to get them.'[63]

There is nothing in the above description to indicate that immemorial right pertains only to Saami reindeer herding. In fact there are legal precedents where Swedes have fished and hunted according to immemorial right. The appropriate application of immemorial right guarantees the right of present and future generations to continue using the traditional resources of their forefathers, assuming this was indisputed and well-grounded. However, there is much that needs clarification. Is immemorial right only an individual right or a collective *Lappby* (now *sameby*) right? If it is a civil right, not merely a privilege, how is it that the state can regulate its practice so as to deny the non-herding Saami access to their immemorial resources without due process or just compensation? Why have Saami immemorial rights to hunting and fishing been ignored, and if they were to be recognized in practice, what would this entail? The questions are many, and one would have thought items for the strict scrutiny of the Swedish Saami Rights Commission established in 1983. Unfortunately, despite the fact that the Commission could have given its directives an interpretation broad enough to grapple with these issues, the Commission chose not to, thereby allowing the problems to fester and pushing the matter over to the courts, national and international.

The same legislation which has just given the Saami their *Sameting* with one hand has struck at their vulnerable resource base with the other. Proposition 1992–93:32 asserts that the Crown possesses hunting and fishing rights on Crown lands parallel to that of the Saami. Regardless as to whether or not the Crown is correct in all its land ownership claims in Saamiland – and as Justice Bertil Bengtsson of the Swedish Supreme Court has taken such pains to point out, the Skattefjäll Case in no way sets a general precedent for such a claim[54] – it has confirmed that in the areas demarcated by the Land Survey, Saami hunting and fishing rights are exclusive. Immemorial rights have legal precedence over newer laws and these cannot expropriate immemorial rights without due process or just compensation. It is all the more disconcerting that the government adopts such tactics in a legislative process which was originally designed to support Saami culture and forms of livelihood. Assuredly it will not be long before the Swedish Saami mount an offensive on the international level to seek support in protecting the minimal hunting and fishing rights they do/did have.

The argument that the state has for many years administered all hunting and fishing licences in these regions is hardly a convincing justification for state rights when it becomes plain that the state has simply taken upon itself the role of administering these licences for the Saami. The fact that the state administers Saami hunting and fishing licences does not mean that the state itself has hunting and fishing rights. The state took over these duties of administration for the Saami with the following motivation:

> *'Should one consider how poorly suited a Lapp association is to hold deliberations and to make decisions as well as to utilize for the collective good incoming funds, it is probably best to hand over duties of this type to the county administration.'*[55]

It seems that the Swedish state desires to cling to the position that it has granted certain special resource privileges to the Saami in order to preserve their unique culture, and Saami culture is then narrowly recognized by the government to mean only reindeer herding. To the extent a Saami strays from this livelihood, to that same extent must he give up his special rights. Paragraph 9 of the Act of 1971 asserts that the *sameby* may engage in no economic activity other than herding. In this manner Saami self-determination has been severely limited. With the increasing pressures of extractive industries on the land, the available grazing land, and by extension the *samebys'* rational herd numbers, constantly decreases. At the same time, the subsistence minimum in terms of the number of reindeer needed per family continues to increase. Thus, the herders are hit from both ends. According to the law, the herder must keep herding as his major income source or leave the *sameby*. Furthermore, the *sameby* as a collective can exercise its special resource privilege only in connection with herding.

The economic realities pressuring the herder from the field – rationalization policies, extractive industries and rising subsistence minimum in reindeer – must be put in relation to Saami category divisions and the closed shop membership of the *sameby*. (Only *sameby* members can herd, hunt and fish.) What emerges is a highly efficient phase-out mechanism.[56]

Once an active herder stops herding, he loses *sameby* membership. His chances of ever re-entering the *sameby* are small. Entrance to the *sameby* is not open; the current *sameby* members decide about the new applicants. Because of the unemployment crisis in the north, he may well be forced to leave the Saami core area and move south. Stockholm now has the second highest population of Saami in Sweden. As one would expect, the population graph for the Swedish Saami shows that while the total number of Saami is rising, the number of herders has been falling steadily.

Surely, one cannot blame state policies for the limited ability of resources to sustain fully an expanding population. Reindeer herding has never been able to support all Saami, and it is only natural that the group controlling access to a resource seek to bar others from it should they find it difficult to meet their own needs. A vital question, however, is – should internal regulatory mechanisms be applied by the state or the Saami?

There are other unforeseen consequences of the emphasis on Saami reindeer herding and the linkage of resource rights to its practice alone. The position of women in the modern Swedish *samebys* is often significantly unequal to that of the men as a result of the administrative policies of the Swedish government. In the traditional bilateral Saami society, women held rank equal to that of men and, before becoming encumbered with the paraphernalia and rhythms of the dominant culture, herded along with the men. However, today, in many *samebys* women are unable to vote in herding affairs or about collective economic matters. Their reindeer property counts as belonging to their husbands or fathers as heads of household for purposes of computing voting strength. A girl does not necessarily enjoy the same official membership status in the *sameby* as her younger brother. These are effects which have their roots in two concepts basic to the Swedish herding law. Firstly, a Saami has rights because he herds. A *sameby* member is one who participates in herding in the *sameby* territory. The wife of the actively herding man is not considered to participate actively in herding herself if she washes his clothes, raises the children and cooks the food. Secondly, it is argued that since the *sameby* administers a communal treasury for herding matters, it is only fair that the true participants in herding have a say in how it is utilized. Moreover, the strength of a herder's 'say' is variable with the size of his (together with his wife's) herd. Similarly, it is argued that since each family is considered as one business enterprise, it would be unfair if a married couple had more say than a bachelor (assuming the two 'enterprises' had the same herd size).[57]

Of course, changes in technology, transportation, and schooling for the children, to name but a few of the more important factors altering the herding family's life style, have greatly affected the position of women in the herding culture. The modern facilities have often caused new kinds of separations in the herding family. Mothers will generally spend the regular school year with their children in or near the larger towns while their men may take care of the deer with the help of helicopters, snowmobiles and herders' cabins. These same transportation and communication devices may bring the men home after a hard day's work, but they mean that the woman and the children are increasingly less an integral part of the herding unit's life in the field. 'How can I train my children to be reindeer herders on summer vacation?' is a common complaint from the herders. Recently, and on a number of occasions, Saami women have come together from all the Saami nations to discuss their situation and to seek general solutions. They have formed the international Saami women's organization *Sáráhkka*.

The linkage of Saami resource rights to reindeer herders alone has not only separated many non-herding Saami from their lands and deprived them of compensation money paid by the state for expropriation, it has also placed Saami culture and identity in an extremely vulnerable position. Certainly the reindeer, as an object of both hunting and herding, has been of central importance for the Saami, not least as a cultural symbol. Nonetheless, crediting reindeer herding with being the only legally empowered expression of Saami traditional culture neglects other important cultural facets. The result of these state policies has been to link Saami identity ever more closely to this single dominant expression. Hence, any threat to reindeer herding like that caused by the April 1986 nuclear reactor disaster at Chernobyl not only jeopardizes the economy and lifestyles of the herders themselves, but it also constitutes a serious threat to Saami native rights in general.

In Finland, a Saami Commission was directed to evaluate the legal position of Saami long before the Saami Rights Commissions of Norway and Sweden were started. The Finnish Saami Commission's report, KM 1973:46, proposed a Saami law, defining Saami on a linguistic criterion (as that discussed above) and attempting to ensure the continuation of Saami resource usage by the acknowledgement of a specific Saami area. This proposal has not been taken up by the Finnish government or Parliament, but as a result the Finnish Saami Parliament was founded and the Saami Homeland defined. According to the Saami Commission, the Saami are the original owners and users of the Saami Homeland. Whatever rights this would secure the Saami have not been examined by the state, and according to the Commission, the Saami do not practise the rights which are their due. As there is no general law governing Saami rights, these are instead regulated in diverse specific laws such as those about water, timber and fishing – none of which is specifically directed towards the Saami. The current reindeer-herding law in Finland dates from 1948, although there have been a number of revisions. As noted earlier, reindeer herding is not a right reserved for the Saami. Ever since 1974 work towards the legislation of a new reindeer-herding law has been in progress, and ever since 1978 a legal section was tied to the Advisory Board on Saami Affairs to research Saami rights to natural resources. The unexamined and unspecified condition of Saami rights in Finland runs contrary to the international agreements Finland has ratified.

Publication of a doctoral dissertation by Kaisa Korpijaakko in 1989 on the legal rights of the Saami in Finland during the period of Swedish rule has had a major effect on Finnish Saami policy formulations which will probably be echoed to some degree in Sweden and Norway as well. Since her research deals with the period when Sweden and Finland were one country, it is plain that her results bear upon the legal rights of the Swedish Saami too. Her research shows that the Swedish/Finnish government recognized that Saami people owned their lands as witnessed by taxation records. Thus, at that time the Saami were not simply considered landless nomads but rather their land titles were incorporated into the state's land tenure system. While the Skattefjäll verdict in Sweden ruled that such ownership was not the case for the Saami with regard to the Skattefjäll lands in Jämtland, it stated clearly the possibility that ownership title could be substantiated for the Saami elsewhere. This has now come to pass. Korpijaakko's work in Finland, following upon the trail blazed by Cramér in Sweden, has documented Saami land claims to an extent which can no longer be ignored. It is hard to imagine that herding rights based on privilege can long stand against immemorial rights and outright ownership rights.

In 1978, Finland's Advisory Board on Saami Affairs decided to establish a section to evaluate which rights should be transferred to the Saami over the natural resources administered by the state. Korpijaakko was appointed secretary to the section in March 1990. This legal section of the Advisory Board is sometimes referred to as the Finnish Saami Rights Commission in the spirit of harmonization with the Commissions in both Norway and – until 1991 – Sweden. In June 1990 the section proposed a Saami Act which would reinstitute the collective Saami ownership to the lands formerly owned by the Saami and which now constitute so-called state forests. The proposed Act would also confirm the rights of Saami to herd reindeer, hunt and fish.

The Saami Homeland was to be divided among Saami villages (*Lapinkylä*) for the administration of these traditional Saami liveli-hoods. This arrangement would not infringe on the property rights of the non-Saami local population nor their traditional rights to fish, hunt and move freely. The present Saami Delegation (*Saamelaisvalutu-uskunta*) would be replaced by a new representative organ, the Saami Thing (*Saamelaiskäräjät*).

During the hearing procedure (*lausuntokierros*) when state and local authorities as well as organizations and associations were asked to pre-sent their views on the proposed Act, the majority of the written opin-ions were in favour of it. Eight opinions were unconditionally in favour; 12 had limited, clearly specified conditions; and 16 wished for additional studies. Fifteen written opinions were negative towards the whole proposed Act. The present government has been somewhat reluctant to push the matter through, while the Finnish Parliament has been more positive towards the proposal. Currently (summer 1993) the situation is the following: The question of Saami land rights has been referred for further studies to the Saami Parliament, whereas the organizational and administrative issues are under investigation by the Finnish Ministry of Justice.[58]

Norway too, through the continued work of its Saami Rights Com-mission, seeks to address the vital issue of Saami land title. Sweden, however, refuses to confront this issue squarely.

In 1991, an amendment was introduced to the Finnish Act of Parlia-ment, making it a responsibility for the Parliament to hear the Saami in matters of special concern to them (Section 52a). However, the idea of reserving a seat in the Parliament for the Saami was rejected.[59]

In conjunction with the establishment of the Norwegian *Sameting*, it should be noted that on 21 April 1988, an addendum (Section 110a) was made to the Norwegian Constitution to the effect that it is the responsibility of the Norwegian state to ensure that conditions are such that the Saami people can secure and develop their language, their culture and their social life. Moreover, on 20 June 1990 Norway ratified the International Labour Organization's (ILO) Convention 169 concerning indigenous and tribal peoples in independent countries. Of the four nations with indigenous Saami populations, Norway is the only one which has ratified ILO 169.

The main obstacle to ratification by Finland and Sweden is Section 14 of this Convention which states among other things that: 'The rights of ownership and possession of the peoples concerned over the lands which they traditionally occupy shall be recognized.' When the text of this Convention was still in draft form, Sweden and a number of other nations sought to have this article changed so as to recognize the peoples' right of *use* rather than right of *ownership*. Failing this, Sweden has declined ratification, despite the fact that the text was adopted by the International Labour Organization before being opened up for ratification by member states. Norway, however, has taken another tack and ratified the Convention, thus accepting its many safeguards for and positive attitude towards indigenous peoples, while at the same time presenting a special interpretation of Section 14. According to Norway's special interpretation, strongly protected rights of usage must be viewed as satisfactorily fulfilling ILO's demand for admission of indigenous land ownership, as the Norwegian state cannot grant ownership rights to the Saami for vast land areas occupied by other people, often in the possession of what would then become conflicting private ownership claims. Norway has thereby taken the risk of being declared in violation of the Convention, and the Swedish Saami minister, Per Unckel, has made it plain in his presentation of the new Swedish Saami policy to the Swedish national Parliament on 15 December 1992, that Sweden intends to let Norway be the guinea pig on this issue.

The Saami Parliaments

Finland
In Finland, resulting from the work of the Finnish Saami Committee (itself established by the government in 1971), proposition 1973:824 which advocated the establishment of a representative Saami Delegation was accepted. This body has commonly been termed by the Finnish Saami the 'Saami Parliament', an unofficial name, but one now used by Finnish administrators and politicians as well. This Parliament, founded by cabinet decree under the Department of the Interior, had its first meeting in 1976. The same legislation defined the so-called Saami Homeland in Finland (the municipalities of Enontekiö, Inari, Utsjoki and the herding area of Sodankylä).

The Saami Parliament, with offices located in Inari, is to concern itself with Saami rights and support Saami economic, social and cultural development. Structurally and functionally it is on par with the Saami Parliaments, *Sametings*, of Norway and Sweden established approximately 15 and 20 years later respectively. It is conjectured that being a bilingual nation already because of its Swedish-speaking minority, Finland was considerably ahead of its Fennoscandian neighbours in establishing a democratically elected representative organization for the Saami. Moreover, the Saami Parliament can take the initiative to present cases to different authorities, although it has no control outside of its own organization.

The Finnish Saami Parliament is composed of 20 representatives, chosen by the Saami, but authorized by the government – at least two representatives from each of the four provinces composing the Saami Homeland, but also 12 representatives regionally unbound and elected by popular support. Elections are held every fourth year. Unlike Norway and Sweden, Finland has kept a registry of its Saami population, pertaining to the homeland area. Later this was broadened to include Saami living outside the Finnish Saami Homeland territories. There is an official list for the Saami electorate which now contains about 3,000 names. To be eligible for this list, one must be 18 years of age or older and conform under the language criterion – that is, have learned Saami as a first language or have a parent or grandparent who has. (Even non-Saami spouses were declared eligible to vote.) Approximately 82 per cent of the defined electorate voted in the first election in October 1972.

The Saami Parliament has five working committees: a legal committee, an industrial-business committee, an educational committee, a cultural and social committee, and a work committee. The Parliament convenes six times a year. Expenses are paid by the Finnish state, although the low working budget has caused difficulties. The Parliament sends delegates to the triennial Nordic Saami Conferences and appoints the Finnish Saami members to the Board of the Nordic Saami Institute in Kautokeino, Norway. The Parliament also nominates the five Saami who, together with Finnish bureaucrats, form an Advisory Board on Saami Affairs (*Saamelaisasiain neuvottelukunta*), founded by the Finnish government in 1960, and not to be confused with the Saami Parliament.

This Advisory Board is composed of the governor of the Lappland province and ten members – five of them from different government departments and five from the Saami Parliament – authorized by the government. The Advisory Board is to prepare the government with respect to the recommendations from the Nordic Council on the Saami, to monitor the development of Saami economic conditions and to give the authorities in the Lappland province statements on questions about the Saami.

Norway
The Norwegian *Sameting* was established according to the new Saami Law of 12 June 1987, No.56, and was inaugurated by the Norwegian King Olav V in Karasjok on 9 October 1989. The new Norwegian Saami

Law gives the *Sameting* the mandate to concern itself with all matters which the *Sameting* considers touch upon the Saami people. The Norwegian *Sameting* has also taken over the functions of the Norwegian Saami Council which since 1964 has advised authorities in economic, cultural, judicial and social issues related to the Saami. In taking over the Council's functions, the *Sameting* also comes to control the Saami Development Fund.

For the Norwegian *Sameting*, with offices based in Karasjok, 39 representatives are elected for four-year terms by the direct votes of the Saami people from 13 constituencies -six in Finnmark, three in Troms, two in north Nordland, one covering south Nordland, Trøndelag and northeast Hedmark, and lastly one regionally unbounded to include all those Saami who have scattered far from their core areas. The law defines those eligible to register for the Saami electorate as those of voting age who feel themselves to be Saami and who speak Saami or have a parent or grandparent who speaks or has spoken Saami. The *Sameting* is meant to be a centre for the Saami political debate, to support the variety within the Saami culture and to take initiatives in Saami concerns. It is to take a stand on difficult political questions, to act as a bridge builder in ethnic conflicts, to ensure that Norway's Saami policies are in accord with the obligations Norway has accepted from international law, and to represent the Saami and to be their voice.

At least once a year, the Norwegian national Parliament has agreed to put Saami matters on the agenda to review its responsibilities towards the realization of its new Saami policy.

In May 1990 the Norwegian *Sameting* established a Praesidium, an Executive Council, an administrative body and six committees: education and research; trade, industry, nature and environment; civil rights; social affairs and health; language and culture; organizational and constitutional affairs. The powers of the Norwegian *Sameting* are expected to expand, largely as a result of its own initiatives. However, there is also the distinct possibility that considerably greater powers will be conferred upon the *Sameting* with regard to resources by the results of the ongoing work of the Norwegian Saami Rights Commission. Unlike the Swedish Saami Rights Commission, which was ended in 1991 before the legislation establishing a *Sameting* was enacted, the Norwegian Saami Rights Commission, led now by its third chairman, Tor Falch, continues with research into Saami land claims in Finnmark and, thereafter, will look into Saami land claims elsewhere in Norway.

Sweden

On 15 December 1992 the Swedish national Parliament voted by an overwhelming majority to pass Proposition 1992–93:32, *The Saami and Saami Culture, etc.*, which set forth both a *Sameting* law and changes in the Reindeer Herding Act. There were 5,390 persons registered to vote for representatives in the Swedish Saami Parliament, *Sameting*, on 16 May 1993, and out of these, 3,808 or 71 per cent actually voted. Thirteen parties campaigned in the election, and of these, 11 parties acquired seats. On 26 August 1993, in Kiruna, where its offices are probably to be based, the *Sameting* was inaugurated with the Royal family in attendance. New elections will be held every four years.

Like its sister assemblies in Norway and Finland, the Swedish *Sameting* is a department of government, subject to government directives and, besides some administrative duties, in possession of only advisory status. For the Saami, this Bill was a disappointment. Not only does the *Sameting* it established lack the power to veto or even delay exploitation of lands important to reindeer herding, the proposition rejected an addendum to the Swedish Constitution similar to that accepted by Norway. (However, Section 2, paragraph 4, of the Swedish Constitution already stipulates in a general way that the cultural and social life of ethnic, linguistic and religious minorities should be promoted.) Nor did the Bill grant official status to the Saami language in any region regarding Saami livelihoods (as the Saami Rights Commission had advocated), and it made plain Sweden's intent not to ratify ILO 169. Moreover, the changes it prescribed for the Reindeer Herding Act were basically a tightening of restrictions and regulations, and to the Saami the most bitter and unexpected blow – a removal of Saami hunting and fishing exclusivity on lands until now reserved for their use alone.

Despite the weak advisory construct of the *Sameting* and its constraint by government directives as a government authority, the creation of a Swedish *Sameting* has been a much-desired goal by the Swedish Saami. Their hope is that the *Sameting* will in time mature into an administrative body with increasing autonomy and respect.

At an extra meeting held by SSR, the largest Swedish Saami organization, following upon the presentation of Proposition 32 and before its acceptance by the Swedish Parliament, the text of the proposition was publicly burned in front of national news TV cameras. The main Saami organizations passed resolutions calling for the acceptance of the *Sameting*, but the rejection of all other suggestions, at least until the newly formed *Sameting* had the opportunity to convene and to discuss them. This, they argued, is the stated goal of such a *Sameting*, and it would be to defeat its own purpose were the state to institutionalize a *Sameting* and then refuse it the chance of expressing itself on, and possibly bring revisions in, the most significant legislative changes for the Saami presented during the last 20 years. Nonetheless, this is precisely what happened. Proposition 32 was accepted in its entirety and hailed by the government as a major victory for the Saami.

The Swedish *Sameting* will make decisions regarding the distribution of government funds, other funds dedicated to Saami collective use, and funds from the Saami Fund (*Samefond*) in support of Saami culture and Saami organizations. It will appoint the members of the Saami School Board. It will lead work concerning the Saami language. It will cooperate in the formulation of social plans, guaranteeing that Saami interests are considered, among them the interests of reindeer herding in plans concerning the use of land and water. Lastly, it will give information about Saami conditions.

The position of the *Sameting* as a government authority is generally buttressed by the motivation that status as a government department will ensure its financial base, guarantee that it be heard in important issues affecting the Saami and assure that it has the proper powers to administer matters given over to its realm of responsibility.

With regard to the definition of the Saami electorate, the Swedish *Sameting* Law follows, in the main, the Finnish and Norwegian model which bases the objective criterion on language. With regard to organizational practicalities, the *Sameting* Law deviates from the Commission's recommendations in that it suggests one rather than six Saami constituencies in Sweden. Moreover, also in contrast to the Commission's recommendation, the *Sameting* Law states that the Sameting president will be appointed by the government after hearing, but not necessarily abiding by, the wishes of the *Sameting*.[60]

Members of various human rights organizations have criticized the *Sameting* Law for constructing the *Sameting* as a government authority, for this will bind the *Sameting* to government directives. It becomes impossible, for example, for the *Sameting* to play any kind of role in legal processes against the state in national or international courts. In fact, the *Sameting* must represent the state in such cases, and obviously there can arise a conflict of interests. The rebuttal that individual Saami and other Saami organizations can still oppose the state in court, and therefore the *Sameting*'s inability to do so need not restrain the judicial process, loses weight when it becomes clear that the state no longer guarantees the Saami the right to free trial. The argument that the Norwegian *Sameting* is also a government department and does not appear to suffer from this position must be balanced against the observation that, unlike Sweden, Norway has made a special addendum to its Constitution to ensure the maintenance of the Saami culture and society, has ratified the ILO Convention 169 on indigenous and tribal peoples and has directed its Saami Rights Commission to investigate Saami land claims.

In general, views about the propriety of the Swedish state's *Sameting* construction have been strongly divided along the lines of trust in the benevolence of the state's Saami policies. Those in favour of the accepted *Sameting* construct stress that the given framework is only the beginning of the path towards greater autonomy and powers and that all fears of being 'bought out' and trapped by government encapsulation are groundless. Those opposed feel that Saami free rein will be either insignificant or non-existent. They argue in effect that if the line on the hook is long enough to start with, it may take time for the fish to realize it is caught.

The political future

While the creation of these Parliaments in Norway and Sweden and, together with the already existing Finnish Saami Parliament, the prospective establishment of a Nordic Saami Assembly with representatives from the three national Saami Parliaments, must be viewed as major victories for the Saami, these developments are not without challenges and risks. The state will now gain the ability to refer to *the* will of the Saami as expressed in their representative organizations. However, many Saami interest groups and organizations are not politically organized or activated to the same extent, and it may take a good deal of time before the new Saami Parliaments actually do represent the full spectrum of Saami. In the meantime, there is always the risk that the small or unorganized group within the general Saami category loses its voice with respect to the state.

The Saami Parliaments hold a promise of improved Saami–state relations, but there may be a cost, at least initially, of internal Saami strife. Of course, this is an unavoidable consequence of the democratic process, and such strife is certainly not something new. However, the bureaucratic parliamentary process itself does not derive from the Saami. The gains from this new model will be brought from within a context of increased cultural encapsulation. The Saami must try to mould their Parliaments to themselves rather than merely to the demands of state processes and to maintain general Saami concerns despite short-sighted gains to be made by any one faction temporarily in a position of power.

Conclusions

The situation of the Saami minority offers valuable lessons for the struggle of indigenous and minority peoples. The encompassing Fennoscandian governments are known for being dedicated to the precepts of human rights and social welfare and, as a result, the Saami suffer but little from official policies of negative discrimination when compared to many other indigenous peoples. The Fennoscandian Saami are not grossly impoverished, and they still inhabit their land. Nonetheless, they face serious problems in the struggle for cultural maintenance. While the linkage of Saami culture to reindeer has provided them with great cultural strength and continuity, the more the northern grazing lands are exploited by modern industrial needs, the more this strength turns towards a liability. In the effort to protect the Saami while at the same time expanding resource extraction and industry, governments implement a welfare-privilege ideology at the expense of acknowledging absolute resource rights. The Saami, a minority people of considerable variety, have been split further by all manner of legislative categorizations (legally and ethnically false), and are now called upon to unite under elected representative organizations with only advisory capacities.

Only a small minority within the Saami minority are directly involved with reindeer herding, which allows them access to their traditional resources and to a great extent maintains the foundations of Saami identity for all Saami. In Norway, as opposed to Sweden for example, there are sizable local populations of Saami who form a majority in their towns or even in their municipalities. While there are many Saami who still live in their traditional home regions, so-called core areas, most have been denied the practice of their immemorial land rights and over the centuries prevented from combining traditional Saami livelihoods with traditional non-Saami livelihoods. As a result of these constraints, and the continuing destruction of their land base, many Saami have been forced (and in various proportions enticed away) from their home regions to settle in urban centres, often far south. Very little is known about this large group of Saami. As noted, they blend smoothly with the majority population. Almost without exception they speak the language of the majority population fluently and are subjected to no blatant formal discrimination by their governments. For many of them, Saami identity has been passive, but the possibility of active participation in the new arena of Saami politics opened up by the establishment of the *Sametings* in Norway and Sweden may change this.

Now that Norway, Sweden and Finland all have Saami Parliaments, it will probably not be long before the Russian Saami also establish a Saami Parliament and participate with their Saami neighbours in an over-arching pan-Saami Parliament with representatives from the four national Saami Parliaments. The charter of the Finnish Saami Parliament has been newly translated into Russian to serve as a model for the creation of a Russian Saami Parliament. As noted, the Russian Saami have joined the Saami Council. A Russian Saami youth organization has just been established, *Samnuras*, as has an organization of Russian Saami artists and workers in handicraft. Despite these political and organizational gains, the Russian Saami face hard times. They have recently founded 15 or so Saami businesses in different branches, but all of these are beset with troubles. For the elderly and for families with many children, famine is not far away. Inflation has now reached 2,500 per cent a year. The Saami Council is considering a programme of economic aid for the Russian Saami.[61]

In Fennoscandia, the Saami have little choice but to revert to litigation. This time, however, the Saami can approach international as well as national forums with a new spirit of unity stretching across Saamiland. The Swedish Saami will undoubtedly contest the state's disregard of their exclusive hunting and fishing rights, and they will most surely seek to revive a dormant piece of litigation on land rights called the Gauto Case. Here they will also be aided by pan-Saami organizations such as the Saami Council which enjoys NGO status at the UN and, in time, by the future Nordic Saami Parliament (or along with the Russian Saami, a Pan-Saami Parliament). To what extent the national Saami Parliaments will be able to participate in such a confrontation with their governments is, of course, unclear, but they will undoubtedly press their advantage to the fullest. A government which invokes its directive to muzzle its Saami Parliament would suffer mightily in international stature.

In Norway, the continuing Saami Rights Commission may well lead to results which staunch the most immediate calls for litigation, just as in Finland the process surrounding the Saami Act may bring concrete improvements for the Saami without litigation. In Sweden, however, alternative courses to litigation seem bankrupt.

In closing, it is important to consider what the Saami are hoping to achieve. Few if any Saami would advocate the building of an independent Saami state as a viable and serious alternative. What they do want, however, is the ability to protect their lands of traditional use against heavy exploitation. This is not to say that they will automatically oppose all development, only they insist on being a decisive part of all negotiations. Similarly, the Saami are not necessarily opposed to allowing a broader use of their hunting and fishing rights. But these must be recognized as *their* rights, the revenues from which should accrue to them. Their main desire is to protect their wildlife resources within a programme of sustainable use. Within that ecological framework, and after their own needs have been met, they have indicated that they would not be averse to allocating a share of the harvestable resource to others.

Even though they are encapsulated by government and minimally empowered, the Saami Parliaments now in all three of the Nordic Saami countries open to the Saami new avenues of action, both within each nation state, and also as a unified transnational entity. With these democratically elected representative Parliaments the Saami will be in a position to clarify their own position and to mount a unified front. These bodies and their future combined manifestation, armed with the recent and emerging body of international indigenous rights, place the Saami in a better position than ever before to force the practical recognition of the rights they already have in each of their separate nation states and to partake in the new rights evolved by the international community. One can only hope that the new Saami parliamentary organizations manage to represent Saami diversity justly and that their voices will be respected even when opposed to state desires.

Internally the Saami face the difficult task of healing the divisions within them caused by the various imposed legal categorizations. While many of these divisions were and are unjust and unjustifiable, there is no doubt that the traditional Saami livelihoods cannot alone sustain the entire Saami population; certain distinctions within the Saami group must be made. The important point is that in these internal matters, within the framework of their rights, the Saami be allowed to make their own allocations. The new *Sametings* may also prove to be the vehicle by which the Saami confront these internal responsibilities. For the Saami this is a time of new political processes, new laws and increased pan-Saami cooperation – a time of extraordinary challenge.

NOTES &
BIBLIOGRAPHIES

Greenland: Emergence of an Inuit Homeland

Notes

[1] For example, see Hart Hansen, J.P., Meldgaard, J. and Nordqvist, J. (eds.), *The Greenland Mummies*, Smithsonian Institution Press, Washington, DC, 1991.

[2] Kleivan, I., 'Studies in the vocabulary of Greenlandic translations of the Bible', in Basse, B. and Jensen, K. (eds.), *Eskimo Languages*, Arkona, Aarhus, 1979.

[3] Nuttall, M., *Arctic Homeland: kinship, community and development in northwest Greenland*, Belhaven Press, London, and University of Toronto Press, Toronto, 1992.

[4] Jenness, D., *Eskimo Administration –IV Greenland*, Arctic Institute of North America, Technical Paper No.19, 1967.

[5] Dahl, J., 'Greenland: political structure of self-government', *Arctic Anthropology*, Vol.23, Nos.1-2, 1986, pp.315-324.

[6] Dahl, J., *op. cit.*, p.317.

[7] Dahl, J., *op. cit.*, p.323.

[8] Kleivan, I., 'Greenland's national symbols', *North Atlantic Studies*, Vol.1, No.2, 1991. pp.4-16.

[9] Petersen, R., 'The role of research in the construction of Greenlandic identity', *North Atlantic Studies*, Vol.1, No.2, 1991, pp.17-22.

[10] Poole, G., 'Fisheries policy and economic development in Greenland in the 1980s', *Polar Record*, Vol.25, No.157, 1990, pp.109-118.

[11] Poole, G., personal communication, July 1993.

[12] Robert-Lamblain, J., 'Ammassalik: end or persistence of an isolate?', *Meddelelser om Grønland* (Man and Society), Vol.10, 1984; Søby, R., 'Language and identity in Thule', in Basse, B. and Jensen, K. (eds.), *Eskimo Languages*, Arkona, Aarhus, 1979.

[13] Rink, H.J., *Eskimoiske Eventyr and Sagn*, Nordiskes Landes Bogforlag, Holsteinsborg, 1974.

[14] Berthelsen, C., 'Greenlandic literature: its traditions and trends', *Arctic Anthropology*, Vol.23, Nos.1-2, 1989, pp.339-46.

[15] Berthelsen, C., *op. cit.*, p.341.

[16] Petersen, R., 'Copenhagen Greenlandic', in Basse, B. and Jensen, K. (eds.), *Eskimo Languages*, Arkona, Aarhus, 1979.

[17] Søby, R., 'Savissivik: West Greenlandic influence on a settlement in Thule', *Inter-Nord*, Vol.17, 1983, pp.181-92.

[18] Bjerregaard, P. and Misfeldt, J., 'Infant mortality in Greenland', *Arctic Medical Research*, Vol.51, 1992, pp.126-35.

[19] Bjerregaard, P., 'Geographic variation of mortality in Greenland', *Arctic Medical Research*, Vol.49, 1990, pp.16-24.

[20] Pedersen, J., 'Substance abuse among Greenlandic schoolchildren', *Arctic Medical Research*, Vol.51, 1992, pp.67-71.

[21] For example, Lynge, I., 'Suicide in Greenland', *Arctic Medical Research*, Vol.40, 1985, pp.53-60.

[22] Briggs, J., 'Socialization, family conflicts and responses to culture change among Canadian Inuit', *Arctic Medical Research*, Vol.40, 1985, pp.40-52.

[23] Nuttall, *op. cit.*

[24] For example, *ibid.*, pp.104-6.

[25] *Greenland Medical Council Annual Report 1991.*

[26] Cruwys, E. and Nuttall, M., 'The cultural impact of AIDS in the circumpolar north', *Polar Record*, Vol.28, No.167, 1992.

[27] Melbye, M. (ed.), 'AIDS and other sexually transmitted diseases in the Arctic regions', *Arctic Medical Research*, Vol.49, Supplement No.3, 1990.

[28] Sontag, S., *AIDS and its Metaphors*, Penguin, Harmondsworth, 1989.

[29] Melbye, *op. cit.*

[30] Dahl, J., 'Beluga hunting in Saqqaq', *North Atlantic Studies*, Vol.2, Nos.1-2, 1990, pp.166-9.

[31] Caulfield, R., *Qerqertuarsuarmi Aarfanniarneq: Greenlandic Inuit whaling in Qerqertarsuaq kommune*, West Greenland, Department of Rural Development, University of Alaska, Fairbanks, 1991.

[32] Airoldi, A., 'The European Communities' legislation and its consequences for Arctic sealing', unpublished M.Phil. thesis, University of Cambridge, 1989.

[33] Lynge, F., 'Conflict treatment old and new', *Folk*, Vol.30, 1988, pp.5-22.

[34] Wenzel, G., *Animal Rights, Human Rights*, Belhaven Press, London, 1991.

[35] Nuttall, *op. cit.*

[36] See Peterson, N. and Matsuyama, T (eds.), *Cash, Commoditization and Changing Foragers*, National Museum of Ethnology, Osaka, 1991.

[37] Faegteborg, M., 'Inuit organizations and whaling policy', *North Atlantic Studies*, Vol.2, Nos.1-2, 1990, pp.124-9.

[38] Wenzel, *op. cit.*

[39] Freeman, M.M.R., 'A commentary on political issues in relation to contemporary whaling', *North Atlantic Studies*, Vol.2, Nos.1-2, 1990, pp.106-16.

Bibliography

Birket-Smith, K., *The Eskimos*, Rhodos, Copenhagen, 1971.

Foighel, I., 'Home Rule in Greenland', *Meddelelser om Grønland* (Man and Society), Vol.1

Gad, F., *The History of Greenland*, Vol.1, C. Hurst & Co., London, 1970.

Kaalund, B., *The Art of Greenland*, Berkeley, University of California Press, 1983.

Nuttall, M., *Arctic Homeland: kinship, community and development in northwest Greenland*, Belhaven Press, London, and University of Toronto Press,Toronto, 1992.

Native Peoples of the Russian Far North

Footnotes

Abbreviations used for journals (j) and newspapers (n) in the notes

I	*Izvestiya* (n)
ZN	*Zhizn' natsional'nostey* ('Life of Nations', 1922–4) (j)
LoP	*Lovozerskaya Pravda* (n)
LR	*Literaturnaya Rossiya* (n)
SA	*Severnaya Asia* ('Northern Asia', journal of the Committee of the North, 1925–31) (j)
SP	*Severnye Prostory* ('Northern Expanses', 1985) (j)
RG	*Rossiyskaya Gazeta* (n)
SAr	*Sovetskaya Arktika* ('Soviet Arctic', journal on Northern peoples and economy – largely Communist Party propaganda – 1936– 41) (j)
SS	*Sovetskiy Sever* ('Soviet North', journal of the Committee of the North, 1930–5) (j)
QS	*Questions siberiennes* (1990), Institut du Monde sovietique et de l'Europe Centrale et Orientale, Edité sous la direction de Boris Chichlo, Paris (j)

[1] Armstrong T., Rogers G. and Rowley G., *The Circumpolar North. A Political and Economic Geography of the Arctic and Subarctic*, Methuen and Co., London, 1978, pp.23-4.

[2] *Etnicheskoye razvitiye narodnostey Severa v sovetskiy period*, Nauka Publishers, Moscow, 1987, pp.32-90.

[3] See also Terletsky, P.E., *Naseleniye Kraynevo Severa (po dannym perepisi 1926–7)*, Institut Narodov Severa, Leningrad, 1932, for the results of another census, the Polar Census of 1926.

[4] Of these, the best is a classification suggested by I.S.Gurvich (Gurvich, 'Eshche raz k voprosu o perekhode malykh narodnostey Severa i Dal'nyevo Vostoka k sotsializmy', *Voprosy Istorii KPSS*, Moscow, No.9, 1964, p.101). This classification has similarities to my own.

[5] Armstrong et al, *op. cit.*, p.24.

[6] Krupnik, I.I., *Arkticheskaya etnoekologiya*, Nauka Publishers, Moscow, 1989, pp.146-64.

[7] Serebrennikov, I., *Inorodcheskiy vopros v Sibiri*, Irkutsk, 1917, p.6.

[8] Gurvich, I.S., 'Severo-vostochnye paleoaziaty i eskimosy' and 'Zaklucheniye', in *Etnicheskaya istoriya narodov Severa*, Nauka Publishers, Moscow, 1982.

[9] Zibarev, V.A., *Sovetskoye stroitel'stvo u malykh narodnostey Severa*

(1917–1932), Tomsk University Press, Tomsk, 1968, pp.21-3; Prutchenko, S., *Sibirskiye okrainy*, St Petersburg, 1899, p.175.

[10] *Svod Zakonov Rossiyskoy Imperii*, Vol. II, unofficial publication, St Petersburg, 1892.

[11] Bakhrushin, S.V., 'Sibirskye tuzemtsy pod russkoy vlas'tyu do revolyutsii 1917 goda', in *Sovetskiy Sever*, eds. Suridovich, P.G.,Buturlin, S.A., Leonov, N.I., Committee of the North Publication, Moscow, 1929, pp. 66-95; Zibarev, *op. cit.* pp.23-5.

[12] Serebrennikov, *op. cit.*, pp.14ff.

[13] *Obrazovaniye SSSR. Sbornik dokumentov.*, Politizdat, Moscow, 1949, p.20.

[14] *Ibid.*, p.57.

[15] *SS*, No.2, 1934, p.10.

[16] Compare Kolarz, W., *The People of the Soviet Far East*, New York, 1954, pp.65-6.

[17] Compare Forsyth, J., 'The indigenous peoples of Siberia in the twentieth century', in Wood, A. and French, R.A. (eds), *The Development of Siberia: Peoples and Resources*, Macmillan Press and the University of London, London, 1989, p.79.

[18] S.V. Bakhrushin states that 'from beginning to end the Code is inspired by the desire to protect not only the economic welfare, but also the traditional way of life of the native peoples. Speransky understood the perils of administrative interference in the native way of life and tried to protect native communities from it'. Bakhrus, in *op. cit.*, p.86.

[19] *ZN*, Nos.3-4, 1923, p.172; *SS*, No.2, 1934, p.9.

[20] *SA*, Nos.5-6, 1925, pp.101-4.

[21] *SA*, Nos.1-2, 1925, p.8.

[22] *SS*, No.1, 1930, pp.21ff.

[23] Drafts were published in SA, No.3, 1926, pp.94-101.

[24] Zibarev, *op. cit.*, p.130.

[25] *Ibid.*, p.160.

[26] Demidov, V.A., *Sovetskoye natsional'no-gosudarstvennoye stroitel'stvo v Sibiri*, Novosibirsk, 1981, p.72.

[27] Zibarev, *op. cit.*, p.113.

[28] *Ibid.*, pp.111-12.

[29] *ZN*, No.1, 1923, pp.251-4.

[30] *ZN*, No.18, 1922, p.153.

[31] Forsyth, *op. cit.*, p.80.

[32] *SS*, No.2, 1930, pp.22ff.

[33] *SA*, No.3, 1925, pp.111-13.

[34] *SS*, No.1, 1930, pp.117-24.

[35] *SS*, No.2, 1930, pp.22ff.
[36] In 1953, the project was moved to Hertzen State Pedagogical Insti-
      tute (which was granted university status in 1990), where teachers
      for Northern schools are being trained to this day.
[37] *SS*, No.1, 1930, p.42.
[38] *SA*, No.3, 1925, p.114.
[39] *SAr*, No.7, 1938, p.106. The Stalinist purges of the 1930s–1950s were
      absolutely devastating for research on the North. W.G. Bogoraz died
      in 1936, luckily too early to witness the arrest of his best and most
      talented friends and colleagues. Ya.P. Al'kor, L.Ya. Shternberg, E.A.
      Kreinovich, G.M. Vasilevich, A.M. Zolotarev, S.I. Rudenko, W.
      Schneider, N. Forstein and many others were murdered. Those who
      survived had their work suppressed for decades. S.N. Stebnitskiy, A.
      Pyrerka, N.G. Schnakenburg, D.G. Verbov, G.M. Korsakov were
      killed during the Second World War. The next wave of purges came
      in 1952 with the publication of Stalin's notorious book, *Marxism and
      Problems of Linguistics*, which was used as a pretext for launching a
      wide campaign against those few remaining linguists and cultural
      and educational workers who still retained some knowledge and
      skills.
[40] *SA*, Nos.5-6, 1929, p.126.
[41] Onishchuk, N.T., *Sozdaniye sovetskoy natstional'noy gosudarstvennosti
      narodnostey Severa*, Tomsk University Press, Tomsk, 1986, pp.132-3.
[42] *SS*, No.5, 1931, p.6.
[43] *SS*, No.2, 1931, pp.5-29.
[44] *SS*, No.1, 1933, p.98.
[45] *SS*, No.2, 1931, pp.5-29.
[46] *SS*, No.4, 1930, pp.7-23.
[47] *SS*, No.2, 1931, p.16.
[48] Forsyth, *op.cit.*, p.84.
[49] Zibarev, *op.cit.*, p.183.
[50] *SS*, No.5, 1931, p.7.
[51] See Chichlo, B., 'La collectivisation en Siberie: un problème de
      nationalités', in *L'expérience sovietique et le problème national dans le
      monde* (1920–1938), Paris, 1981, pp.297-307, for details.
[52] Gurvich, I.S., 'Printsipy leninskoy natsional'noy politiki i prime-
      neniye ikh na Kraynem Severe', in *Osushchestvleniye Leninskoy nat-
      sional'noy politiki u narodov Kraynevo Severa*, Nauka Publishers,
      Moscow, 1971, pp.30-4.
[53] *SAr*, No.11, 1936, pp.37-9.
[54] *SS*, No.5, 1931, pp.20-1.

[55] *SS*, No.4, 1930, pp.7-23.

[56] The first signs of it in the North came as early as 1939 – cf. *SAr*, No.6, 1939, pp.17-24, an article called 'On Russian investigation of the Arctic and cringing to the West'.

[57] *SP*, No.1, 1988, p.5.

[58] *SP*, No.6, 1988, p.19.

[59] Chichlo, B., 'La Tchoukotka: une autre civilisation obligatoire. Quelques observations sur le terrain', in *Objets et mondes, La revue du Musee de l'Homme*, Nos.3-4, Vol.25, Paris, 1988, p.150.

[60] *Osvoyeniye bez otchuzhdeniya, Materialy expertnovo oprosa*, Tyumen, 1989, Parts 1 and 2, p.45.

[61] Forsyth, *op.cit.*, p.91.

[62] 'Distaste for traditional occupations among young people, and an aspiration towards a place in modern Russian urban culture, may reflect a desire for "progress", but also betokens a loss of self-esteem on the part of native people', Forsyth, *op. cit.*, p.90.

[63] *KPSS v resolyutsiakh 1986*, Vol.9, Moscow, 1986.

[64] *SP*, No.1, 1989, pp.10-11.

[65] Chichlo, *op. cit.* (1988), p.150.

[66] *LR*, 1/6/90, p.16.

[67] *LoP*, 5/11/88.

[68] Kimeyev, V., *Shortsy, kto oni? Etnograficheskye ocherki*, Kemerovo Literary Press, Kemerovo, 1990, p.138.

[69] Smolyak, A.V., and Krupnik, I.I., 'Sovremennoye polozheniye korennovo naseleniya Sakhalinskoy oblasti', unpublished report based on fieldwork in Okha and Nogliki regions, September 1982.

[70] *SP*, No.4, 1988, pp.4-6.

[71] *SP*, No.5, 1988.

[72] *I*, No.166, 15 June 1990.

[73] *SP*, No.1, 1991, p.4.

[74] Krupnik, I.I., 'Demograficheskoye razvitiye asiatskikh eskimosov v 1970-e gg (osnovniye tendentsii i etnosocial'niye usloviya)', in *Regionalnye problemy sotsial'no-demograficheskovo razvitiya*, Institute of Sociological Research and Soviet Sociological Association Publication, Moscow, 1987, p.109.

[75] Krupnik, I., personal communication, February 1991.

[76] *I*, No. 194, 13 July 1990, p.3.

[77] *Zakon Rossiyskoy Sovetskoy Federativnoy Sotsialisticheskoy Respubliki ob avtonomnykh okrugakh RSFSR*, Passed by the Supreme Soviet, 20/11/80, Moscow, 1980.

[78] See Nemtsev, V.A., *Pravoviye i organizatsionnye problemy administra-*

tivno-territorial'novo deleniya soyuznoy respubliki, Irkutsk State University, Irkutsk, 1974, for details.

[79] *Osvoyeniye, op. cit.*, p.15.

[80] Tchlenov, M.A., 'Quel destin attend les peuples du nord?', *QS*, Bulletin 1, Paris, 1990, p.36.

[81] *SP*, No.4, 1988, p.6.

[82] Kimeyev, *op.cit.*, p.139.

[83] *SP*, No.1, 1990, p.17.

[84] *SP*, No.5, 1988, p.16.

[85] *SP*, No.6, 1988, p.11.

[86] *SP*, No.3, 1990, p.27.

[37] *SP*, No.1, 1989, p.4.

[88] *SP*, No.3, 1988, p.2.

[89] *SP*, No.4, 1988, p.10.

[90] *SP*, No.2, 1988, pp.18-9.

[91] *SP*, No.2, 1988, pp.6-9.

[92] *SP*, No.3, 1989, p.2.

[93] Kimeyev, *op.cit.*, p.137.

[94] *SP*, No.3, 1989, p.6.

[95] About 13 million hectares of hunting grounds and pastures were destroyed as a result of its activities. The total damage for the Okrug was approximately 98 million rubles, *RG*, 20 April 1991.

[96] See p.47 of this chapter.

[97] *SP*, No.6, 1988, p.10.

[98] Smolyak and Krupnik, *op. cit.*

[99] *SP*, No.1, 1988, p.9.

[100] *SP*, No.2, 1988, pp.9-10.

[101] Vasiliev, V.I., and Malinovskaya, S.M., 'The Sel'kups' problems of national construction: history and modern times', conference paper, Seventh Inuit Studies Conference, 19–24/8/90, University of Alaska, Fairbanks.

[102] *APN (Agenstvo pechati 'Novosti')*, typescript, December 1989.

[103] *SP*, No.3, 1990, pp. 2-3. For a detailed account of the Congress, its declaration and status, see IWGIA Document 67, *Indigenous Peoples of the Soviet North*, Copenhagen, 1990.

[104] See a chronological survey of the principal publications on and events in the life of the Northern Minorities in *QS*, No.1, 1990, pp.51-6.

[105] Kozlov, V., 'Kak nam sokhranit' samobytnost' narodov Severa?' in APN, typescript, 27/12/89.

[106] *Novye Zakony SSSR, Vypusk I*, Yuridicheskaya Literatura, Moscow, 1990, pp.91-104.

[107] *Ibid.*, pp.167-72.
[108] Krauss, M., 'The world languages in crisis', conference paper, Symposium on 'Endangered Languages and their Preservation', Meeting of the Linguistic Society of America, Chicago, 3/1/91.
[109] *I*, No.166, 15 June 1990.
[110] Gracheva, G., personal communication, January 1992.
[111] *SP*, No.1, 1989, p.11.
[112] Osvoyeniye, *op. cit.*
[113] *SP*, No.5, 1988, pp.4-5.
[114] Dorais, L-J., 'Knowledge, identity and the future of Inuktitut in Canada', conference paper, Seventh Inuit Studies Conference, 19-24/8/90, University of Alaska, Fairbanks.
[115] Vasiliev, V.I., 'Osobennosti razvitiya etnicheskikh i yazykovykh protsessov v etnokontaktnykh zonakh Evropeyskovo Severa i Severnoy Azii', in *Etnokul'turnye protsessy u narodov Sibiri i Severa*, ed. Gurvich, I.S., Nauka Publishers, Moscow, 1985.

Bibliography
(In languages other than Russian)

For background on nationalities and Soviet nationality policy see:

Bialer, S. (ed.), *Politics, Society and Nationality inside Gorbachev's Russia*, Westview Press, Boulder, 1989.
Conquest, R. (ed.), *Soviet Nationalities Policy in Practice*, Bodley Head, London, 1967.
Hosking, G., *A History of the Soviet Union*, revised edition: Collins/Fontana, London, 1990.
Karklins, E., *Ethnic Relations in the USSR: the Perspective from Below*, Allen & Unwin, Boston, 1986.
Katz, Z. (ed.), *A Handbook of Major Soviet Nationalities*, Free Press, New York, 1975.
Kozlov, V.I., *The Peoples of the Soviet Union*, Hutchinson, London, 1988.
Nahajlo, B. and Swoboda, V., *Soviet Disunion: A History of the Nationalities Problem in the USSR*, Hamish Hamilton, London, 1990.
Smith, G., 'Gorbachev's greatest challenge: perestroika and the national question', *Political Geography Quarterly*, Vol.8, No.1 1989, pp. 7-20.

On the peoples of the North:

Armstrong, T., Rogers, G. and Rowley, G., *The Circumpolar North. A Political and Economic Geography of the Arctic and Sub-Arctic*, Methuen and Co., London, 1978.

Armstrong, T., 'Soviet policy towards northern peoples of the USSR', in *Arctic Policy. Papers presented at the Arctic Policy Conference*, M.A. Stenbaek (ed.), Centre for Northern Studies and Research, McGill University, Montreal, 1987.

Armstrong, T., *Russian Settlement in the North*, Cambridge University Press, Cambridge, 1983.

Chichlo, B., 'La collectivisation en Siberie: un problème de nationalités', in *L'expérience sovietique et le problème national dans le monde* (1920-1938), Paris, 1981, pp.279–307.

Czaplicka, M.A., *Aboriginal Siberia: A Study in Siberian Anthropology*, Clarendon Press, Oxford, 1914.

Jochelson, W., *Peoples of Asiatic Russia*, The American Museum of Natural History, 1928.

Kolarz, W., *The People of the Soviet Far East*, New York, 1954.

Komarov, B., *The Destruction of Nature in the Soviet Union*, Pluto Press, London, 1980.

Levin, M. and Potapov, L., (ed), *The Peoples of Siberia*, Chicago University Press, Chicago, 1964.

Mark, R., *Die Voelker der Sowjetunionen, Ein Lexicon*, Westdeutsches Verlag, Opland, 1989.

Wood, A. and French, R.A., (eds.), *The Development of Siberia: Peoples and Resources*, Macmillan Press and University of London, London, 1989.

The Alaska Natives

Footnotes

[1] State of Alaska, Department of Labor, 'Alaska population by sex, race and Hispanic origin: 1990 Census', Juneau, 1991.

[2] Krauss, Michael, *Alaska Native Languages*, University of Alaska, Fairbanks, 1980.

[3] State of Alaska, Department of Labor, *Alaska Population Overview*, Juneau, 1991, p.58.

[4] State of Alaska, Department of Labor, 'Alaska Population', *op. cit.*

[5] Alaska Federation of Natives, *The AFN Report on the Status of Alaska Natives: A Call for Action*, Anchorage, 1989; Napoleon, Harold, *Yuuyaraq: The Way of the Human Being*, Center for Cross-Cultural Studies, College of Rural Alaska, University of Alaska, Fairbanks, 1991.

[6] Fortuine, Robert, *Chills and Fever: Health and Disease in the Early History of Alaska*, University of Alaska Press, Fairbanks, 1989, pp.115-16; Gibson, James R., 'Colonial Russian America', in Mangusso, M.C. and Haycox, S.W. (eds.), *Interpreting Alaska's History*, Alaska Pacific University Press, Anchorage, 1989, p.113; Veltre, Douglas W., 'Perspectives on Aleut culture change during the Russian period', in *Russian America: The Forgotten Frontier*, Washington State Historical Society, Tacoma, 1990, p.178.

[7] This paragraph, unless otherwise noted, drives from Veltre, *op. cit.*

[8] Crowell, Aron, 'Prehistory of Alaska's Pacific coast', in Fitzhugh, W.W. and Crowell, A. (eds.), *Crossroads of the Continents*, Smithsonian Institution Press, Washington, DC, 1988, pp.132-6.

[9] The Inuit of Alaska can be classified into two ethnolinguistic categories: the North Alaskan Inuit, who speak Inupiag, and the Yupik-speaking groups. The latter include Siberian (encompassing St Lawrence Island), Bering Sea (including Nunivak Island) and Pacific (Koniag and Chugach). The Kenaitze, on the other hand, have been grouped in the Athabaskan–Eyak family of languages. See Fitzhugh, William W., 'Eskimos: hunters of the frozen coasts', in Fitzhugh and Crowell, *op. cit.*; and Kraus, Michael, *Alaska Native Languages* (map), University of Alaska, Fairbanks, 1980.

[10] Fiennup-Riordan, Ann, *Yup'ik Lives and How We See Them*, Rutgers University Press, New Brunswick and London, 1990, pp.8-10.

[11] Black, Lydia T., 'The story of Russian America', in Fitzhugh and Crowell, *op. cit.*, pp.76-7.

[12] De Laguna, Frederica, 'Tlingit: people of the wolf and raven', in Fitzhugh and Crowell, *op. cit.*, pp.58-61.

[13] US Library of Congress, Law Library, *Russian Administration of Alaska*

and the Status of Alaska Natives, Appendix 3, Senate Document No.152, 81st Congress, 2nd Session, Washington, DC, 1950, pp.56-6.

[14] Chance, Norman A., *The Inupiat and Arctic Alaska: An Ethnography of Development*, Holt, Rinehart & Winston, Fort Worth, 1990, pp.21-33.

[15] US Library of Congress, Law Library, *op. cit.*, p.55.

[16] For a more detailed treatment of Athabaskan culture, see VanStone, James W., *Athapaskan Adaptations: Hunters and Fishermen of the Subarctic Forests*, Aldine, Chicago, 1974.

[17] Chance, *op. cit.*, pp.21-33.

[18] Black, Lydia T., 'Ivan Pan'kov: architect of Aleut literacy', in Mangusso and Haycox, *op. cit.*, Dauenhauer, Richard L., 'Orthodoxy and education', paper presented at the Symposium on Russian America, Anchorage Museum, 17 November 1990.

[19] Svensson, Frances, 'The final crisis of tribalism: comparative ethnic policy on the American and Russian Frontiers', *Ethnic and Racial Studies*, Vol.1, No.1, January 1978, pp.100-23.

[20] US Library of Congress, Law Library, op. cit., pp.11-16; Jones, Richard S., *Alaska Native Claims Settlement Act of 1971 (Public Law 92-203): History and Analysis*, Congressional Research Service, Washington, DC, 1972, pp.6-7.

[21] Pullar, Gordon, presentation to the Cook Inlet Historical Society Anchorage, 18 October 1991.

[22] Treaty of Cession (15 Stat. 539), Article III, as quoted in *United States v. Berrigan*, 2 Alaska Reports, 445 (1905). Note that the Alaska Natives never signed a treaty with Russia or the United States surrendering their aboriginal rights.

[23] Naske, Klaus M., *A History of Alaska Statehood*, University Press of America, Lanham, 1985, pp.9-18.

[24] Haycox, Stephen, 'Racism, Indians and territorial politics', in Mangusso and Haycox, *op. cit.*, p.289.

[25] Organic Act of 17 May 1884, 23 Stat. 24, sec. 8.

[26] Two early Alaskan cases affirming aboriginal title were *United States v. Berrigan*, Alaska Reports 442 (1905) and *United States v. Cadzow*, Alaska Reports 125 (1914). For more detailed discussion of aboriginal title, see Berman, Howard R., 'The concept of aboriginal rights in the early legal history of the United States', *Buffalo Law Review*, No.27, 1978, pp.637-67; and Slattery, Brian, *Ancestral Lands, Alien Laws: Judicial Perspectives on Aboriginal Title*, Studies on Aboriginal Rights No.2, University of Saskatchewan Native Law Centre, Saskatchewan, 1983.

[27] Slattery, *op. cit.*, pp.38-9; Case, David, *Alaska Natives and American*

Laws, University of Alaska Press, Fairbanks, 1984, p.65.

[28] Cases making this argument included *Sutter* v. *Heckman*, Alaska Reports 188 (1901), and *Worthen Lumber Mills* v. *Alaska-Juneau Gold Mining Company*, 229 F. 966 (9th Cir., 1916).

[29] Otis, D.S., *The Dawes Act and the Allotment of Indian Lands*, University of Oklahoma Press, Norman, 1973, pp.152-3.

[30] Gruening, Ernest, *The State of Alaska*, Random House, New York, 1954, pp.96-9.

[31] Case, *op. cit.*, pp.85-98. Prior to 1936 Congress created only one reservation in Alaska: Metlakatla. Metlakatla was considered an exception. A group of Tsimshian Indians from British Columbia and missionary William Duncan obtained permission from US President Grover Cleveland to settle on the Annette Islands in 1887, after the Canadian government disputed the Tsimshians' land claims. Four years later Congress established a reservation for them. See *ibid.*, p.116, note 26.

[32] Philip, Kenneth R., 'The New Deal and Alaskan Natives, 1936-1945', Pacific Historical *Review*, Vol.50, No.3, 1981, pp.309-27.

[33] Case, *op. cit.*, pp.12, 100.

[34] State of Alaska, Governor's Task Force, *Report of the Governor's Task Force on Federal–State–Tribal Relations*, submitted to Governor Sheffield, Anchorage, 14 February 1986, p.121.

[35] Gruening, *op. cit.*, pp.460-92.

[36] Wilkinson, Charles F. and Biggs, Eric R., 'The evolution of the termination policy', *American Indian Law Review*, No.5, 1977, pp.139-84.

[37] Gruening, *op. cit.*, pp.460-92

[38] Naske, Klaus M., and Slotnick, Herman E., *Alaska – A History of the 49th State*, 2nd edn., University of Oklahoma Press, Norman, 1987, p.297.

[39] Arnold, Robert D., *Alaska Native Land Claims*, Alaska Native Foundation, Anchorage, 1978, p.100.

[40] Federal Field Committee for Development Planning in Alaska, *Alaska Natives and the Land*, US Government Printing Office, Washington, DC, 1968, p.454.

[41] Ellana, Linda J., *Bering-Norton Petroleum Development Scenarios and Sociocultural Impacts Analysis*, Vol.1, Minerals Management Service Social and Economic Studies, Anchorage, 1980, pp.256, 350.

[42] Langdon, Steve J., 'Alaskan Native subsistence: current regulatory regimes and issues', paper presented at the Roundtable Discussions of Subsistence, Vol.19, Alaska Native Review Commission Herings, Inuit Circumpolar Conference, Anchorage, 10–13 October 1984, p.11.

[43] With respect to aboriginal title, see Cohen, Felix S., *Handbook of Federal Indian Law*, Michie Bobbs-Merrill, Charlottesville, 1982, p.492; and Berman, *op. cit.*

[44] Among the Marshall opinions, see *Cherokee Nation v. Georgia*, 30 US (5 Pet.) 1 (1831), and *Worcester v. Georgia*, 31 US (6 Pet.) 515 (1832).

[45] Cohen, *op. cit.*, pp.247-50.

[46] The state's postion summarized here is taken from the report on federal–state–tribal relations, State of Alaska, Governor's Task Force, *op. cit.*

[47] Williams, Andy, 'Natives get cash but little land in first decade', *Fairbanks Daily News-Miner*, 16 November 1981, p.1.

[48] Berger, Thomas R., Village Journey: *The Report of the Alaska Native Review Commission*, Hill & Wang, New York, 1985, pp.18-19.

[49] *Ibid.*, p.167.

[50] '1991 resolutions', *Alaska Native News*, June 1986, pp.28-35.

[51] Alaska Federation of Natives, *1991: Making It Work: A Guide to Public Law 100-241*, Anchorage, 1991.

[52] Bernton, Hal, 'Native firm OKs new stock plan', *Anchorage Daily News*, 10 November 1989, pp.C1, C5.

[53] The ANCSA did provide for revenue sharing between regional corporations, a hastily drafted section known as 7 (i) which has been the subject of considerable litigation. See Bernton, Hal, 'Robin Hood clause shares the wealth', *Anchorage Daily News*, 15 December 1991, p.E3.

[54] Case, *op. cit.*, p.295; Caulfield, Richard A., 'Alaska's subsistence management regimes', *Polar Record*, Vol.22, No.164, 1992, p.25.

[55] Smith, Eric, 'McDowell decision and ANILCA: what's next?', *Alaska Marine Resource Quarterly*, No.5, Winter, 1990, p.6.

[56] *Kenaitze Indian Tribe v. State of Alaska*, 860 F. 2d. 312 (9th Cir., 1988), p.318.

[57] Caulfield, *op. cit.*, p.26; *McDowell v. State of Alaska*, 785 p. 2d. 1 (Alaska, 1989).

[58] Caulfield, *op. cit.*, pp.30-1.

[59] Native American Rights Fund, 'Petition for rule-making by the Secretaries of Interior and Agriculture that navigable waters and federal reserved waters are "public lands" subject to Title VIII of ANILCA's subsistence priority', 15 July 1993, Anchorage.

[60] Hulen, David, 'Fishing ban irks Natives', *Anchorage Daily News*, 4 September 1993, pp.A1, A10.

[61] Fienup-Riordan, Ann, *Eskimo Essays*, Rutgers University Press, New Brunswick and London, p.181.

[62] McBeath, Gerald A. and Morehouse, Thomas A., *The Dynamics of Alaska Native Self-Government*, University Press of America, Washington, DC, 1980.

[63] State of Alaska, Department of Labor, *Alaska Population Overview*, 1991, *op. cit.*, p.42.

[64] In fact, several villages would like to disband their municipal governments in favour of traditional tribal councils. Elders may feel that the tribal councils are more culturally appropriate forms of governance. Seven years ago the village of Kasigluk disbanded the municipality and it has since been governed by a council that runs a tribal court, collects a sales tax, employs tribal police and has a tribal gaol. See 'Five villages eager for tribal councils', *Fairbanks Daily News-Miner*, 22 October 1993, p.B2.

[65] Morehouse, Thomas A., The *Dual Political Status of Alaska Natives under US Policy*, Institute of Social and Economic Research, Anchorage, 1992.

[66] O'Brien, Sharon, *American Indian Tribal Governments*, University of Oklahoma Press, Norman and London, 1989, pp.86-90.

[67] US Department of the Interior, Bureau of Indian Affairs, 'Indian entities recognized and eligible to receive services from the United States Bureau of Indian Affairs', Washington, DC, 15 October 1993.

[68] *In Re Delinquent Property Taxes Owed to the City of Nome*, 780 P. 2. 363 (Alaska, 1989); Jaeger, Lisa, personal communication, Fairbanks, 5 October 1993.

[69] This issue is currently before the federal court in *Alyeska* v. *Kluti Kaah*, Case No. A87-201 CIV.

[70] Kleinfeld, Judith, *Alaska Native Education: Issues in the Nineties*, University of Alaska, Anchorage, Institute of Social and Economic Research, April 1992, p.13.

[71] Krauss, Michael, 'Many tongues – ancient tales', in Fitzhugh and Crowell, *op. cit.*, pp.145-50.

[72] McBeath, Gerald A., personal communication, Fairbanks, 6 September 1993.

[73] Barnhardt, Carol, 'History of schooling for Alaska Native people', unpublished manuscript, University of Alaska Fairbanks, 1993.

[74] Memorandum from Heather Dendall, Native American Rights Fund, Anchorage, 4 October 1993.

[75] Native American Rights Fund, *Indian Education Legal Support Project: Tribalizing Indian Education*, presentation/workshop materials, September 1993, section 4.

[76] Huskey, Lee, *The Economy of Village Alaska*, Institute of Social and

Economic Research, University of Alaska, Anchorage, 1992.
[77] 'The Alaska congressional delegation's report to AFN', Anchorage, October 1993, pp.1,4.
[78] *Ibid.*, p.4.
[79] *The AFN Report on the Status of Alaska Natives: A Call for Action*, Anchorage, January 1989, p.65.
[80] Colt, Steve, 'Financial performance of Native regional corporations', *Alaska Review of Social and Economic Conditions*, No.28, December 1991, pp.1-24.
[81] State of Alaska, Department of Labor, Research and Analysis, State Data Center, 'Income data for the State of Alaska', Juneau, 1990.

Bibliography

Alaska Federation of Natives, *The AFN Report on the Status of Alaska Natives: A Call for Action*, Anchorage, 1989.

Arnold, Robert D., *Alaska Native Land Claims*, Alaska Native Foundation, Anchorage, 1978.

Barsh, Russel Lawrence and Henderson, James Youngblood, *The Road: Indian Tribes and Political Liberty*, University of California Press, Berkeley, 1980.

Berger, Thomas R., *Village Journey: The Report of the Alaska Native Review Commission*, Hill & Wang, New York, 1985.

Case, David, *Alaska Natives and American Laws*, University of Alaska Press, Fairbanks, 1984.

Caulfield, Richard A., 'Alaska's subsistence management regimes', *Polar Record*, Vol.22, No.164, p.23-32, 1992.

Chance, Norman A., *The Inupiat and Arctic Alaska: An Ethnography of Development*, Holt, Rinehart & Winston, Fort Worth, 1990.

Cohen, Felix S., *Handbook of Federal Indian Law*, Michie Bobbs-Merrill, Charlottesville, 1982.

Federal Field Committee for Development Planning in Alaska, *Alaska Natives and the Land*, US Government Printing Office, Washington DC, 1968.

Fienup-Riordan, Ann, *Yup'ik Lives and How We See Them*, Rutgers University Press, New Brunswick and London, 1990.

Fitzhugh, William W., and Crowell, Aron (eds.), *Crossroads of the Continents: Cultures of Siberia and Alaska*, Smithsonian Institution Press, Washington DC, 1988.

Fortuine, Robert, *Chills and Fever: Health and Disease in the Early History of Alaska,*. University of Alaska Press, Fairbanks, 1989.

Gruening, Ernest. 1954, *The State of Alaska*, Random House, New York, 1954.

Huntington, Sidney, *Shadows on the Koyukuk: An Alaskan Native's Life along the River*, Alaska Northwest Books, Anchorage, Seattle and Portland, 1993.

Huskey, Lee, *The Economy of Village Alaska*, Institute of Social and Economic Research, Anchorage, 1992.

Kleinfeld, Judith, Alaska Native Education: Issues in the Nineties, Institute of Social and Economic Research, Anchorage, 1992.

Langdon, Steve J., (ed.), *Contemporary Alaskan Native Economies*, University Press of America, Lanham, 1986.

McBeath, Gerald A., and Morehouse, Thomas A., *The Dynamics of Alaska Native Self-Government*, University Press of America, Washington DC, 1980.

Mangusso, Mary Childers, and Haycox, Stephen W., (eds.), *Interpreting Alaska's History: An Anthology*, Alaska Pacific University Press, Anchorage, 1989.

Morehouse, Thomas A., *The Alaska Native Claims Settlement Act, 1991, and Tribal Government*, Occasional Paper No.19, Institute of Social and Economic Research, Anchorage, 1988.

Moorhouse, Thomas A., *The Dual Political Status of Alaska Natives under US Policy*, Institute of Social and Economic Research, Anchorage, 1992.

Napoleon, Harold, *Yuuyaraq: The Way of the Human Being*, Center for Cross-Cultural Studies, College of Rural Alaska, University of Alaska, Fairbanks, 1991.

Naske, Klaus M., and Slotnick, Herman E., *Alaska – A History of the 49th State*, 2nd edn., University of Oklahoma Press, Norman, 1987.

Nelson, Richard K., *Hunters of the Northern Forest*, 2nd edn., University of Chicago Press, Chicago, 1986.

Smith, Barbara Sweetland, and Barnett, Redmond J., *Russian America: The Forgotten Frontier*, Washington State Historical Society, Tacoma, 1990.

Smith, Eric, and Kancewick, Mary, 'The tribal status of Alaska Natives', *University of Colorado Law Review*, No.61, pp.455-516.

Wilkinson, Charles F., *American Indians, Time, and the Law*, Yale University Press, New Haven and London, 1987.

The Inuit of Canada

Footnotes

[1] McGhee, Robert, *Canadian Arctic Pre-history*, National Museum of Man, Ottawa, and Van Nostrand Reinhold, Toronto, 1978, p. 80.

[2] *Ibid.*, p. 118.

[3] Rasmussen, Knud, *Intellectual Culture of the Iglulik Eskimos*, report of the Fifth Thule Expedition 1921–4, Vol.7, No.1, Gyldendalske Boghandel, Nordisk Forlag, Copenhagen, 1929.

[4] Usher, Peter, 'Fur trade posts of the Northwest Territories: 1870–1970', *Inuit Land Use And Occupancy Study*, Vol.2, Department of Indian and Northern Affairs, Ottawa, 1976, p. 154.

[5] Crowe, Keith J., *A History of the Original Peoples of Northern Canada*, McGill-Queens University Press (revised edition), Montreal, 1991, p.97.

[6] Berger, Thomas R., *Northern Frontier, Northern Homeland: The Report of the Mackenzie Valley Pipeline Inquiry*, Supply and Services, Canada, 1977, Vol.2.

[7] Crowe, Keith J., 'Claims on the land', *Arctic Circle* magazine, Nortext, Iqaluit, January/February 1991, p.33.

[8] *Ibid.*, pp. 156-60.

[9] President Paul Quassa in *News/North*, 25 February 1991.

[10] Fleras, Augie and Elliott, Jean Leonard, *The Nations Within: Aboriginal–State Relations in Canada, the United States and New Zealand*, OUP, Toronto, 1992, p.64.

[11] The 'Meech Lake Accord' was the document which resulted from an attempt by Prime Minister Brian Mulroney to amend the Constitution with the help of all ten provincial premiers, but without the participation or approval of aboriginal peoples. For reasons too complex to explain here, two provincial legislatures failed to ratify the Accord and it was therefore never implemented.

[12] Irwin, Colin, 'Lords of the Arctic: wards of the state – the growing Inuit population, Arctic resettlement, and their effects on social and economic change', report prepared for *Health And Welfare Canada*, Ottawa, 1989, p.9.

[13] Amagoalik, John, article in *Inuit Today*, Inuit Tapirisat of Canada, Ottawa, Vol.6, No.4, 1977, p.52.

Bibliography

Abele, Frances, *Gathering Strength*, Arctic Institute of North America, Calgary, 1989.

Ames, Randy, Axford, Don, Usher, Peter J., Weick, Edward R. and Wenzel, George W. *Keeping on the Land: A Study of the feasibility of a comprehensive Wildlife Harvest Support Programme in the Northwest Territories*, Canadian Arctic Resources Committee, Ottawa, 1988.

Arctic Circle, Iqaluit: Nortext, 1990.

Berger, Thomas R., *Northern Frontier, Northern Homeland: The Report of the Mackenzie Valley Pipeline Inquiry*, Douglas and McIntyre (revised edition, originally published in two volumes by Supply and Services, Canada, 1977), Vancouver, 1988.

Berger, Thomas R., *Village Journey: The Report of the Alaska Native Review Commission*, Hill and Wang, New York, 1985.

Bone, Robert M., *The Geography of the Canadian North: Issues and Challenges*, OUP, Toronto, 1992.

Briggs, Jean, *Never in Anger: Portrait of an Eskimo Family*, Harvard University Press, Cambridge, MA, 1970.

Brody, Hugh, *Living Arctic: Hunters of the Canadian North*, Faber and Faber, London, 1987.

Brody, Hugh, *The People's Land: Eskimos and Whites in the Eastern Arctic*, Douglas and McIntyre (originally published in 1975), Vancouver, 1991.

Canada, DIAND, *Comprehensive Land Claims Policy*, 1987.

Canada, DIAND, Constitutional Development and Strategic Planning Branch, *A Northern Political and Economic Framework*, 1988.

Canada, DIAND, *The Western Arctic Claim: The Inuvialuit Final Agreement*, 1984.

Canada, et al., *The James Bay and Northern Québec Agreement*, Editeur Officiel (agreement between the Government of Québec, the Société d'énergie de la Baie James, the Société de développement de la Baie James, the Commission hydroélectrique de Québec [Hydro-Québec], the Grand Council of the Crees [of Québec], the Northern Québec Inuit Association, and the Government of Canada), 1976.

Coates, Kenneth S. and Morrison, William R. (eds.), *Interpreting Canada's North: Selected Readings*, Copp Clark Pitman, Toronto, 1989.

Cox, Bruce A. (ed.), Native Peoples, *Native Lands: Canadian Indians, Inuit and Métis*, Carleton University Press, Toronto, 1989.

Crnkovich, Mary (ed.), 'Gossip': *A Spoken History of Women in the North*, Canadian Arctic Resources Committee, Ottawa, 1990.

Crowe, Keith J., *A History of the Original Peoples of Northern Canada*, McGill-Queens University Press (revised edition), Montreal, 1991.

Dacks, Gurston (ed.), *Devolution and Constitutional Development in the Canadian North*, Carleton University Press, Ottawa, 1990.

Damas, David J. (vol. ed.), *Arctic*, Vol.5 of *Handbook of North American Indians* series, gen. ed. William C. Sturtevant, Smithsonian Institution, Washington, 1984.

Dickerson, Mark O., *Whose North? Political Change, Political Development, and Self-government in the Northwest Territories*, UBC Press and the Arctic Institute of North America, Vancouver, 1992.

Duffy, R. Quinn, *The Road To Nunavut: The Progress of the Eastern Arctic Inuit since the Second World War*, McGill-Queens University Press, Kingston, 1988.

Eber, Dorothy H., *When the Whalers Were Up North: Inuit Memories from the Eastern Arctic*, McGill-Queens University Press, Kingston, 1989.

Études/Inuit/Studies, Laval: Inuit and Circumpolar Study Group (GETIC), UniversitÄ Laval/Inuksiutiit Katimajiit Association.

Freeman, Milton M.R. (ed.), *Inuit Land Use and Occupancy Project*, Supply and Services, Canada, 3 vols.: 1) Land Use and Occupancy, 2) Supporting Studies and 3) Land Use Atlas, Ottawa, 1976.

Freeman, Milton M.R., Wein, Eleanor E. and Keith, Darren E. *Recovering Rights: Bowhead Whales and Inuvialuit Subsistence in The Western Canadian Arctic*, Canadian Circumpolar Institute/Fisheries Joint Management Committee. (Studies in Whaling No.2), Edmonton, 1992.

Grant, Shelagh D., *Sovereignty or Security? Government Policy in the Canadian North 1936–50*, University of British Columbia Press, Vancouver, 1988.

Hall, Sam, *The Fourth World: The Heritage of the Arctic and its Destruction*, Knopf, New York, 1987.

Inuit Ratification Committee, Agreement between the Inuit of the Nunavut Settlement Area and Her Majesty in Right of Canada, Yellowknife, 1992.

Irwin, Colin, 'Lords of the Arctic: wards of the state – the growing Inuit population, Arctic resettlement, and their effects on social and economic change' (report prepared for *Health and Welfare Canada*, reprinted in *Northern Perspectives,* Vol.17, No.1), Ottawa, 1989.

McGhee, Robert, *Canadian Arctic Pre-history*, National Museum of Man, Ottawa, and Van Nostrand Reinhold, Toronto, 1978.

Marcus, Alan R., *Out in the Cold: The Legacy of Canada's Inuit Relocation Experiment in the High Arctic*, International Work Group for Indigenous Affairs (IWGIA), Document No.71, Copenhagen, 1992.

Merritt, John, Ames, Randy, Fenge, Terry, and Jull, Peter, *Nunavut: Political Choices and Manifest Destiny*, Canadian Arctic Resources Committee, Ottawa, 1989.

Petrone, Penny, *Northern Voices: Inuit Writing in English*, University of Toronto Press, Toronto, 1988.

Pitseolak, Peter, and Dorothy H. Eber, *People from our Side: The Land of The People of Cape Dorset*, Hurtig, Edmonton, 1975.

Purich, Donald J., *The Inuit and Their Land: The Story of Nunavut*, James Lorimer, Toronto, 1992.

Richardson, Boyce, *Strangers Devour the Land: The Cree Hunters of the James Bay Area versus Premier Bourassa and the James Bay Development Corporation*, Douglas and McIntyre, (revised edition), Vancouver, 1991.

Riewe, Roderick R. (ed.), *Nunavut Atlas*, Canadian Circumpolar Institute, Tungavik Federation of Nunavut, Edmonton; 1992.

Usher, Peter J., Tough, Frank J. and Galois, Robert M., 'Reclaiming the land: aboriginal title, treaty rights, and land claims in Canada', *Applied Geography* Vol.12, No.2, 1992.

Wenzel, George W., *Animal Rights, Human Rights: Ecology, Economy and Ideology in the Canadian Arctic*, University of Toronto Press, Toronto, 1991.

The Saami of Lapland

Footnotes

[1] Manker, 1947:11-13.
[2] Wiklund, 1899:5.
[3] Ruong, 1951:113; Söderström, 1984:36.
[4] Beckman, 1964; cf. Fjellström, 1985:137-8.
[5] Sammallahti, 1991:117 ff.
[6] Collinder, 1949:34.
[7] Wickman in Manker, 1947:52.
[8] Collinder, 1949:92.
[9] Hansegård, 1974.
[10] Marjut Aikio, 1991.
[11] Magga, 1986; cf. Wickman in Manker, 1947:56-7.
[12] Ruong, 1975:202.
[13] Collinder, 1949:37.
[14] Helander, 1984.
[15] Magga, 1986:7.
[16] Collinder, 1949:180.
[17] Aikio, 1986:16.
[18] SOU 1975:100, 344.
[19] Aikio, 1986:16.
[20] Guttorm, 1986.
[21] Helander, 1986:14.
[22] Magga, 1986:14-15.
[23] Aikio, 1986:11.
[24] Aikio, 1986:14.
[25] Beach, 1981:418.
[26] Svensson, 1985.
[27] Collinder, 1949:181.
[28] Magga, 1986:18.
[29] Aikio, 1986:19.
[30] Cf. Fjellström, 1985:69-71.
[31] Wiklund, 1918:270; Hultblad, 1968:73.
[32] Hultblad, 1968:58, 127.
[33] Fjellström, 1985:92.
[34] Ruong, 1982:57.
[35] For example, Tornaeus in Schefferus, 1956 edn, 168-9.
[36] Beach *et al.*, 1991:62.
[37] The Swedish School 'Reform', 1913.
[38] Cramér, 1986.
[39] Haraldson, 1962.

[40] Beach, 1981:454 ff.
[41] SFS 1971:437.
[42] Dunfjeld, 1979:35.
[43] Eidlitz, 1979.
[44] Beach, 1986a.
[45] Andrejev, 1977.
[46] Beach, 1981, 1986b.
[47] Beach, 1990.
[48] NOU 1984:18.
[49] See the Norwegian Government Bill, Ot prp nr 33, 1986-7.
[50] Dir 1982:71.
[51] Beach, 1986.
[52] Beach, 1985:24; Cramér, 1986.
[53] *Jordabalken*:15; Promulgation of the new *Jordabalken*, SFS 1970:995; cf. Undén, 1969:142.
[54] Bengtsson, 1991:40.
[55] Special Parliamentary Committee of 1886.
[56] Beach, 1986c.
[57] Beach, 1982.
[58] Personal communication, Frank Horn; cf. Sillanpää, 1992.
[59] Report of the Committee for the Revision of the Election Acts, KM 1989:38, p.81.
[60] Proposition 1992/93:32, pp.62 f.
[61] Personal communication, Leif Rantala.

Bibliography

Aikio, M., 'The Status of the Sami language in the Nordic countries: the Finnish perspective – Language and Ethnicity', in *Languages of the Arctic Peoples*, UNESCO, 1986.

Aikio, M., *The Saami Language in Finland: Problems and Progress*, Rovaniemi Conference on the Linguistic Rights of Minorities, 30 May–1 June, 1991.

Andrejev, V., Reindeer herding in the world and its classification, *Ekologija*, No.4, 1977.

Beach, H., *Reindeer-Herd Management in Transition: The Case of Tuorpon Saameby in Northern Sweden*, Acta Univ. Ups., Uppsala Studies in Cultural Anthropology, No.3, Uppsala, 1981.

Beach, H., 'The place of women in the modern Saameby: an issue in legal anthropology', in *Antropologisk Forskning, Ymer*, årgång 102, ed. Margareta Elg. Svenska Sällskapet för Antropologi och Geographi, Borgströms Tryckeri AB, Motala, 1982.

Beach, H., 'Moose poaching or native minority rights: a struggle for definition in Swedish Saamiland', in *Nord Nytt*, Nordisk Tidskrift for Folkelivsforskning, 26, Kulturer i Norr. udgivet af NEFA-Norden, Special-Trykkeriet Viborg a-s, Denmark, 1985.

Beach, H., 'The reindeer-caribou conflict in the NANA region of Alaska: A case study for native minority rights issues', in *Nomadic Peoples*, 17, February, ed. Philip C. Salzman, Commission on Nomadic Peoples, McGill Univ., Canada.

Beach, H., 'Visit to a Siberian Sovkhoz', in *Antropologiska Studier*, 38-39, ed. T. Gerholm, Dept. Social Anthropology, Stockholm, 1986a.

Beach, H., 'Three complementary processes that alienate the Saami from their land in Sweden (the IUAES Inter-Congress)' in *Nomadic Peoples*, No.20, March, ed. Philip C. Salzman, Commission on Nomadic Peoples, McGill University, Canada. 1986b.

Beach, H., 'The phase-out clause in minority rights legislation: a comparison of the Swedish and Alaskan methods', in *Nordisk Tidsskrift for International Ret*, Vol.55, Fasc.1-2, Copenhagen, 1986c.

Beach, H., 'The Saami in Alaska: ethnic relations and reindeer herding', in *Contributions to Circumpolar Studies*, ed., Hugh Beach, Uppsala Research Reports in Cultural Anthropology, No.7, Department of Cultural Anthropology, Uppsala University, Sweden, 1986.

Beach, H., 'Perceptions of risk, dilemmas of policy: nuclear fallout in Swedish Lapland', in *Social Science & Medicine*, Vol.30, No.6, 1990, pp. 729-738. 1991, with Myrdene Anderson and Pekka Aikio, 'Dynamics of Saami territoriality within the nation-states of Norway, Sweden and Finland', in *Mobility and Territoriality: Social and Spatial Boundaries among Foragers, Fishers, Pastoralists and Peripatetics*, ed. Michael Casimir and Aparna Rao. Berg Publishers, New York.

Beckman, L., *On the Anthropology of the Swedish Lapps*, Studia Ethnographica Upsaliensa, XXI, Lund, 1964.

Bengtsson, B. (1991), 'Skattefjällsmålet och dess efterverkningar' in *Samesymposium*, eds. Marjut Aikio and Kaisa Korpijaakko, eds. Lapin Yliopiston Hallintoviraston Julkaisuja, Lapplands Universitet, Förvaltningsämbetetes publikationer 15, Rovaniemi, 1991.

Collinder, B., *The Lapps*, Princeton University press, New York, 1949.

Cramér, T., *Volym 22. Samernas Vita Bok*, utg Landsförbundet Svenska Samer, Samenytt 1-2, Tärnaby, 1986.

Dir, 1982:71, *Vissa frågor om samernas ställning i Sverige*, Kimmittedirektiv, Beslut vid regeringssammanträde 1982-09-02, Chefen för justitiedepartementet, statsrädet Petri, anför. Sweden.

Dunfjeld, E., *Reindrift:Samisk Naering, Samisk Fremtid*, Bodo, Norway, 1979.

Eidlitz, K., *Revolutionen i Norr*, Uppsala Research Ueports in Cultural Anthropology No.1, Uppsala, 1979. English translation: Kuoljok, K., *The Revolution in the North*, Acta Universitatis Upsaliensis, Studia Multiethnica Upsaliensia 1, 1985.

Fjellstöm, P., *Samernas Samhälle i Tradition och Nutid*, Norstedts, Stockholm, 1985.

Guttorm, J., 'Alle kouluikäisten saamelaislasten kasvuolosuhteet ja niiden kehittämismahdollisuudet Utssjoen kunnassa', *Sosiaalihallituksen julkaisuja* 2/1986, Helsinki, 1986.

Hansegård, N.E., 'Samernas sprak', in *Samerna: ett folk i fyra länder*, ed. Lars Svonni, Prisma, Falköping, 1974.

Haraldson, S., 'Levnads-och dödlighetsförhållanden i de nordligaste svenska lappbyarna', *Svenska Lükartidningen*, 59th year, No.40, 1962, p.2829.

Helander, E., *Om Trespråkighet: en undersökning av språkvalet hos samerna i Övre Soppero*, Acta Universitatis Umensis, Umcå studies in the Humanitics No.67, Umeå, 1984.

Helander, F., 'The Situation of the Sami Language in Sweden', in *Languages of the Arctic Peoples*, UNESCO, 1986.

Hultblad, F., *Övergång från Nomadism till Agrar Bosüttning i Jokkmokks Socken*, Nordiska Museet, Acta Lapponice XIV, Lund 1980.

Jordabalken from 1734, sections regarding immemorial rights (Chapter 15), see the 1971 or earlier editions of the semi-official Swedish Law Book, *Sveriges Rikes Lag*.

Magga, O.H., 'The Sami language in Norway', in *Languages of the Arctic Peoples*, UNESCO, 1986.

Manker, E., *Det Svenska Fjällapparna*, Svenska Turistföreningens handböcker om det svenska fjället 4, Stockholm, 1947.

NOU 1984:18, *Om samenes rettsstilling*, Norges Offentlige Utredninger, Avgitt til Justisdepartementet 15 juni 1984, Universitetsforlaget, Oslo.

Ot prp nr 33, *Om lov om Sametinget og andre samiske rettsforhold (sameloven)*, Justis- og politidepartementet, Norway 1986–7.

Proposition 1992/93:32, *Samerna och samisk kultur m.m.*, 1 Riksdagen 1992/93, 1 samling. Nr.32. Sweden.

Ruong, I., *Samerna*, Stockholm, 1975.

Ruong. I., *Samerna: i historien och nutiden*, Bonniers, Stockholm, 1982 edn.

Sammallahti, P., 'The Origin of the Saami (Lapps)', in *Academia Scientiarium Fennica*, yearbook, 1990–1.

Schcffcrus, J., *Lappland*, trans. from Latin by Henrik Sundin, first published in 1673, Acta Lapponica 8, Stockholm, 1956 edition. English edition 1674, facsimile 1971.

SFS 1970:995 (Svensk Författningssamling 1970:995), *Lag om införande av nya jordabalken.* (Swedish Statute-Book)

SFS 1971:437, *Rennäringslagen*, Stockholm.

Sillanpüü, L., *The Development of Sami Assemblies in Fennoscandia: Towards Aboriginal Self-Government*, Circumpolar and Scientific Affairs, Indian and Northern Affairs, Canada, 1992.

Söderström, S., 'Från den sydsamiska ordboken', in *Svenska Landsmål och Svenskt Folkliv*, Uppsala, 1984.

SOU 1975:99 and 100, *Samerna i Sverige* and *Bilagor*, Stockholm.

Svensson, T., *Asa Kitok och hennes döttrar: en studie om samisk rotslöjd*, Acta Lapponica, 21, Nordiska Museet, Arlöv, 1985.

Undén, O., *Svensk Sakrätt, Fast Egendom*, Gleerupa Förlag, Lund, 1969.

Wickman, B., Sprak, in *Det Svenska Fjällapparna*, Svenska Turistföreningens handböcker om det svenska fjöllet 4, ed. Ernst Manker, Stockholm, 1947.

Wiklund, K., 'Om renskotselns uppkomst', *Ymer*, tidskrift utgiven av Svenska Sallskapet for Antrpologi och Geografi Vol.38, No.3, 1918,pp. 249-73.

INDEX

Home Rule: *see* Greenland Home Rule
Home Rule Act, 8, 10
Hootch, Molly, 101
Hudson's Bay Company, 110, 111
Hultblad, 171
human rights issues, 32, 158, 203
hunter-gatherer societies, 23, 85
hunting,
   commercial, 4, 6, 17, 59, 86, 110, 111, 112, 125
   cultural significance, 5, 20-22, 126
   disruption of, 57, 58, 76
   marine mammal, 58, 59, 83, 86, 107
   seal, 20, 22, 25, 128-29
   skills of, 107-8, 126
   poaching, 64, 67-68
   regulation of, 23-25, 100, 120
   subsistence, 3, 7, 14, 60, 64, 81, 85, 92, 97-99, 128-29, 139
    opposition to, 2, 22-23:
   see also whaling
hunting rights, 92, 172, 174, 190, 191-92, 205
hydro-electric power, 66, 116-19, 182-83

Iceland, 3, 25, 109
Icelandic sagas, 3
Ickes, Harold, 89
Idre region, Dalecarlia, 157
Igloolik Inuit, 109
Ilismatusarfik (University of Greenland), 16
illiteracy, 45
ILO: *see* International Labour Organization
Ilulissat, Greenland, 19, 21
Inari, Finland, 164, 187, 197
Indian Brotherhood, 119-20
Indian Child Welfare Act (1978), 100
Indian Civil Rights Act (1968), 100
'Indian Country', 92, 93-95, 101, 104
Indian Reorganization Act, 89, 90
Indian Self-Determination and Educational Assistance Act (1975), 100
Indigenous languages, 75, 130
   alphabetization, 16, 46-47, 55, 124, 135-36, 159
   education in, 45-47, 55, 62, 73, 79, 102, 124, 132, 137, 145, 146, 159, 160-62

About Minority Rights Group Reports

Minority Rights Group began publishing in 1970. Over two decades and ninety titles later, MRG's series of reports are widely recognized internationally as authoritative, accurate and objective documents on the rights of minorities worldwide.

Over the years, subscribers to the series have received a wealth of unique material on ethnic, religious, linguistic and social minorities. The reports are seen as an important reference by researchers, students, and campaigners and provide readers all over the world with valuable background data on many topical issues.

Around six reports are published every year. Each title, expertly researched and written, is approximately 30 pages and 20,000 words long and covers a specific minority issue.

Recent titles in our report series include:

Africa
The Sahel
Somalia

Americas
Maya of Guatemala
Inuit (Eskimo) of Canada

Asia
The Chinese of SE Asia
The Adivasis of Bangladesh
Lumad and Moro of Mindanao

Europe
Minorities in Central/Eastern
    Europe

General
Language, Literacy and Minorities
New Approaches to Minority
    Protection

Middle East
The Kurds
Minorities in the Middle East

Southern Oceans
Maori of Aotearoa-New Zealand
The Pacific: Nuclear Testing
    and Minorities

Women
Female Genital Mutilation

If you have found this book informative and stimulating, and would like to learn more about minority issues, please do subscribe to our report series. It is only with the help of our supporters that we are able to pursue our aims and objectives – to secure justice for disadvantaged groups around the world.

We currently offer a reduced annual rate for individual subscribers – please ring our Subscription Desk on +44 (71) 978 9498 for details. Payment can be easily made by MasterCard or Visa by either telephone or post.

All enquiries to:

> Sales Department
> Minority Rights Group
> 379 Brixton Road
> London
> SW9 7DE
> UK

Customers in North America wishing to purchase copies of our *reports* should contact:

> ism Press
> PO Box 12447
> San Francisco
> CA 94112
> USA
> TEL/FAX: 415 333 7641

> Cultural Survival
> 215 First Street
> Cambridge
> MA 02142
> USA
> TEL: 617 621 3818
> FAX: 617 621 3814

For *books* contact:

> Paul and Co.
> c/o PCS Data Processing Inc
> 360 West 31 Street
> New York
> NY 10001
> TEL: 212 564 3730
> FAX: 212 971 7200